SOCIAL SCIENTIST
AS INNOVATOR

SOCIAL SCIENTIST AS INNOVATOR

Michael Young

Abt Books
Cambridge, Massachusetts

Library of Congress Cataloging in Publication Data

Young, Michael Dunlop, 1915–
  Social scientist as innovator.

  Includes index.
  1. Sociology—Addresses, essays, lectures. 2. Social prediction—Great Britain—Addresses, essays, lectures. 3. Great Britain—Social policy—Addresses, essays, lectures. 4. Education and state—Great Britain—Addresses, essays, lectures. I. Title.
  HM51.Y625 1983   301   83-21387
  ISBN 0-89011-593-1

© Abt Associates Inc., 1983

All rights reserved. No part of this publication may be reproduced or transmitted in any form or by any means, electronic or mechanical, including photocopying, recording, or any information storage or retrieval system, without specific permission in writing from the publisher: Abt Books, 55 Wheeler Street, Cambridge, MA 02138.

Printed in the United States of America

Contents

Acknowledgements		vii
Introduction Daniel Bell		ix
Part I:	**An Approach to Forecasting**	1
Chapter 1:	Forecasting and the Social Sciences	3
Chapter 2:	Cycles in Social Behaviour	27
Part II:	**Educational Policy**	43
Chapter 3:	The Meritocracy	45
Chapter 4:	The Need for an Open University	63
Chapter 5:	Third World Alternative to Schools	73
Part III:	**Family and Social Policy**	97
Chapter 6:	Conservation of Family Life	99
Chapter 7:	The Old World to Redress the Balance of the New	119
Chapter 8:	The Mortality of Widowers	138
Chapter 9:	Leisure and the Family	146
Part IV:	**Sociology and Politics**	175
Chapter 10:	The Meaning of the Coronation	177
Chapter 11:	Small Man, Big World	195
Chapter 12:	The Chipped White Cups of Dover	210
Chapter 13:	Consumers and the Quality of Life	233
Chapter 14:	Somali Radio Service	238
Chapter 15:	The Middle of the Night	242
Epilogue Michael Young		253
Index		256

Acknowledgements

The author would like to acknowledge his debt to the co-authors of several of the contributions in this book, and to their original publishers.

1. "Forecasting and the Social Sciences" was originally published in a book with the same title, by Michael Young (London: Heinemann Educational Books, 1968).

2. "Cycles in Social Behaviour", written jointly with John Ziman, was published in *Nature* (London: MacMillan Journals, Ltd., 1971).

3. "The Meritocracy" is the last chapter of *The Meritocracy* by Michael Young (London: Thames and Hudson, 1958), a book which has subsequently been republished in 13 editions in English, French, German, Italian, Dutch, Danish, Norwegian, Swedish, Finnish, Japanese, and Spanish.

4. "The Need for an Open University" is an essay which appeared in 1962 in the educational magazine *Where?*, started by the author soon after he had launched *Which?* as a magazine for consumers.

5. "Third World Alternative to Schools" was co-authored with Tony Dodds, Hilary Perraton, and Janet Jenkins and originally appeared in the book *Distance Teaching for the Third World* (London: Routledge and Kegan Paul, Ltd., 1980).

6. "Conservation of Family Life" was originally published in Michael Young and Peter Willmott's *Family and Kinship in East London* (London: Routledge and Kegan Paul, Ltd., 1957).

7. "The Old World to Redress the Balance of the New" is from a study written with Hildred Geertz in Menlo Park, CA and published in the *British Journal of Sociology* (Henley-on-Thames; Routledge and Kegan Paul, Ltd., 1961).

8. "The Mortality of Widowers" is from a joint paper published in *The Lancet* (London: The Lancet, Ltd., 1963).

9. "Leisure and the Family" is republished from *The Symmetrical Family* (London: Routledge and Kegan Paul, Ltd., 1973), co-authored by Peter Willmott.

10. "The Meaning of the Coronation" was co-authored with Edward Shils and published in *Sociological Review* (Staffordshire: The University of Keele, 1953).

11. "Small Man, Big World" is from a pamphlet published by the Labour Party in 1948.

12. "The Chipped White Cups of Dover" is a plea for a new progressive party published privately by the author in 1960.

13. "Consumers and the Quality of Life" is a speech made to the International Organization of Consumers Unions, Oslo, Norway, 1964.

14. "Somali Radio Service" is a speech made in the House of Lords on 31 July 1981.

15. "The Middle of the Night" is a 1982 policy pamphlet for the new Social Democratic Party.

Introduction

If one were introducing Michael Young to an English audience—where he needs little introduction—one would say that he is a modern blend of Charles Booth, Charles Babbage, Edwin Chadwick, and Isambard Kingdom Brunel, with a sprinkling of William Morris or H. G. Wells thrown in for spice. Why invoke these names, many of them, unfortunately, unfamiliar to an American audience? Simply because there is no American figure like Michael Young, yet he is one of the most imaginative, innovative, and unique sociologists in the world today.

Perhaps the best way of establishing this claim is to look at the Victorian forebears I have named, not because he repeats their work, but because he embodies the inquisitive spirit which animated them, and the realistic utopianism which marked their achievements. Charles Booth wrote the great *Life and Labor of the People in London* (1903), an eighteen-year investigation of the London neighborhoods, which is the prototype of the modern social survey. Charles Babbage built the first calculating machine, the first practical application of the mathematics he taught at Cambridge. Edwin Chadwick, the leading social reformer of his day, wrote the famous report on sanitation which led to the modern system of public health inspection of housing conditions and sewage. And Isambard Kingdom Brunel was the pioneering English engineer largely responsible for the railway tunnel, bridge, and viaduct construction and the great iron train sheds of Victorian England.

Michael Young is not a technologist or a planner, as these terms are commonly understood, but a social designer, an architect, in the metaphorical sense of the term, whose passions lie in the social use of social knowledge, a devotion to empirical research and the application of that research to social practice, and a sophisticated awareness of the political process through which social policy and new social institutions have to be guided.

John Stuart Mill once observed that the critic was the lowest order among the potentates of the human mind. To be critical is always necessary. But if one is only critical, who is to take the responsibility to create and implement what we need or want to do? Too often the sociologist has remained only the critic, and evaded the larger responsibility.

There is a second kind of sociologist, who often has ideas for social reform, but who rarely does the necessary research to find out if the reforms are viable. And there are the sociologists who, to their credit, will do both. Yet as Adam Yarmolinsky noted twenty years ago—drawing upon his experiences as one of the designers of the war on poverty in the Kennedy/Johnson administrations—if one is to effectuate ideas, there is a series of many further steps which few persons understand, and even fewer take. It is relatively easy to spout ideas, but it is much more difficult to translate these ideas into specific policy, and even more difficult to translate that policy into legislation. The next step involves mastering the political process to get that legislation passed and then, the most difficult of all, the tasks of creating the necessary institutions and agencies within the bureaucracy to carry out those initial ideas and policies.

Michael Young is that rare sociologist, a man who has done pathbreaking empirical and survey research, has applied that research to practical social policy, and has moved on to the more demanding challenge of building institutions—and successful ones, at that—to carry out social practice. In England he has made distinctive and enduring contributions in the areas of family, education, the consumers' movement, social forecasting—and even in the building of a new political party.

Michael Young came to larger public recognition with the publication of the book (co-authored with Peter Willmott) *Family and Kinship in East London* (1957), which sold a staggering number of copies. The book dealt largely with the consequences of the new social planning of the London Labour governments, which had resulted in the creation of the great blocks of tower flats in East London, one of the oldest and most dilapidated sections of the metropolis. The immediate problem was the dissatisfaction of the residents with this housing, even though there were some amenities such as green space, open vistas and fresh air, none of which had been present in the crowded London described by Charles Dickens and sketched by Gustave Doré. The reason for the dissatisfaction was that the planners who built these flats had never actually considered the nature of English working-class life, in particular the continuing closeness of the family, and the desire of many English workers to have their parents living near them. In effect, the new housing was breaking up both kinship ties and community. But it was more than the shortsightedness of planners that was the thrust of the Young-Willmott book. They were also destroying one of the most cherished—and invidious—and unfortunately still persistent myths in contemporary sociology: the ideas embodied in the terms *Gemeinschaft* and *Gesellschaft*.

Much of sociology, in moving away from history, created a set of ideal types which, unfortunately, most persons have accepted as a historical or literal reality. This was the idea that "the past" was orderly, settled, traditional, intimate, and personal, the notions summed up in the word *Gemeinschaft* (or community), and that the present is anomic, impersonal, bureaucratic, a world in which individuals are rootless or anomic or depersonalized. This is a myth derived from romanticism, and often shared by left and right alike. But it is a dubious myth in two ways. One is that no "past" has ever been settled, its inhabitants' lives unravaged by plagues, epidemics, migrations, conquests, war, or even simply the monotonous brutalities of farming life, a picture depicted so vividly in Ronald Blythe's book *Akenfield*. Nor is the present as fragmented and impersonal as the reverse side of that myth suggests. In a cosmopolitan world, individuals can escape from the conformity of small-town life, while in the large metropolises there are also strong and enduring family-kinship and communal ties. These are some of the truths which Michael Young, along with others like Richard Hoggart, have been able to demonstrate. It was the neglect of this "practical" social knowledge which had led the planners astray.

Michael Young's work on the family was derived from the Institute of Community Studies, which he founded and which still continues. It has sponsored the work of Peter Willmott, Peter Marris, and other imaginative social researchers, and remains one of the main resources for English social policy today.

In the field of education, Michael Young was one of those responsible for the creation of the comprehensive schools, one of the most sweeping and controversial reforms in English society in the last fifteen years. English class society, as everyone knows, has been buttressed and reinforced not only by the "public" schools (which in England, of course, means the elite private schools) but by the "streaming" system of the state schools, which after age eleven divided students among different educational tracks, the brighter ones going into the grammar schools, which were primarily academic and prepared students for universities, the others streamed into different vocational tracks. (The nearest analogy in the United States was the creation, in cities such as Boston, of the older Latin schools, which served the same purpose as the English grammar schools.)

Critics of English class structure have argued that one of the ways to "democratize" the system and to reduce the inequalities generated by a rigid streaming would be to create secondary schools on the model of the American high school, in which all students would get a "comprehensive education." These experiments gathered force in England when Anthony Crosland was Secretary of State for Education, and Michael Young one of his principal advisers.

Whether the comprehensive schools have achieved their purposes is one of the most hotly disputed questions in England today. Critics charge that they have become a form of "levelling," in which academic excellence is downgraded. Defenders of the idea point to the fact that most of the comprehensive schools have not been adequately funded from the start, and that resources have been cut even more sharply, particularly in the last five years. But it is still an experiment which any social scientist has to watch.

A more distinctive contribution made by Michael Young was the creation of the Open University, a wide-reaching enterprise wherein systematic instruction is supplied by radio, television and correspondence courses. A full-time core of academics organizes courses, receives material from enrolled students, and guides their work. Given its present budget of £73 million and the 92,000 students enrolled, (67,000 undergraduates, 25,000 continuing education students) it is probably one of the largest educational projects of this kind in the world.

Given the extraordinary number of such initiatives—it is not farfetched to say that Michael Young is probably the most successful "entrepreneur" of social enterprises in the world—one is tempted to continue this inventory of achievements. However, I will mention only two others. One was the creation of the Consumers Association, which now has a turnover of £14.5, the largest of its kind in England, and which publishes *Which*, a guide to consumer products and practices in the society. (The Association has helped to sustain the consumer advisory councils attached to public institutions, such as Heathrow Airport, to present the consumer viewpoint in the development of day-to-day policy.) The second was the creation of the Social Science Research Council as an official government body, and which Michael Young served as the first chairman. Until the creation of that S.S.R.C., there had been no central public source in the U.K. to fund social research and to initiate social investigations. One of the first such groups was the Committee on the Next Thirty Years, which Young founded with Mark Abrams in 1969, to develop social forecasting.

What is most characteristic of Michael Young, however, is his intellectual restlessness and extraordinary energy. Most persons might be content to set up a successful institution, remain at its head, and reap the kudos and benefits from that position. It has been Young's practice, once an institution has been launched, to make sure that it can keep going, and then to move on to other fields through the unique combination of new social research to be translated into new social policies and into new social institutions. One fruit of this singular career was the recognition of these achievements by the Labour government of James Callaghan, which in 1977 named him a life peer. He is now Lord Young of Dartington.

Michael Young was born in August, 1915, in Manchester, England, of an Australian father and an Irish mother. He was educated at Dartington Hall School, a unique progressive school which had been founded by Leonard Elmhirst and his American wife, Dorothy Whitney Straight Elmhirst. Some people have seen Dartington as a kind of forerunner of the counter-culture alternative-schools movement which flourished in the late '60s and early '70s in the United States, but the resemblances are superficial. The animating impulse of Dartington was aesthetic and naturist, and bore closer resemblance to the German youth movement before World War I, the Wandervöget; to the spiritualism of Hermann Hesse; and to the anarchist Ferrer Schools which took occasional root in Europe and the United States. (Interestingly, Bertrand Russell and his then wife, Dora, started such a school in England; its great notoriety arose from the fact that all the children were allowed to romp naked. In a different vein, Dartington was a parallel to schools such as A. S. Neill's Summerhill.) But Leonard Elmhirst was more interested in stressing a union of agricultural and aesthetic pursuits, and the students were taught rustic skills, as well as encouraged to develop imaginative and artistic talents. It may well be that Michael Young's intellectual restlessness as well as his practicality have reflected that environment. In any event, Dartington left its imprint on Young in many ways. He became a trustee of Dartington Hall in 1942, and still holds that position at present. He has also published a book about the Elmhirsts and Dartington Hall (1982), and in homage to that place designated his title as Young of Dartington.

His further education was at Grays Inn in law, and at London University, where he took his Ph.D. in social administration under Richard Titmuss. Social administration in the U.K. embraces both sociology and social work, and it is the cornerstone of much of the research and writing on social policy and social welfare. Young's contemporaries include some of the best-known names in social administration, such as those associated with him in the Institute of Contemporary Studies, as well as such other well-known persons as A. H. Halsey, of Nuffield College, who is Professor of Sociology at Oxford; Peter Townsend, Professor of Sociology at the University of Bristol; and Brian Abel-Smith, Professor of Social Administration at the London School of Economics.

During the war, Young was director of P.E.P. (Political and Economic Planning), the leading such body of the time, and in 1945 he became the secretary and key figure in the research department of the British Labour Party. He was influential in drafting the postwar election program of the Labour Party, and was one of the principal aides of Clement Attlee in helping shape the major welfare-state program which undergirds the U.K. today.

While Young retained an interest in politics and served as an adviser in several Labour governments, particularly to Anthony Crosland—some of that close association is recounted in the extraordinary and moving memoir of Crosland written by his widow, Susan Crosland—he was also tempted by the academic life. In 1961, when Cambridge established, for the first time, a degree program in sociology, Young was named as the first lecturer, to organize and direct the program. But living in the closed world of Cambridge soon palled, and Young resigned, to return to active research and policy activities through the Institute of Community Studies, which has long been his base. Over the years, he has published eight books within the field of social policy.

Young's unique strength lies not only in research and social practice, but in his intimacy with the political process, an intimacy gained by close association with the Labour Party and its several governments. In 1960, Young began to feel that the Labour Party was becoming more and more ineffectual, and would continue to be so, in large measure because of its increasing dependence on the trade-union bureaucracy. He believed that the interest groups and the corporatist character of the unions were inhibiting innovation in British society. In 1960, he drafted a unique proposal for a new "consumer party," which would speak for the broader interests of British society, rather than the enclaved industrialist-and-trade-unionist combination, which emphasized the syndicalist features of British society. It is a prescient document, for what Young was proposing has in fact come into being with the formation of the new Social Democratic Party in Great Britain. Young has been one of the leaders of this new party, and in 1982, to help give it a strong intellectual direction, he created the Tawney Society, as a competitor to the old Fabian Society, which had been the intellectual ginger-group of the Labour Party. The symbolism of the new organization is obvious. It is named for the great intellectual figure of British socialism, R. H. Tawney, and derives its purposes from the two books which defined Tawney's attitude toward the negative and positive features of contemporary life; namely, *The Acquisitive Society* and *Equality*.

I said at the start that Michael Young embodied the spirit of a number of Victorian forebears. It is now time, perhaps, to vindicate my references to William Morris and H. G. Wells. For Michael Young is also a novelist, and the author of one of the most imaginative social-science fictions of the 20th century, *The Rise of the Meritocracy* (1958)—the word itself now part of the common tongue of political reference.

The Rise of the Meritocracy is a utopian fable, an account of English society in the year 2033. It is a picture of a society in which everyone has achieved his place on the basis of merit, rather than by inheritance. Since Britain could no longer afford a ruling class without the necessary technical skills, the principle of merit has become the primary criterion of advancement in school and position in society. Each person acquires his place in the social order on the basis of "I.Q. and effort." By 1990 or thereabouts, all adults with I.Q.s over 125 belonged to the meritocracy.

My references to William Morris and to H. G. Wells are not intended to indicate distinct lineages. (If anything, Michael Young's idea of meritocracy is more a realization of R. H. Tawney's idea of "function" as the just principle to replace the acquisitive society.) However, the mood of Morris is there in the novel's idealization of a just society and the hoped-for gentle temper which the abolition of privilege would bring. (In fact, Morris's *News from Nowhere,* published in 1890, actually seems to anticipate the intentions of Dartington Hall.) The echo of H. G. Wells is more distinct, in that Wells believed in an aristocracy of talent, which he quaintly called the samurai, and who by their superior talents, scientific knowledge, and organization would overcome the social divisions of a brawling society, and create a new harmony—a scenario sketched most elaborately in Wells' *The Shape of Things to Come* (1933).

Young's meritocracy has its own delicious dénouement. Since all men of talent had been given recognition, those below had no excuses for failure, and had only the stigma of rejection. And so, in 2034, the Populists revolted. Yet they could only succeed because of their alliance with "a new class," the high-status women who were the wives of the leading scientists. Relegated to the household because of the need to nurture high-I.Q. children, the activist women demand equality between the sexes and a view of life which would not be determined by "a mathematical measure." The good life that is demanded—but would it emerge?—is one which would emphasize each person's diverse capacity for diversity.

What, then, of this volume of essays? It is, to put it most simply, a Michael Young sampler: a selection of some of his best essays and of chapters from some of his books. They indicate not only the astonishing range of Michael Young but are illustrations of the relationship of social research to social practice, of ideas to policy, and of policy to social planning—planning not dictated by social technologists, but planning responsive to the diverse natures of human society and the efforts to achieve a more rational coordination of the interconnections and interdependencies of these communities.

The reader of these essays will meet a unique man. But, equally important, he or she may also begin to understand the nature of sociology as a practice, and the possibilities of thinking about utopia in a realistic way.

> Daniel Bell
> Henry Ford II Professor
>   of Sociology, Harvard
>   University
> Cambridge, March 1983

PART I
An Approach to Forecasting

1

Forecasting and the Social Sciences

No competent decision–maker would make forecasts (or have them made for him) unless he had to. But he has to, just as anyone has continuously to reconstruct the past and future in their minds in order to do service in a moving present, bearing out the words of T.S. Eliot:

And every moment is a new and shocking
Valuation of all we have been.

This essay, written in 1968 while the author was the founding Chairman of the Social Science Research Council in Britain, suggests how the social sciences could help to avoid some of the pitfalls in the exercise of the 'art of conjecture'.

If there were not so many examples of predictions falsified, and of so few confirmed, one would immediately make the confident assertion that the overall demand for professional forecasters is going to grow steadily for the next thirty years and beyond, with their forecasts increasingly incorporated in budgets and forward programmes, and all being continuously revised in the light of experience. But until much more is known about the pressures and counter–pressures for division of labour in decision–making—particularly when the exercise of foresight is, and when it is not, treated as a specialized function separate from other administrative functions—it would no doubt be wise to be as sceptical about this prediction as about any other.

Even so, some of the reasons for expecting demand in general to increase may still be worth stating with due hesitance. By demand is meant *effective* demand, that is, backed by money to pay professionals. Latent demand has always been intense. All decision–makers at all times must have wanted to know what was going to happen in the future and, more to the point, what the effects of their own decisions would be so that they could ponder the consequences of any alternative courses of action open to them. But the extent to which they have been ready to pay astrologers and other oracles to trench on the indeterminacies of the future has varied from time to time, and place to place, depending upon their views of the usefulness of contemporary prophets either as seers or propagandists.

In modern times latent demand has perhaps become even more marked. This is not necessarily because social change in general has increased. One cannot, it is true, measure it *in general,* but, since one can still make judgments about things that are not measurable, I would say it is quite arguable that social change has in a sense slowed down in Britain as in other industrial countries if the comparison is with the great upheaval when people not armoured against the shocks of change (as modern man in some degree is) moved out of agriculture into industry, out of villages into towns or from the Old to the New World. The sorts of 'forecasts' that were comforting then were the 'almanacs for the Millennium' of which George Eliot spoke. Since that time change in a multitude of particulars, mostly stemming from the advance of science and technology, has become less fitful, more continuous and perhaps more confusing. Another way of talking about what has happened is to say that in pre—industrial society the individual's future (with high mortality and fluctuating harvests) was less predictable both for himself and other individuals than society's future, which remained much the same over a period. In industrial society the situation may have been reversed—with the future for the individual in important respects more predictable than for society. Hence, perhaps, the growing interest in the future of society.

Social change today is more confusing in part because the improvement in communications has multiplied the speed with which new ideas are picked up from all over the world and spread around it. People are not ordinarily affected in their overt behavior by what goes on at the other end of a continent (though they sometimes are), but more of them than ever before at least know about the changes that are happening there. One of the most important developments of all is that it has become accepted that decision—makers, especially in government, have a duty to cope with changes and control them. This they can hardly do unless they make an attempt to foresee them.

This is of course an extremely hazardous undertaking since it is (far more happily than unhappily for mankind) part of the definition of the future that it is unknown. The job becomes more difficult rather than easier (and at the same time a job more necessary to tackle) just because men have gained increasing control of their environment. What happens does in other words depend more than it did upon the conscious decisions of policy–makers, especially the ones who are in and around governments. So if the future is to be charted, guesses have to be made about the decisions that policy–makers will take. This is obviously very risky since decisions depend upon quirk and temperament as well as reason, and even if it were only reason that was at play the task would not be all that much simpler. The difficulties are at any rate so great that no competent decision–maker would make forecasts (or have them made for him) unless he had to. His objective is flexibility. The more that can be done to preserve flexibility, the more is his power of initiative retained and the greater his capacity to adapt to changing circumstances. But forecasts cannot in practice be avoided. Every time an investment is made an implicit or explicit forecast is made about its yield over a term of years to come, and the same goes for practically all other decisions whose consequences will obviously spill out into the future. Recognizing this, the competent administrator is bound to make forecasts (and, preferably, to make his assumptions explicit so that they can be quizzically debated, especially where decisions cannot be reversed) and yet at the same time to arrange that the forecasts shall be continuously or periodically recast in the light of changing circumstances. A budget, whether for a nation or for a company, is the simplest example of a forecast which is a guide to action but one which is adjusted as events alter the assumptions on which it rests.

Latent demand for forecasting is especially great in a democracy. Since much is left to the private decisions of the multitude of individual citizens, governments and other organizations are very much concerned with the nature of those decisions, and can hardly discharge the duties to those citizens which they are obliged to perform unless they do make some forecast about the choices that will be made. In a totalitarian state where far less choice is left to the individual and decisions are to a greater extent political, those who walk the commanding heights can imagine (and with more justification) that they do not need to predict what others are going to do so much as tell them.

Although Stalin could not hide major failures to attain Five–Year–Plan targets (due to setting unrealistic objectives) he could at least conceal the sort of minor mistakes which are liable to get notice in a country like Britain. The latent demand for forecasting is expected to be made manifest on an increasing scale because so many of these mistakes are made and known. This is less paradoxical than it may sound. Wherever it is accepted that governments, and others with power, should to some extent plan—which means everywhere—a mistaken forecast does not so often produce the reaction, 'if we cannot get it right let us not try at all,' (though it does sometimes) as it produces the ever–hopeful opposite, 'let us try again and do it better'. This proposition underlies the argument of this section; seven illustrations from recent British experience are sketched in to show how mistakes and the criticism which they evoke do not necessarily prompt a demand for the abandonment of explicit forecasting.

(a) Economic Plans

The volume of criticism depends for the most part upon how much the mistake matters. The outcome of such a 'commitment to action by the government' as was contained in the British National Plan was bound to invite complaint; it did not, however, lead to any proposal that the whole apparatus for planning should be disbanded. The same murmurs are heard when a single industry goes wrong. In electricity supply, for instance, forecasts were at one time repeatedly belied—the forecast demand was 9.6% too low in 1961/62, 11% too low in 1962/63 and 10% too low in 1963/64. The investment in new generating plants made six years before on the basis of these forecasts was therefore too low and consumers suffered from consequential load–shedding. As a result the economist Chairman of the Electricity Council brought in other economists to improve their forecasting effort. This does not, and cannot, prevent their going wrong when their expectations for the economy in general are not fulfilled. The general economic setback in the last few years could not easily have been foreseen. Nor, presumably, could North Sea gas have been known about in advance.

(b) Birth–rate and Education

Criticism is sometimes directed at the forecasting method itself, or the lack of it. It is easiest to criticize when the course of events seems so obvious (at any rate with the benefit of hindsight) as not to have called for any but the bluntest sort of anticipation. An example is the first post–war bulge in the birth–rate, in 1946 and 1947. The extra children were already born but, at any rate in the planning of higher education, there was a failure to take account of them. There was eventually what the Robbins Report referred to as an 'emergency'. In 1965/66 to 1967/68 'the very large numbers of boys and girls who were born just after the war will reach the age of entry to higher education. Their numbers are so great as to make it certain that those qualified and wanting to enter higher education will far outnumber the places that, on present plans, will be available to them. Institutions will suddenly be faced with pressures almost different in kind from those that they have faced hitherto.' The warning was sounded just in time. Experience has not been all that happier with the second post–war bulge which started in 1955. The Crowther Report proposed that the school–leaving age should be raised to 16 in the period between 1965 and 1969, the valley during which the 15–year–olds from the first post–war bulge would be moving out of the schools before those from the second would have arrived; the proposal was not acted upon.

(c) Age Structure of New Settlements

Somewhat similar mistakes have been repeatedly made about the demand for houses in new settlements. Migrants are usually married couples of child–bearing age—indeed the houses provided have nearly always been built expressly for them. It is obvious enough that many of them already have children who will grow up to marry and need houses, and that more are going to be born. Yet housing authorities have customarily planned only for the first wave, and not for the bulge caused by their descendants. The warning is of long standing. An estate like that at Dagenham was started in the 1920s. Since land had not been left for expansion, the second generation had, though much against the wishes of many of them, to move off again. But the consequences for housing demand of an unbalanced age–structure have been disregarded in most later new towns and housing estates. It is only recently that more sophisticated forecasting has been attempted, and it is only a pity that with such blessings behind it expectations were frustrated and the town in question, at Hook, never built. The report on it not only stated:

> Conclusions from the study of the experience of present new towns are: first, that serious efforts must be made to arrive at a more balanced initial population intake; and secondly, that it is especially necessary to foresee clearly and plan as early as possible for likely developments arising from the nature of the immigrant population.[1]

It also produced a population projection for the first seventy–five years in the life of the town that was not to be.

(d) Manpower Forecasting

Forecasts about the number of people there are going to be in particular occupations, or that are going to be 'needed' in them, are far more difficult to make. Those responsible cannot here be blamed for overlooking the obvious, because nothing is. That has not altogether protected them from criticism. In 1957 the Willink Committee forecast a falling demand for doctors and accordingly recommended that the intake of medical students be reduced. The subsequent shortage, and reliance on immigrant doctors from countries with health needs rather greater than ours, has naturally been blamed on the Committee. Likewise with the 1961 Zuckerman Committee on scientific manpower. Its forecast that 'by 1965 supply and demand of scientific manpower should not be much out of balance and that a surplus may exist after that date' may have helped to produce the swing amongst school–children towards the social sciences and arts and away from science and mathematics. The resulting criticism has prompted efforts to prepare more exacting forecasts—at least as exacting as the predictions in the Robbins Report for the 'demand' for places in higher education or for schoolteachers up to the 1980s.

(e) Cars

Another series of mistakes, about the prospective population of cars, has become flagrantly obvious, and not just to specialists. Since the planners apparently did not expect that car ownership would spread downwards at such speed from one class to another, almost no housing estate or new town has been supplied with enough garages or even enough street–room for parking. Nor were the main roads generously enough planned; the result is that in new towns, whenever the factories empty, traffic jams are caused by cars belonging to workers who were expected to come by bus. At Croydon offices were developed 'because of fine rail transport' only to find that employees do not relish rail; and Croydon is not alone. The lesson is slowly being learned. Vehicles are now expected to multiply at a faster rate than people to travel in them, from a 1964 actual figure of 12 million to 40 million in 2010. In France the expectation is much the same; indeed in all industrial countries it is the same. The resulting dilemma was discussed in the Buchanan Report—how are such numbers of people to exercise the will they have so far evidenced to own and use cars without defeating each other's implicit predictions that there will be road space for each and all of them?

(f) Development Costs

Public authorities have sometimes embarked on new developments on the basis of forecasts of their cost which have turned out wrong. If estimates had been more nearly right, the initial decision might never have been taken. The best–known examples have been in aviation. The Anglo–French Concorde is one. Estimated costs (not at constant prices) have risen as follows:

1962 estimate   £150–£170 million

1964 estimate   £280 million
1966 estimate   £500 million.

Students of military and industrial forecasting in the United States believe that such 'learning curves' about likely costs often have the same configuration. 'In general, intuitive expert forecasting will tend to be over–optimistic for the near future and too pessimistic for the more distant future.'[2] Whenever it is realized that such habits of thought have led to under–estimation (initial over–estimation is very rare) attempts are likely to be made, whether in private industry or in government, to improve methods of forecasting. This should be particularly well worth doing for defence equipment—not only because of the usual under–estimation of costs but because it is only too easy to order the wrong thing. There are both very long lead times for investment—ten years is not unusual—and uniquely rapid rates of obsolescence. The economic return on a good forecast of the international political environment of the 1980s could be enormous. This is not the sort of thing that political scientists in England have much done.

(g) Competitive Predictions

Failure to allow for other people doing the same thing as oneself is rather general. Developers of shopping centres may not bank on other people building competing ones—so much so that some time ago it was estimated that schemes planned for shopping centres in Britain would serve a population of 300 million, and the Government Actuary has not raised his projections to that height. It was perhaps not altogether surprising when so much was being done inside cities that no one came, even by car, to the first major out–of–town shopping centre in Britain, at Nottingham. Manufacturers are liable in the same way to plan on the assumption that their competitors are not going to build a new plant for making nylon or fertilizers or machine tools, although this sort of over–optimism in forecasting is perhaps not a charge that can be generally levelled at British industry so much as can its opposite. But whenever double or multiple counting is obvious, the case for centralizing, or at any rate coordinating, foresight is bound to be pressed, just as are the advantages of having many competitive and perhaps offsetting forecasts (with errors possibly cancelling each other out) when a mistake is made by a single government body.

(h) An Accelerating Demand

Mistakes will not become all that less prevalent; their inevitability is one reason for expecting demand to increase. Another is that any serious forecasting generates further demand for the same thing to be done by others. The process is cumulative.

The planning of new towns provides as good an example as any of the way forecasts interweave. It may start with demographic projection. When the Government Actuary raised an earlier figure, as he did in 1964, and forecast a population for Britain by the year 2000 higher than in 1964 by about 20 million, it stimulated discussion about where all the extra people were to be housed. Projects for new conurbations on Humberside and Severnside were canvassed. At the political level, partly because projections for the regional distribution of population are if anything even more treacherous than for the total population, the decision to consider one site rather than another may be more determined by the desire to minimize immediate political opposition, or maximize political advantage, than by anything else. But once the prospective sites are chosen, those responsible for the detailed prospecting cannot proceed without a bevy of assumptions for periods up to maybe a hundred years ahead.

To start with, even though the initial size of the new settlement is laid down by authorities 'forecasting' at a higher level of generality, the town planners need to come to a great many decisions about the character of the expected population. They need to have estimates for future age–structure and for the division into households of different sizes, and these should preferably be based not just on the Registrar General's figures for the country at large but be specific to the kind of migrant families anticipated. They need to adapt Ministry of Labour projections for the composition of the labour force, and to make new ones which will show what the influence is likely to be on the proportion of married women at work of providing nurseries or of siting new factories nearer or further from homes (that is, either clustered or diffused more widely). They need to anticipate preferences about the same issue, that is whether to concentrate or disperse, as it affects shops, pubs, clinics and, above all, open space. They need to make a guess about the amount of shift–working there will be; the more there is, the less land will be required for factories and car parks around them. They need to anticipate what people's standards for household amenities are going to be fifty years hence. Even though present economic restrictions may force standards which are below today's, let alone tomorrow's, they can still attempt to allow for later improvements to be made both to houses and their environment so that the new towns will not have to be pulled down as out of date before the end of the century.

They can also hardly avoid speculating about still broader questions. Long before the houses springing out of the planners' anticipations of the future have to be replaced there is likely to be more

Forecasting and the Social Sciences 11

'leisure'. But how will it be divided? By adding still more to the time spent not working at either end of life, in education or retirement? By having longer 'sabbatical' periods in mid–life? By longer annual holidays? By longer weekends? By shorter working days? The expected outcome is of obvious relevance. If, for example, people continue to prefer longer weekends and holidays to a shorter working day, and, linked with that, recreation further from the home rather than nearer—for sailing, fishing, camping and the 'driving for pleasure' which is already America's favourite recreation, rather than team games, walks in the park or gardening—it will affect the tolerated density of settlements and almost everything else about them as well. At present it is usually taken as given that people will continue to want more space around their houses. Buchanan in *The South Hampshire Study* proposed that density in the proposed new 'city' should be only 15–20 persons per acre. But this trend may be reversed; there are some signs from the U.S.A. that it is beginning to happen there. People may prefer much more densely populated cities than at present planned for, partly because it will be easier to get out of them to the lower density places where they will take their leisure. The half–country, half–town of the suburbs may gradually disappear. May, may, may! The planner has to decide, and in doing so the more help he can get from specialized forecasters, the better he is pleased. He creates a demand and in some slight degree others respond.

The same sort of reactions are set going by anyone who has to take a long–term decision and thinks there might be some approach which is a little better than hunch, or which will at any rate supplement it. A company like I.C.I. has many different lines of research it might pursue. Each may lead in say twenty years' time to a distinct kind of product. It cannot sensibly choose between them until the saleability of each has been estimated, and this means preparing, or seeking out, elaborate forecasts of the course of consumption behaviour. The General Post Office has to consider the future demand for postal services because it has to settle on the kind of equipment to be installed. It is therefore concerned with almost everything the town planner is interested in. A particular question is whether people will continue to be willing to work unusual hours as postmen, in the early morning and at night. If not, the postal service might change so much that householders would not be able to benefit nearly so much from the privacy of communication which the post gives more easily than electronic communication. A water authority—the newly created Water Resources Board—picks up the forecast made by the General Register Office, and featured in one report, that the population of the South East region might grow by 3,500,000 between

1961 and 1981. On the basis the extra demand for water is estimated. It is evident that the extra population will make the South East even more of a 'water deficiency zone' than it already looks like being. The Board does not stop at 1981. It forecasts demand up to 2001 as well in order to stress that very expensive capital works like atomic desalination plants may by that time be necessary, and that preliminary research is justified now. The forecasters of the Electricity Council need to estimate how future demand for electricity is to be distributed geographically. They do as best they can. They could do better if predictions of regional population were fuller and firmer.

At the other extreme from the social scientists who work directly for decision–makers are the ones who are for the most part forecasters' forecasters. We have already mentioned population projections several times. Because they are basic to a hundred and one other forecasts, there is a rather general demand for them to be made more sophisticated. Something has been done. The Census has been made quinquennial rather than decennial. A little more is being spent on research at the G.R.O. But the pressure is bound to mount, for the importance of the work is obvious. It has been calculated that, as things are, the projections for the end of the century could easily be out by ±10 million. The difference this makes to the cost of investment in road systems, new towns and new services, some of which will be started well in advance, could easily be very large indeed.

The other basic forecast is for total production. It is a good deal more important for many purposes; but far more difficult to prepare with any assurance even than a population projection. Undated forecasts can be made. These are in the form that if and when the Gross National Product rises by 5% or 10% the pattern of consumption will change in such and such a way. Dated estimates are more hazardous. Which does not, and will not, prevent the job being done, and with increasing sophistication.

Another reason for the increase in demand for this skill, as for any other, is that its supply has been growing. Administrators would not have reacted as they have unless social scientists and others had been able to provide useful advice. This they have begun to do.

They cannot, let us be clear, ordinarily even speculate more intelligently than many other people (perhaps less so) about what decisions are going to be taken by individuals. One would not expect a social scientist, unless a psychologist (and perhaps not even then), to be able to guess any more sagely than anyone else what deGaulle or Ho Chi–Minh is going to do next month. Nor would he necessarily be any more spry about particular events. His skill in dealing with 'facts relating to communities which are capable of being expressed by numbers'[3] is what provides him with his framework for prediction.

There is little hope of saying whether a particular Mr. Jones is going to buy a television set in 1970. Something may be said with a little more assurance about what consumers in general may do.

Naturally enough, the usefulness of the counsel depends upon how much is known about the past. It is the sole guide to the future as much for the social scientist as for anyone else, and at root the 'reasoning' employed by each is not so different. Extrapolation in some form is used to begin with by almost everybody, if with varying degrees of finesse. In its crudest guise the supposition is that the future will differ from the present in the same way as the present differs from the past. This simple idea exerts a strong sway over almost all minds. 'The life span of man has become longer; it will become longer still. The number of work hours has decreased; it will decrease yet further. The standard of living has risen; it will rise even more.'[4] Extrapolation *ad absurdum* is also used in the same simple way to show that extrapolation is not justified, or, rather, that decisions must be taken which will stop it coming about.

> Thus world population, and also the available labour force in industrial countries, is doubling every 50 years. The gross national product is doubling every 20 years and so are the number of major scientific discoveries. The whole scientific and engineering establishment, including for instance numbers of graduates, membership of learned societies and scientific publications, is doubling every 15 years. The money spent on applied research is doubling every 7 years, and so also is the demand for electronics and aviation. If all these processes were to continue unchecked we should certainly be heading for catastrophe. Within about 100 years every one of us would be a scientist, the entire national output would be absorbed in research, and we should be spending most of our lives airborne at 40,000 feet.[5]

The social scientist can only be more sophisticated than this if he knows a good deal about the influences which have operated upon the particular trend being extrapolated. Why has the past betrayed the pattern it has if, that is, it has betrayed one at all? There is little hope of finding out without nicely judged disaggregation. The transport planner for a city cannot well estimate how much traffic a new system of roads will be required to carry unless to start with he knows a great deal about past traffic generation of different kinds. The demographer cannot begin to estimate what the birth–rate will be in the future unless he first calculates the number of women of child–bearing age who will survive out of each cohort of women already born; net migration; the proportions of women of child–bearing age who will be married, since this still affects fertility; and, much more treacherous, the numbers of children they will have. The results, with these as with a hundred other projections, hang to a large extent upon the judgment with which this sort of disaggregation is carried out, before the trends for each of the components are estimated. How far disaggregation can go depends, of course, on what data are available.

How much further can the forecaster go? It depends as we have said upon how much more is known. If influences upon (or if not influences upon, associations with) the size of family were known, each of these could perhaps be extrapolated as guides to the general outcome. The more that past and present interrelationships are understood the more discriminate their extension. This is partly why short–term economic forecasts are relatively so refined.

The achievement of economics with the national accounts is to have analysed a certain set of interdependencies in terms of a system of mutually interrelated variables. The basic idea is that of the 'wheel of wealth', or rather 'the circular flow of income'. Production leads to incomes, which lead to expenditure, which leads back to production again. There are therefore separate ways of measuring the Gross Domestic Product which should give the same answer, so that each can be used to check the other. The advantage of such a scheme is that forecasts of each main variable, and all the intermediary variables, can be to some extent made consistent with each other. Thus, where a start is made with output, preliminary estimates can be made for exports, investment, consumption and so forth, giving a first–round output estimate. Such a level of output implies a certain level of incomes. With given tax rates and levels of saving this will show what consumption follows from such incomes. If the two estimates of consumption are not the same, it is necessary to start all over again. The model also means that not all the variables are ones whose value will not be altered by changes in other variables (the exogenous); others (the endogenous) can within limits be derived. Consumption, for instance, is assumed to be very much dependent on the general level of production. But most estimates take account of both types of variable.

The apparatus of thought is there, and so is the need for it. No government now considers that the economic system, however nicely articulated it may be, is self–adjusting. All believe that a touch or more on the brake or accelerator is almost continuously needed in order to secure the best balance between the sometimes contradictory objectives of maximum employment, maximum economic growth, maximum price stability and equilibrium in the balance of payments. But to decide whether brake or accelerator, and how much, always requires that a forecast be made of what will happen if nothing is done. To prepare forecasts most governments employ economists. The methods six of them use—Canada, France, Holland, Sweden, Britain and the United States—have recently been described. They are very similar, which is not perhaps surprising since the theoretical framework is also. There are minor differences, and some more major, like the extent of dependence upon econometric models.

Two issues faced by economists are common to all forecasters. The first is about validation. The best ways to check upon the efficacy of a method is clearly to see whether the prediction it leads to is borne out by events. It is much easier said than done. A forecast of this sort is not like a gamble which can be verified by the event: a horse either wins or loses. The forecast is a 'primary stage' one, that is a forecast of what will happen without policy changes (while a 'secondary stage' forecast is of the results of policy changes), although its purpose is to guide such changes. Usually there are policy changes, whether guided or not by the forecasts. It is comparatively rare for professional forecasters to parallel a primary stage prediction with a series of secondary stage ones about the consequences of a variety of particular policy decisions, though of course administrators have in effect to do this. Whenever there are policy changes, there is no way of knowing whether the forecast would without them have been right or not. Another difficulty is that statistics referring to the past and present are always being revised, so that without going through the whole exercise again and making a whole series of elaborate adjustments the forecast often cannot be put in a form which can be compared explicitly with the outcome. Still, a good deal can be learned from post–mortems and obviously all that can, should be.

The second issue is about publication. The implication of all that has been said so far in this paper is that alternative forecasts should be independently prepared. There is then less danger that they will be treated, just because they have a lot of figures in them, as though they are 'accurate'; and also much more chance that in the course of the debate about methods which is bound to arise, these may be improved, partly because publication obliges the forecaster to state what his methods are. It follows that there should be publication. The practical question is how much. In Britain private forecasts are published in full, notably the ones made by the National Institute of Economic and Social Research, but the government publishes less than in many other countries. In the U.S.A. the President's Council of Economic Advisers, even if it is not exactly generous in what it publishes, does at least provide more than in Britain. The argument is presumably that the 'announcement effect' of an official prediction might be too great—the forecast of a fall in private investment might, for example, bring it about, and in much larger measure than expected in the primary stage forecast. But in other countries where governments publish more, the level of discussion about economic policy is raised and the publication in any case does not take account of action the government will take. It is surely time that the British government adopted a more generous attitude.

Forecasting can be of value to administration—that is why we expect demand to increase. Can it also be to the social sciences? It is a difficult question. Demography apart, there is no long experience on which to draw. The four linked arguments set out below suggest all the same that engagement with forecasting is likely to be fruitful for the social sciences as well.

(1) It is possible, but not easy, for a social scientist to be concerned only with the past, at any rate in his professional capacity. For the more that is known about the past, particularly if it is about change over time, the more readily do questions about the future spring to mind. Every statistical time series has an open end—what is going to happen to it from now on?

But it is not possible for a social scientist to be concerned only with the future, though he may of course be obsessed by it. If he ventures to predict, he knows that his ability to do so convincingly depends upon the data he has about the past and present. To know where we are going, we first have to know where we are and where we have come from. To do his job better he needs more and better data. The 'better' is perhaps even more important than the 'more'. Every forecaster is aware of the deficiencies. Almost all figures, especially about aggregates, stand at the end of a long process of collection and calculation and therefore at the end of a process of possible and actual distortion. Awareness of faults leads to calls for improvement.

All researchers do the same. It is rare for an inquiry of any sort not to refer to others which need to be made. The audience for such pleas is a select one, ordinarily limited to other specialists. When the entreaty comes from the forecaster it is addressed as much to the administrator, whose support is often needed if data are to be improved. The plea has special force in so far as better data will improve the forecasts he needs. Forecasting can make him an ally of social science.

(2) Another inclination favoured by forecasting is for movement across the boundaries of disciplines. This is least evident with short–term forecasting, most wherever it is medium– or long–term. The physical planner wants to know what spatial configuration he should give to a complex of buildings, roads and open spaces. The decision should not be reached, as we have seen, without a wide–ranging inquiry. The demographer has to estimate on the basis of the little

that is known about the motivations for procreation how many children people will choose to have. There is hardly any feature of society, from incomes to education, which may not be relevant. The demographer is dependent on the economist: the economist is dependent upon the demographer. In his forecast for ten years ahead[6] Beckerman needed, before he could arrive at a growth rate for the economy, to make an estimate for net migration, for the population of working age, for the active labour force (which depends, among other things, on how many people the educational system retains and on the number of wives who choose to go to work) and the preference for leisure in various forms as against income. He had too to take up other questions as slippery as they are important—the extent to which optimism or pessimism might govern the expectations that businessmen have about the future.

The old platitude is, in other words, constantly being confronted. Society is a whole. Its parts are interrelated even if the manner is still not understood. Engagement with forecasting is therefore some counterweight to all the other pressures bearing the other way, towards institutional specialization. If one believes these pressures need to be resisted, the conclusion is clear.

The same point has been made before by de Jouvenel. Referring to the moral or social sciences he says:

> I wish to emphasise that the common task of forecasting will cause them to converge again. None of these human disciplines, each fixed on one aspect of human behaviour and relations, can make forecasts in its field without drawing support from the other disciplines. As data are compiled and methods compared, each discipline will undergo an internal transformation arising from the new orientation toward forecasting.[7]

(3) The purpose of science, either natural or social, is explanation, not prediction. But prediction is one of the best means of testing explanation, although not the only one. An explanatory theory about geological sedimentation as it occurred one million years ago, or the evolution of man, or the rise of feudalism may be perfectly satisfactory if it fits the facts about the past, and is only predictive insofar as it implies that anyone in the future who tries to test it by reference to the past will acknowledge its explanatory power.

But many theories are not so limited. Deductions from them can be tested in the future in another sense beyond the one just mentioned—that is, by the theoriser or others proceeding in the future to check whether future events do turn out as deduced or predicted. The social scientist cannot ordinarily manipulate events by means of experiments, but events as they unfold can still be used to test his theories. Wherever theories can be translated into the form of predictions and checked in this way, they should be. The test is an acid one. It is also peculiarly impressive if the prediction comes off sufficiently often for 'accident' to be ruled out or assigned a very low probability. It is so too wherever the outcome is unexpected—that is, not partly or wholly taken for granted by laymen or even colleagues (until they have recovered their composure and profess to have known it all along). If it is particularly impressive to others, so also is it liable to impress the person who succeeds in bringing it off. Students of society should not be deprived of such satisfaction, or at any rate the possibility of it.

Prediction is also essential to many other sorts of power. The natural sciences are useful because they have thrown up so many predictions on which they and other men can lean in order to control the environment. It is the same with the social sciences. They are and will be useful, and in that measure supported, insofar as they add to mankind's span of control. To reduce, or at any rate specify, the margins of error in predictions is one way to advance.

(4) Perhaps most vital of all, forecasting forces us to focus on social change and hence on the main point of weakness in almost all branches of social science. Crude extrapolation is, as we have seen, no good guide. It is only when some regularities can be discerned in the processes of change as they have happened in the past that one may be able to guess a little more confidently.

There are two main, though connected, approaches that can be adopted. One is to scan the fluctuations in any particular variable or set of variables in search of a pattern. The simplest is a cycle, that is a fluctuation upwards and downwards over time which is both regular and recurrent. The relevance for forecasting is obvious. If, oscillating from one limit to another, events did follow an orderly sequence, then once the present position in the cycle were known the succeeding position could be forecast with some rigour. A bevy of 'amplitudes' and 'wavelengths' could be measured and parallels sought with the physical sciences. The trouble is that the fluctuations seldom do dispose themselves in such an orderly way.

Yet they sometimes do. The most strongly marked cycles affecting human society are, of course, biological or due to the rotation of the earth on its own axis and around the sun. The manifestations of these three cycles have naturally changed. The length of the life cycle from birth to death has become more standardized in the industrial countries, partly because digestive cycles have become more regular. Greater proportions of people survive to a full span—with the consequence that people can more safely predict that they will need support from insurance or other sources after their retirement; and of course that they are likely to have a retirement. There have been changes like the long–term fall in the age of menarche by an average of about four months per decade. Though there is here as elsewhere probably an ultimate threshold, the prediction can be made 'that the average menarcheal age will decrease at least to about 12 years 6 months during the next twenty to thirty years'.[8] The effects of seasonal and daily cycles have also changed: there is less dependence on a single harvest, indoor temperatures have become more stabilized as between one season and another, and electric light has made night more like day. But in a thousand ways these fundamental cycles still influence human behaviour and provide the framework within which people make the humdrum predictions, about the time of rising, the period of their holidays or the duration of their earning capacity, which give order to their lives.

Though other fluctuations are less regular they sometimes do take a cyclical form. Business cycles are a stock example. Economists and historians have charted alternations of contraction and expansion in economic activity over long periods. Alvin Hansen, for instance, revealed at least two types of such cycle—this without the longer cycles which some economists have claimed to identify.

> The American experience indicates that the major business cycle has had an average duration of a little over eight years. Thus, from 1795 to 1937 there were seventeen cycles of an average duration of 8.35 years. . . . Since one or two minor peaks regularly occur between the major peaks, it is clear that the minor cycle is something less than half the duration of the major cycle. In the one hundred and thirty year period 1807 to 1937 there were thirty-seven minor cycles with an average duration of 3.51 years.[9]

In the post-Keynes era the amplitude and duration of recognizable cycles has changed. In Britain the amplitude of the business cycle has been mixed up with, and affected by, another sort of cycle, the four– or five–year interval between elections. The efficiency of control has in other words somewhat increased. The social and other sciences have repeatedly been used to free man from the grip of cycles by reducing the unregulated variability of his environment— a proposition which itself can be used for prediction. But, control or not, there is clearly still a tendency for certain series of events to follow each other in sequence, first in an upwards and then in a downwards phase of production.

Another example of a cycle is class imitation. Practically all known societies are stratified, and it is not uncommon for a change in behaviour to spread from one layer to another in sequence. The rule enunciated by Bell is that 'What the few have today, the many will demand tomorrow'.[10] The change is then sometimes abandoned at the top (and succeeded by another) when it has spread so far as to cease to be a mark of distinction. Although most such changes start at the top and work down, the movement may also be the other way round, as it was with men's clothing in the 1950s. The length of the cycle, or rate of diffusion, obviously varies a great deal. With something as fundamental as family size the period may have been long. What is at any rate plausible, if speculative, is that patterns of procreation may have been subject to a double wave, each with an interval of about a century between them, and each set moving at the upper end of the class continuum and spreading slowly down through it. The upper middle classes began to limit the size of their families in the middle of the last century, and other classes followed successively, as with other kinds of domestic technology, by also making use of contraceptives. The first wave has engulfed the 'lower middle class' whose families are currently the smallest of all and has greatly influenced the 'lower classes'. But before the first wave has spent itself, the reduction in family size at the top seems to have reached a limit. The direction has been reversed, or at least had been before the arrival of the pill and the intra–uterine contraceptive device. If there is a new vogue and if it is going to spread downwards (and especially if it does so at a faster pace than the previous one, given the faster speed of communication of ideas) the consequences for the future size of population in general are going to be great. We would have a better idea about probabilities if we knew more about the basic factors—whether economic, social or biological—which influence human fertility, and it is worth trying to increase our understanding even though we accept that the more conception becomes subject to human will and decision, the more unsure predictions are likely to become. It would also help if we knew more about the processes of diffusion of different practices from one class to another. What, for instance, is the mode of interaction between rises in standard of living, putting class B in the same position as class A used to be, and the influence of class A as a model?

There appears to have been a somewhat similar cycle, with a shorter duration, in the demand for education, and others, still shorter, in the downward spread in the demand for many commodities. This happened, for instance, with consumer durables. In 1960 Needleman[11] predicted (and with unusual success) that the rate of increase in the demand for TV sets, refrigerators, vacuum cleaners and washing machines was about to fall. First one class and then another purchased them, until a degree of 'saturation' was reached, so that first–time buying became less frequent and replacement demand relatively more important. 'Taken literally, saturation is the point at which the consumer does not want any more, and this point is never reached. But for a period like a decade it is reasonable to say, for instance, that the majority of households will not want more than one washing machine, and it is easier to guess what this temporary saturation limit might be for durable goods—where there is a big jump from owning one to owning two—than for a commodity like whisky, whose consumption can rise gradually.' An upswing can now be forecast because the appliances bought in the 1950s are going to fall due for replacement; the new boom will be a shadow of the earlier one.

The other, related main approach in the search for pattern is to single out associations between different sequences, whether or not these follow a cyclical form. Attempts have, for instance, been made to do this with fashion, even though no one would yet claim to have deciphered the language of symbols that a style comprises. Laver has, for instance, suggested not only that there have been cycles in aesthetic styles: seventy years for dress, about ninety for interior decoration and even longer for architecture—determined, he thinks, by the time it took for the memory of a previous fashion to be submerged—but also that changes in one sphere regularly preceded another, dress coming first, followed after a lag by interior decoration and architecture.[12] Within each sphere some changes are also held to be the prelude to others—changes in children's clothing preceding adults; women's evening dress, shoes, hats and coiffeurs preceding changes in other forms of dress; and colour trends in furnishings being one year behind colour trends in dress among the pioneer manufacturers and two years amongst the rest. Further study of long and short cycles in fashion, and their connections with each other, as well as with the 'turbulence' of society at different periods, might throw a good deal of light on the dynamics of change.

Another like attempt has been made to relate different time series bearing on the state of the economy. In the U.S.A. the National Bureau of Economic Research has spent more than forty years comparing fluctuations in time series with each other. As a result forecasters have available to them a range of 'leading indicators', that is a series whose turning points frequently come before turning points in other series. The leading indicators sometimes give false signals or oscillate too much to act as guides. But they are still of some value to forecasters, when used along with the other information they have available.

Such attempts point to one path of advance for the social sciences. The task is to relate rates of change to each other. We cannot say that society is, like a biological organism, made up on 'some orderly array of inequalities of growth rates'[13] The array is not so orderly, or at any rate does not apear to be if we go by what has been measured so far. But this does not make it any the less important to investigate the connection between one rate of change and another. The commonest problem of this type that has been posed is about the consequences if a particular rate in an array is growing faster than others. With simple organisms the outcome may be simple to picture. 'The horny plates of the tortoise grow, to begin with, a trifle faster than the bony carapace below, and are consequently wrinkled into folds.' A society is not so easy to visualize. But one knows, of course, that if the growth of any one economic sector (or any kind of growth at all which is competitive with others) continues indefinitely at a rate higher than that of other sectors, that sector will in the end swallow up the whole economy, rather as a cancer might consume a whole body if it did not cause death before. The population of the world cannot go on increasing indefinitely within its finite space. Consequently one is always on the alert for the countervailing forces which may check growth and produce the common S–shaped (or logistic or Verhulst) curve, which has its kinetic analogue in the motion of a pendulum and its legal in the prohibition of the protracted accumulation of compound interest. The social scientist, particularly if his interest is in forecasting, is in other words always on the lookout for limits to trends. In this he is certainly not alone. People will continue to speculate about the dire consequences of allowing the growth of scientists, or the population of cars or people, or the mining of scarce minerals, or the proliferation of communications or the rise in the standard of living,[14] to go on as they have been going. But to do so is only to focus at one extreme that relationship between rates of change which is very much a proper study for the social sciences, and one to which attempts at forecasting direct attention.

This search for patterns in events is far from the be–all and end–all of social science. Social scientists are not 'chartists', or at any rate not only. Once a pattern has been revealed, the next step is to explain it, which means constructing suitable theories to account for the apparent facts. Theory should give rise to predictions, and attempts to produce predictions in an empirical way can give rise to theory, indeed they need to if the predictions are to be soundly based.

We will not get far without bearing in mind a rather fundamental question. On what evidence do people base their expectations about what is to come? Only when we know more about that will we know what reliance to place on statements made by people about the future. No doubt, as I said at the beginning of this paper, sensible men do not forecast unless they have to, and when they have to, they retain flexibility and allow as far as they can for things turning out differently from what they expect.[15] But the more choice there is, and the more the 'decisions' that have to be made, the more often people have to commit themselves to a specific forecast about the consequences which will attend their decisions. Whenever people are making stochastic estimates about the future they could fall within the suggested field of study.

Businessmen are of special interest. How their minds work can be assessed to some extent from the decisions they actually take in different circumstances. But in addition direct inquiry into the psychology as distinct from the logic of probability could be rewarding. We might then know how far Frank Knight's account holds true today, particularly in large businesses employing specialist prophets.

> So when we try to decide what to expect in a certain situation, and how to behave ourselves accordingly, we are likely to do a lot of irrelevant mental rambling, and then first thing we know we find that we have made up our minds, and our course of action is settled . . . there is doubtless some analysis of a crude type involved, but in the main it seems that we infer largely from our experience of the past as a whole, somewhat in the same way as we deal with intrinsically simple (analysable) problems like estimating distances, weights, etc., when measuring instruments are not to hand.[16]

Knight comes very close here to the view that Bartlett took about memory. The past, Bartlett said, is seldom isolated from the present in people's minds, but used in order to fill out an 'attitude towards a whole active mass of unorganised past reactions or experience'. According to such a view, future, along with past, merge into a continuous present, rather than being nicely separated in the way the professional forecaster divides up time. Both past and future are being continuously reconstructed in the mind in order to do service in a moving present.[17] It was much the same with Eliot:

> 'There is, it seems to us,
> At best, only a limited value
> In the knowledge derived from experience,
> The knowledge imposes a pattern, and falsifies,
> For the pattern is new in every moment
> And every moment is a new and shocking
> Valuation of all we have been.'

Professional forecasters will be in the dark anyway, but to take up again a point referred to several times, they could be a little less so, in one particular, if they knew more about the influence of their predictions upon the behaviour they were trying to predict. How much do they have? Sometimes a forecast is deliberately intended to be self–fulfilling. The last British National Plan was an instance. As Beckerman pointed out, 'In an economy that has been growing slowly, it is difficult to expect acceleration if future growth expectations are simply extrapolations of the past'; and, in the absence of evidence, that is what expectations are supposed to be. The Plan therefore committed itself to a higher growth rate than had been achieved in the past, and went some way towards committing businessmen by asking them what their investment would be on the assumption that this higher rate were attained. If it were not for the balance of payments, the Plan might have been judged highly persuasive. Usually, though, the 'announcement effect' is not sought after. The psephologists who have on the whole had such success in forecasting election results would not welcome it if the voters' behaviour (or more plausibly, the politicians') were influenced by publication. It has been the same with the 11+ test for the ability of schoolchildren. The Spens Report, leaning on the support of knowledge in the social sciences as it then was, said that it was 'possible at a very early age to predict with some degree of accuracy the ultimate level of a child's intellectual powers'.[18] The element of self–fulfilling prophecy in the 11+—the tendency for children who are told they are expected to do well to conform to the expectation—was not thought to be a merit in the prediction. But whether welcomed or not, the influence of predictions on the behaviour of those whose future behaviour is being forecast is clearly one subject well deserving of inquiry.

Of particular interest is the influence of forecasts about cyclical or other fluctuations upon their amplitude. One purpose of short–term economic forecasting is presumably to damp down the oscillations that would otherwise occur. Speculation in a well–organized commodity or share market is supposed to do this. If speculators expect the price to fall they will sell more now and have to buy more later, thus raising the price above what it would otherwise be; and vice versa. One of the functions of a manpower forecaster, say, is to play the same role as such speculators. The entrance of people into engineering, for example, may lag well behind a turnaround in the incomes of engineers so that incomes rise even more than they would otherwise do; medium–term projections of incomes may help to produce a quicker reaction and a smoother curve. But sometimes professional predictions may not offset the laymen's (which sometimes produce such violent swings as the pig cycle) but aggravate them.

REFERENCES

1. *The Planning of a New Town*, London County Council, 1961
2. E. Jantsch, 'Technological forecasting in perspective' O.E.C.D., Paris, 1966
3. The concern suggested in 1833 for the Statistical Section of the British Association for the Advancement of Science
4. De Jouvenel, *The Art of Conjecture*, Weidenfeld & Nicholson, 1967
5. R. Cockburn, 'Science, defence and society', Trueman Wood Memorial Lecture, Royal Society of Arts, 1967
6. W. Beckerman et al., *The British Economy in 1975*, Cambridge University Press, 1965
7. De Jouvenel.
8. Knowledge about critical periods in the development of children as in animals would make prediction easier, and also guide action to avert the prediction. It appears, for example, that the facility for discriminating speech sounds declines after early childhood, and that babies who do not receive warmth and affection are liable to develop into pathological adults. Psychoanalysts have detected a range of 'repetition compulsions', that is, the repeated, predictable and irrational display by adults of basically the same stock reactions to situations that in some crucial ways resemble similar ones in childhood. *Children and their Primary Schools* (Plowden Report), Central Advisory Council for Education—England, Her Majesty's Stationery Office, 1967
9. A. H. Hansen, *Fiscal Policies and Business Cycles,* Norton, 1941. A discussion of the longer cycles discerned by Schumpeter, Kondratieff and others was contained in B. Thomas, 'The rhythm of growth in the Atlantic economy', *Money, Growth and Methodology,* ed. H. Hegeland, Lund, Sweden, 1961
10. D. Bell, 'The year 2000—the trajectory of an idea', in *Towards the Year 2000: Work in Progress,* Daedalus, 1967, American Academy of Arts and Sciences
11. L. Needleman, 'The demand for domestic appliances', *National Institute Economic Review,* November, 1960
12. J. Laver, *Taste and Fashion,* Harrap, 1945 and *Style in Costume,* Oxford University Press, 1949
13. P. B. Medawar, 'D'Arcy Thompson and Growth and Form', *The Art of the Soluble,* Methuen, 1967
14. See Boulding, for example. 'The evolutionary process, throughout its whole vast span of time, has been characterised by short periods of very rapid change followed by rather long periods of slow change, and one sees this also in human history. . . . To me, the real significance of this transition is that it represents a change from an "open society" with an "input" of

material from mines and ores and fossil fuels, and with pollutable reservoirs as recipients of "outputs"—to a closed society in the material sense, in which there are no longer any mines or pollutable reservoirs, and in which, therefore, all materials have to be recycled. This is what I have called the "space ship earth". In a space ship, clearly there are no mines and no sewers. Everything has to be recycled; and man has to find a place in the middle of this cycle.' K. E. Boulding, 'Is scarcity dead?', *Public Interest*, No. 5, Fall, 1966

15. It would be of interest to know how far different 'gambling' strategies are adopted by people of different personality and social groups. Cohn has suggested that it has been the uprooted who most fervently accept millennial predictions. N. Cohn, *The Pursuit of the Millennium*, Secker and Warburg, 1957

16. F. H. Knight, *Risk, Uncertainty and Profit*, Hart, Schaffner and Marx, 1921

17. F. C. Bartlett, *Remembering*, Cambridge University Press, 1952

18. Consultative Committee on Secondary Education (Spens Report), His Majesty's Stationery Office, 1938

2

Cycles in Social Behaviour

The last essay pinned some faith on cycles, being fluctuations which are both regular and recurrent. Ride a cycle and there is as good a chance of making a reputable forecast as any social scientist will usually ever have. The terminology and a bit more of the subject is explored in this paper, written jointly with Professor John Ziman, a physicist.

Sequences that are repeated again and again are as obvious in the social behaviour of human beings as in the physiological behaviour of organisms. They have been studied extensively in the one case and not the other. One generation of biologists has followed another in noticing the phasing of the rhythms of life to such astronomical influences as the rotation of the Earth, the orbit of the Moon about the Earth, and the orbit of the Earth about the Sun. They have repeatedly produced and pondered over descriptions like that by Brown of fiddler crabs in their intertidal habitat. 'The crabs spend much of their lives in burrows that they dig for themselves, but as each tide ebbs and exposes the burrow entrances the crabs come milling out to feed. While the times of foraging for food vary rhythmically with the tides the crab's skin colour varies with time of day. As the day dawns the crabs darken and as the Sun sets they become pale.'[1]

Many cyclic phenomena in society are also related to astronomical events, and some of them have been for long stretches of time. In Britain there are, for example, three principal ways of reckoning the beginning of 'a year' and three sets of associated cycles. There is first of all the official financial year. The year in ancient Rome began in March (hence September, October and so on). March 25 was for a long time the beginning of the financial year; it was at the point in what had once been the first month which more or less coincided with the vernal equinox, which is as good an astronomical peg for the new year as the winter solstice. The start of the financial year was shifted forward into April when England finally accepted the Gregorian Calendar in 1752 and had to subtract eleven days from the year in order to fall in line with Europe. Hence the Chancellor of the Exchequer usually comes out to introduce his Budget on a Tuesday (which is the traditional day, just as Thursday is the traditional day for altering the bank rate) in April soon after the closing of the previous financial year.

Second, there is the civil or calendar year, which is also of Roman origin. One of Julius Caesar's predecessors added two more months, January and February, to the year, and Caesar himself confirmed that the calendar year should begin on January 1, and incidentally gave his name to the month which had until then been called Quintilis. The guidance came as much from the Moon as the Sun. 'Caesar was swayed by the fact that the date happened to be the day of the occurrence of the new Moon following the winter solstice of the preceding year.'[2] It was particularly appropriate because January took its name from the two–faced Roman god, Janus, who presided over the beginnings of all enterprises and events and who was there to be seen in sculpted form over the entrances to Roman houses.

And third, there is the academic year. Its origins are obscure. The standard explanation is that no mediaeval student could take up residence until he had helped to gather in a harvest which had to wait on the Sun. Whatever its origin, the academic year is clearly of great import, affecting as it does not just the round of events in colleges and schools but also the timing of the peak holiday period for parents and others in the summer.

Without behavioural sequences strictly geared to years like these, to months and to days, and also to the week as a time interval without an astronomical tie; and without hundreds of others which are not regulated by the common calendar of society, the social order could scarcely exist. But sociologists have not yet imitated the biologists; they have hardly begun to describe, let alone to analyse, these sequential chains of recurrent behaviour which are sufficiently similar (in spite of the element of uniqueness about the form which the behaviour takes on each occasion) to justify talking about recurrences. In this respect, a great deal more is known about fiddler crabs than about chancellors of the exchequer or vice–chancellors of universities.

The omission should surely be remedied. Time is no less important as a coordinate for social than it is for biological or physical phenomena. Though the sense of duration of time varies from person to person and minute to minute, it is almost universally agreed that time does 'pass' and that it is more precisely measurable than most of the other variables which have engaged the attention of sociologists. Systematic study of social behaviour in terms of time may bring to light various patterns which would merit investigation.

If this hope is to be realized, attention must be given to terminology. Without a set of terms it is difficult to discuss the subject at all, let alone to decide what may be worth observation or measurement. Classical physics and applied mathematics provide a very extensive set of such terms, some of which have been borrowed and found useful in biology.[3] Our question is whether this kind of language could also serve in sociology. In an attempt to answer this question, we suggest a terminological scheme, with examples of specific usages in various social contexts which indicate the kind of general approach to the subject that might be fruitful. The words in italics are those for which definitions are suggested. The meaning of the terms suggested is also illustrated in the attached diagrams.

We first consider three different mathematical characterizations of the time coordinate, moving from the less to the more sophisticated, which correspond in a very general way to historical developments in conceptions of time as an objectively measurable quantity. (There is an excellent review of historical changes in the concept of time in ref. 4, which consists of papers delivered at the first conference of the International Society for the Study of Time.) We then consider some temporal patterns of behaviour at three different levels of social organization. In each case the more complex includes within itself the less complex concept, while at the same time adding to it. We shall be particularly concerned with patterns that eventually repeat themselves in time, although the sociology of time need not be confined to such regularities.

At its most fundamental, time implies little more than the notions of 'before' and 'after'—of one event following another irreversibly. Whether or not these events are linked causally, the chain may only be traversed in one direction. Consciousness implies memory, and with memory previous successions of events may be reviewed in retrospect, and the sequence of future events to some extent anticipated. This way of representing time we call *episodic* (Fig. 1a); mathematically speaking, time is merely the relation defining the ordering of a set of discrete *episodes* or *events*.

An individual may, for example, remember a series of climatic events, such as a drought, a cyclone, or a freeze–up; a series of births, marriages and deaths in the Royal House (such as 'In the year that King Uzziah died . . .'); or a series of events in his own personal life. Although the events in each series may follow one another in correct chronological order, the important events are likely to be drawn out,

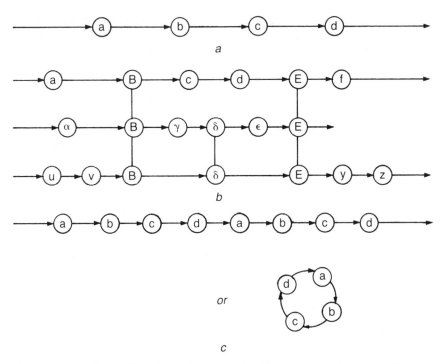

Figure 1. *a,* Episodic time; *b,* an episodic time scale; *c,* cyclic sequences.

and the less important compressed or eliminated (as in compiling a history of almost anything), almost without respect to their actual duration. Episodic time thus has no quantitative measure, and can seem to be purely subjective.

Nevertheless, by correlating such individual sequences, an objective episodic time scale can be established for a whole society. One of the methods used to obtain information for census purposes about the age distribution in societies in which most people do not know how old they are is to ask them to recall what was happening in their own lives at various points of time simultaneous with events that can be dated from more general historical evidence.[5] By this device, the census takers are trying to quantify the general episodic time scale (Fig. 1*b*) which serves most people in the society well enough. Similarly, the cultural sequences of the archaeologist based on potsherds excavated from successive levels at various sites have only recently been dated absolutely by the radio carbon technique.

It is only a step from consciousness that events occur in sequence to noticing that many such sequences repeat themselves. It is difficult now to disentangle a purely episodic view of time from this cyclic characteristic, a *cycle* being defined as a sequence which is repeated (Fig. 1c). The notion that *all* time sequences are essentially cyclic is widely held. This attitude seems to be deeply entrenched in primitive societies, where no doubt the cycle of the seasons matters more than in modern societies: this may be one of the reasons for the neglect of the whole subject by most social scientists in such societies; Goody[6] and Leach being two of the exceptions. Leach has described the primitive attitude to time. 'Time can be regarded as a recurring cycle. Certain events repeat themselves in definite sequence. This sequence is a continuity without beginning or end, and thus without any clear distinction between past and present. The most important time–sequences are seasonal activities and the passage of human life. Both these cycles are conceived as of the same kind.'[7] Eliade, speaking more of ancient societies, says that archaic man 'acknowledges no act which has not been previously posited and lived by someone else, some other being who was not a man. What he does has been done before. His life is the ceaseless repetition of gestures initiated by others.'[8]

The quotation from Leach raises a question about the 'passage of human life'. In ordinary language we refer to a 'life cycle': is this usage consistent with our present definition? A particular human life, as it progresses through various stages in its biological, psychological and social dimensions, is certainly a sequence of events (Fig. 2a). But these events are unique to the person who lives them. The individual cannot repeat his whole life pattern, from birth to death,

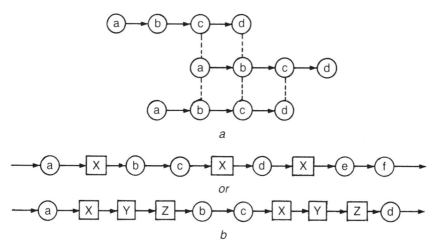

Figure 2. *a*, Life cycles; *b*, recurrences.

in the same way, say, that he repeats himself in one respect by going to sleep on each ordinary night. Nevertheless, it is useful to retain the word 'cycle' in this context, without an attendant adjective to distinguish a sequence of behaviour repeated by the *same* individual from an identical sequence repeated by *another* individual. The common usage of the term 'life cycle' is justified if one does not think of it from the point of view of an individual as he sees himself, but rather as he sees others (including himself) as a member of a society or species. Everyone is in some degree repeating the sequences of behaviour of other people who have preceded him, doing the same kinds of things at the same age, always doing what others have done before. This is a characteristic of biological systems with almost no analogy in the world of physics.

It is convenient, on the other hand, to distinguish a relatively complete cycle, repeating as a closed loop, from a mere *recurrence* (Fig. 2*b*), or repetition of some characteristic type of event in otherwise different circumstances. An eclipse, or the return of a comet, a cyclic phenomenon astronomically, is seen by most men as a historically recurrent event, scarcely to be distinguished in principle from the occasional eruptions of a volcano or one of the military campaigns that has ravaged Flanders over the centuries. It is true that the recurrence of a particular event may imply its repetition in a sequence containing several other events with which it is correlated or causally connected. Each eruption, for example, would be followed by the flight of the population, the sporadic return of refugees, the rebuilding of houses, the restocking of farms and the eventual return to normal life. Such sequences of social or psychological behaviour are obviously of great interest as patterns in time, but we should prefer not to use such phrases as 'the cycle of resettlement' to describe them. We want to say 'History repeats itself, but is not cyclic.'

At the next level of sophistication, time becomes a numerical variable. The interval between notable episodes, such as the death of two successive kings, is given a measure by counting regular astronomical events like the passing of the seasons, or full Moons, or days (Fig. 3*a*). This interpolation is done with greater or less accuracy in all but the most primitive societies, so that any event or sequence of events can be assigned an epoch or a duration. Less precise schemes of counting have gradually given way to more precise, as the years have become ordered into a series starting from zero, say, at the supposed foundation of Rome, or at the birth of Christ, as the days are assigned their places in an annual calendar, and as each day is divided into hours, minutes, seconds, milliseconds, microseconds,

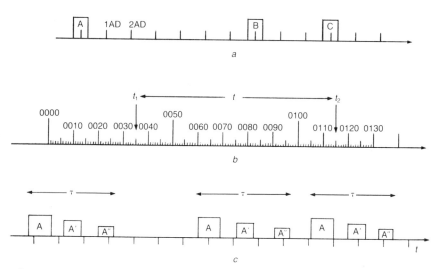

Figure 3. *a*, Measured time; *b*, clock time; *c*, a relaxation time.

nanoseconds, by successive refinements of the clock—a device which Mumford[9] saw outranking the steam engine as the key machine of the modern industrial age.

Clock time thus becomes, by successive subdivision, a continuous variable, analogous to the length coordinate along a line in space (Fig. 3*b*). It is the one dimension of material existence that is both universal and quantified. Ignoring the subtleties of relativity theory, which are irrelevant to human activities on the earthly scale, we can properly assign to any event an exact number—at 27 seconds past 18 minutes past 7 p.m. on the 31st day of October in the year 1970 Clare Ziman began her piano practice, and at 10 seconds past 10 minutes past 8 p.m. on the same day Sophie Young began hers—from which can be computed the exact duration of any particular sequence in which we are interested—a lesson, a task, a journey, a marriage, or a life.

It is not our present purpose to discuss the physics or metaphysics of the measurement of time. The important fact is that human behaviour, individual or social, is to some extent governed by biophysical processes which have their characteristic rates on the clock time scale, and cannot therefore be described completely in the language of episodic time. Many phenomena, for example, may be assigned their typical *relaxation times*—the average time for an effect to fade away (Fig. 3*c*). Thus, a fit of temper may have a relaxation time of a few minutes, the satiation of hunger by a meal lasts for a few hours, a week is said to be a long time in politics, while great political revolutions have consequences over a century or more. Notice that these statements imply recurrences of similar events for comparison, but carry no implications of periodicity.

Another typical time measurement would be the *mean free time* between recurrences of some characteristic event—for example, between changes of job or between strikes (Fig. 4a). This may be, in itself, a meaningful psychologial or social parameter—at one factory, say, the mean free time between strikes might be twice that at another—without being directly related to a particular relaxation effect or referring to a strictly cyclic phenomenon.

The adaptation of our definition of cyclic behaviour to clock time is not unambiguous. It is necessary to introduce a term such as *periodic* to refer to any event or sequence of events that recurs at regular intervals—typically, Christmas, that comes but once a year, or breakfast, that recurs within a *period* of 24 hours ± 10 minutes in any well–ordered household (Fig. 4b). The calendar of the saints days, or the daily round of domestic life, can then be called a *periodic cycle*. In any case it will be as well to follow the convention of physics and regard the *frequency* as the reciprocal of the period, that is, the number of recurrences of a periodic event or cycle in a longer interval—for example, Quarter Days occur with a frequency of four per year.

In considering a genuine periodic cycle, it is natural to close up

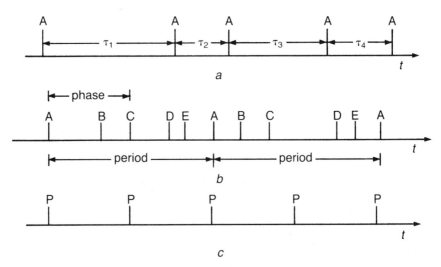

Figure 4. *a*, Mean free time: $\bar{\tau} = \frac{1}{n}(\tau_1 + \tau_2 + \ldots \tau_a)$; *b*, a periodic cycle; *c*, a periodic recurrence, or pulsation.

the ends of the 'circle', and to view time as flowing continuously from one event to the next without a break. Where this is done it becomes necessary to adopt a convention for marking a beginning to each repeated period by reference to one or other of the events in the sequence. Calendar years, for example, begin at 0001 h on January 1. The relative position in time of some other event in the cycle would then be the *phase* of that other event—for example, the various phases in the cycle of the Moon.

These definitions obviously merge into one another. The intervals between recurrences of some sudden, sharp event may become so nearly equal that we should cease to think in terms of mean free times and begin to talk of periods. In such cases, we could perhaps regard the time behaviour as *pulsating*—the nearly regular repetition of a well–defined event in the manner of the pressure of the blood in the body (Fig. 4c). On the other hand, we should still recognize some cycles as essentially periodic, even when they do not repeat at precisely equal intervals. On a camping holiday, for example, meal times tend to wander, while still preserving the essential pattern of the domestic cycle dominated by work and school: in the absence of strong clock cues, the basic relaxation mechanism of our digestive system would still encourage us to keep the cycle fairly regular.

The next stage in precision is to measure not only time in numbers but also the 'events' which are related in time, such as changes in the price of food, or the level of wages, the numbers of unemployed, or the number of members of parliament commanded by a particular party (Fig. 5a). One can then observe whether some quantity depends on time. If such a number varies irregularly with time we should call it a *fluctuating* function of time; if it varies regularly then it can properly be termed *oscillating* (Fig. 5b). A cyclic movement of a measurable quantity up and down would thus be defined as an *oscillation*. Such cycles are, of course, of paramount importance in physics.

Within the social sciences, this approach is less typical of sociology than of economics, where money is a common measure of the value or price of different goods and services, which would be almost as precise in its way as the measure of time itself if it were not for continuous changes in price. Trade cycles or stock exchange cycles are patterns that can emerge from such a scrutiny. The behaviour with which sociology is chiefly concerned—demography apart—does not lend itself so readily to such an approach. But this does not mean, of course, that cycles, pulsations, and other time–dependent phenomena cannot be detected. One can decide on the basis of observation whether a series of events that precede, or follow, say, the annual budget, are sufficiently similar over a period of years to justify

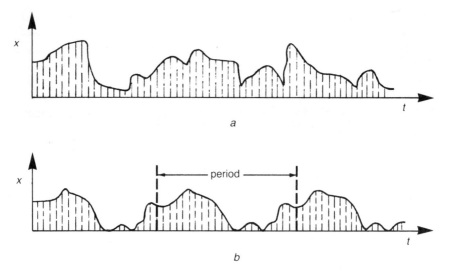

Figure 5. *a*, A fluctuating function of time; *b*, an oscillating function of time.

speaking of cyclic phenomena, even though one cannot represent these observations as mathematical functions. The behaviour of civil servants or government ministers is amenable to observation, description, and comparison, even though only the time dimension can be expressed in numerical terms. If there is any novelty in our present approach, it is in stressing the significance of this sort of analysis, which makes full use of the quantitative character of time itself without attempting to bend the time–dependent observables to a numerical representation.

So far we have been discussing time–dependent phenomena at three levels of formal mathematical sophistication. We now consider cyclic behaviour at three different levels of social organization in order of increasing complexity. The three levels are those of the individual, of the small group, and of a society as a whole. Since people operate at all levels simultaneously, the subdivision is no more than a convenient simplification for our present purposes.

Cycles of personal behaviour or *routines* (which, we suggest, could be used as an alternative word for cycles that appertain to the behaviour of an individual), are partly governed by endogenous biological mechanisms which need to be sustained by food and sleep at more or less regular intervals. These endogenous cycles are, in their turn, geared fairly tightly to exogenous astronomical cycles. Such *circadian* cycles—to use the biological term for cycles with a period of about 24 hours—provide the framework within which the individual can establish his own routines for times of rising, eating his meals, travelling to and from work, working, shopping, watching television, gardening, or whatever it may be. The degree to which people arrange their lives in a cyclical pattern varies from person to person; the amount and correlates of variation is one of the topics which require investigation. But clearly almost everyone does adopt a series of routines, partly to save himself from having to decide afresh each day how to organize his time and partly in the interest of cooperation with others. People can become so conditioned to their routines that these become habits which are hard, indeed uncomfortable, to break. A feature of modern society, in which astronomical events are not all-important, is that the individual may become so conscious of clock time that he even regulates his private behaviour to strict periodicity—always going to bed at 11:15 p.m., say, whether he is sleepy or not.

By his existence in society, the individual is geared to many more routines than the circadian. There are weekly cycles—each Monday may have its peculiarities which make it different from Tuesday, and Saturday in any one week may be much more like Saturday in another than it is like any Friday. Even in an industrial society, there may be monthly cycles, related, for example, to the dates on which salaries (as distinct from wages) are paid and mortgage interest remitted; and there are many annual cycles tied in with the seasons and the influences they exert over work and leisure, as well as all the changes implicit in the life cycle itself. For most people there are also many other more idiosyncratic cycles, to do with their work or their family life, which are not so closely related to the standard periodicities of the calendar.

The point we are making is that at any given moment a person is locked into several different cycles with different periods, and his behaviour from moment to moment is the result of influences drawn from all the different cycles, in a manner reminiscent of Fourier's theorem in physics. On a particular Friday afternoon in November 1970, a senior civil servant at the Treasury, who has just had his monthly salary paid into his bank, may be hurrying to finish the work he is doing on some departmental estimates, which are at a particular position in the pipeline leading to the annual budget, so that he can get away before the rush hour to drive down to the country to spend the half-term weekend with his daughter. Perhaps he does not mind 'getting behind' as much as he used to because he is not so far from retirement and has got as high in the civil service hierarchy as he is ever likely to. A constant problem for him, as for anyone else with some freedom in the allocation of his time, is to decide the relative priorities of action in cycles that do not neatly mesh—particularly the priority of long–period cycles over shorter ones. This means, of course, that Fourier's theorem is not strictly applicable, since the various cycles are not additive in any arithmetical sense; the 'behavioural resultant' often reflects the strongest influence at the moment and is not an averaged response to them all.

The final relationship of all the cycles, with their different periods, all operating simultaneously, we call a *rhythm*. Although this is a musical term, without significance in physics, it is much used in biology, and carries many suggestive analogies. The aesthetic appeal of musical rhythm is not necessarily the same as the satisfaction to be obtained from a complex pattern of routines with periods of hours, days or years. The psychology of this whole subject, including attitudes to 'punctuality', is of at least as much interest as its sociology. In this context the word, rhythm, is intended to be value–neutral, without specially favourable connotations.

The example of the civil servant illustrates the interaction of individuals within a group as well as the interactions between the various cycles in a personal routine. Membership of a small group, just as much as of a large one, means that individual cycles need to be *synchronized* or *harmonized* (Fig. 6)—brought into agreement, changed in phase or period, so that significant events may always occur simultaneously. In other words, the *periods* of the routines of the two individuals must be made equal, or else must stand in some simple integral ('harmonic') ratio.

This can be achieved in various ways, of which the commonest is to subordinate a *dependent* cycle to a *dominant* one (the latter controlling the former). Typically, this occurs by the *entrainment* of a cycle of variable period to the more precise period of the dominant routine. Thus, a schoolchild may be required to get up to have his breakfast with his father, and to take about as long over it, the whole being determined by the father's need to catch a particular bus to work. The work cycle entrains the getting up cycle of the father, which does the same, in turn, for that of the child. With very young children the relationship is inverted; their digestive cycles entrain the domestic cycles of the parents. Dominance is, however, seldom complete. Each individual's routine acts back on and changes the timing of the others, just as two physical pendulums change each other's frequency when coupled together.

As individuals and small groups are built into more complex social organizations, their cyclic behaviour patterns combine into a *system*— an assembly of many interacting cycles—which has its own charac-

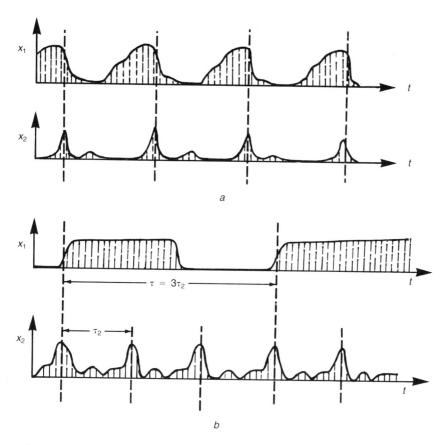

Figure 6. *a*, Synchronized cycles; *b*, harmonized cycles.

teristic time–like properties. In such a system, multiple synchronization, so as to keep a particular phase of one cycle strictly in step with a particular phase of another, becomes essential (Fig. 7).

A school is an example of a relatively simple system. The caretaker, who had to clean the school the evening before, has to open the school gates at 8:15 a.m. The children arrive between 8:30 and 9 (some brought by parents who have gone through standard and carefully timed sequences in order to be punctual at school). The head teacher arrives at 8:40, the teachers from 8:45 on, the van from the school meals service at 11:30 with the containers of dinners cooked the night before, the cook at 11:30, the dinner–ladies from 11:45. Each teacher and each batch of children have to make their appear-

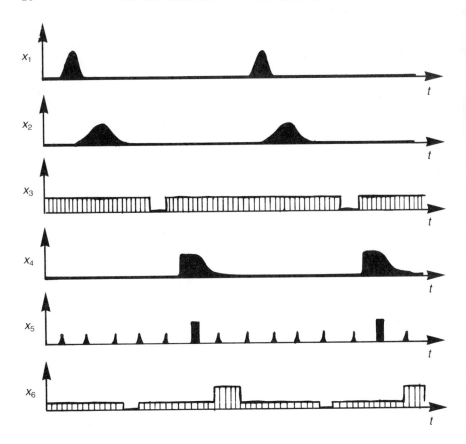

Figure 7. A system of cycles.

ances in the right points in space at the right points in time and to scatter and re-assemble in the right conjunctions or the whole organization will cease to hold together. We are regarding the interconnected cycles as synchronized although they do not necessarily start and end at the same time or have the same period. The caretaker has to begin work before the teachers and the teachers may have to continue with their marking and preparation after the children have left the premises. The engagement of one cycle after another into the assembly in the correct order at the correct time is vital to the coherence of the whole. *Antecedent* cycles (which precede others in their starting times) can be distinguished from *postcedent* cycles.

A school is, as we said, an example of a relatively simple system. It belongs to the larger system of the local education authority which lays down rules for the starting and finishing times of days, weeks and terms; the dates when new staff have to be advertised for, interviewed and take up their appointments; the dates by which requests for additional capital expenditure have to be put up to the office ready for particular meetings, first of the education committee, then of the finance committee, then of the whole council; and hundreds of other matters besides. The operations of the authority are as much timetabled as the school. As the school has to fit into the timetable of the authority, so does the authority have to fit into the timetable of the Department of Education and Science as far as approvals for capital expenditure are concerned. The DES in its turn is bound by the general timetables of the government, including, above all, those of the chancellor of the exchequer and his advisers. Chinese boxes are not the right analogy, for all the subsystems which go to make up, say, the educational system, which goes to make up the society, are composed of moving parts, the cycles to which we have been drawing attention in this paper. An orchestra or a corps de ballet is a more apt analogy, with Greenwich Mean Time and the calendar as the conductor's beats.

We are not claiming that the individual, unless perhaps he is employed in a mass production factory, ordinarily sees his life in the way we have presented it; he might find it 'boring' if he did. He observes rather the deviations from the rule, the differences which, in the nature of time, make each 'repetition' unique. The message is evidently carried (as in radio) by the *modulation*, or variations from regularity, in the cycles of his perennial existence. But whether they see it in this light or not, people are caught up in innumerable, interlocking cycles at the level of the individual, the small group and the system. In the background is the music of the spheres: the astronomical cycles partially entrain the biological cycles and the biological forces entrain or stimulate individual routines. Society builds on this propensity. Although social behaviour, outside a range of occupations to do with the land and the sea, is not directly subject to astronomical forces, it is convenient to use them symbolically to orchestrate the ensemble, even in an industrial society. The actors learn by repetition to become more proficient in their parts. The regularity of cycles that are taken for granted allows a collective endeavour which would be impossible if the whole interlocking series of systems had to be devised deliberately in every particular instead of only in some.

This, then, is the picture—but only in the most general outline, It will become more differentiated and exact only as study proceeds, not only of the various sorts of cycles in behaviour, of the rituals which are embodied in them, of the information feedback cycles which help to maintain synchronization, and of the psychological and biological mechanisms underlying the social routines, but also of the variations in the extent to which behaviour is cyclical at all, between one person and another, one group and another, one class and another and one institution and another. Nor should non–cyclical behaviour patterns be neglected, as typified by relaxation phenomena at the individual and social level. The social sciences will have to take a look at their stock in trade—human behaviour—in its time dimension.

REFERENCES

1. Brown, F. A., in *The Biological Clock*, (edit. by Brown, F. A., Hastings, J. D., and Palmer, J. D.), 16 Academic Press, New York and London, 1970

2. Black, F. A., *The Calendar and its Reform*, Gall and Inglis, London and Edinburgh, 1933

3. Aschoff, J., *Circadian Clocks*, North-Holland, Amsterdam, 1965

4. Whitrow, G. J., in *Studium Generale*, 23, 498 (1970).

5. Quaim, B., *Fiji Village*, 142 (Chicago, 1948), quoted by Scott, C., and Sabagh, G., *Population Studies*, (March, 1970).

6. Goody, J., in *International Encyclopaedia of the Social Sciences*, 16, Macmillan, New York, 1968

7. Leach, E. R., in *A History of Technology* (edit. by Singer, C., et al.), 110 Clarendon, Oxford, 1954

8. Eliade, M., *The Myth of the Eternal Return*, 5, Routledge, London, 1955

9. Mumford, L., *Technics and Civilisation*, Harcourt Brace, New York, 1934

PART II
Educational Policy

3

The Meritocracy

> This is the last chapter from *The Rise of the Meritocracy 1870–2033*, published in 1958 but purporting to be written in 2034, by which time the brilliant new meritocracy would be firmly established. Or would it? The end of this satirical 'essay on education and equality' is also a question mark. One almost immediate outcome was that the new word coined by the author slipped smoothly into the language, or rather, into many languages.

I have been trying to describe the growth of our society, particularly since 1944, in such a way as to reveal some of the deep-rooted causes of our present discontents. I do not gainsay the achievements of social engineering. I do not deny the fact of progress. I do maintain, however, that society never works smoothly. Despite all the advances of the last century, sociology is still in its infancy, and until it has reached the eminence of its fellow sciences, we shall not know with any certainty the muster of laws which social engineering must obey. The Nature of human beings is still the most mysterious of all. As it is, the society we have contrived is no more than a counterpoise of opposing forces held in always delicate equilibrium. Every change creates its counter. The opening of schools to talent was bound to anger some of the old cast down from their seats. Demotion for the stupid children of upper-class origin was bound to grieve their parents, and so forth—all the reactions I have mentioned before. My submission is that these at present inescapable strains account in some measure for the support upon which the extremists have been able to draw. I readily agree, however, that while this historical analysis may go some way to explain the possibility of such a movement, it does not explain why the movement has cohered in this particular form. What is the immediate pattern of organization? And what the spark?

The first and most obvious point to make is that the most prominent present leaders of the Populists are all women, and have been so since the first decade of the century. That was the time when women first began to come to the fore in left–wing politics, and, as one would expect, their first essay was in the romantic style that suits them best. Taking their cue from the Russian Populists[1] of the previous century after whom the modern movement is named, shaggy young girls from Newnham and Somerville, instead of taking the jobs as surgeons and scientists for which their education fitted them, scattered to Salford and Newcastle to become factory workers, ticket collectors, and air hostesses. They used lipstick, watched football matches, and went to Butlins for their holidays. They believed it was their mission to live as common technicians and by so doing to rouse them to a sense of the indignities from which they should feel they suffered. They joined the technical unions, stood for office, and agitated for strike action. They chained themselves to the seats of the British Productivity Council. They petitioned the Trades Union Congress to commit itself to 'Socialism'. They sent propaganda far and wide. Perhaps their strangest achievement was the capture of *The Times* and its conversion, for a few months in 2009, into a popular newspaper. Even so, all their efforts were in vain. For the spark there was no tinder. The girls went home to Tunbridge Wells and Bath, and the great majority of the technicians continued to go calmly about their daily occasions, sharing in the general stability of employment, intent on the interests of their children. They were tolerantly amused by these antics; they were not moved to action. There is ordinarily no one so stolid as ordinary British technicians. They are the salt of the earth.

But before they all went home the girls struck up a strange alliance which has left a permanent mark on our subsequent political affairs. In the inner councils of the Technicians Party there were still some aged men who, after having received their early training in the ancient Labour Party, had never emerged from their political adolescence. The old men were attracted to the young girls, and perhaps now and then it happened the other way round as well. They began to draft programmes and policies. Why, they asked, did the girls fail? They failed, went the answer, because they were not really technicians themselves. Their minds worked differently. They thought in the idiom of Somerville, not Salford. They had no feeling for the technicians' real problems. And therefore they were distrusted. But what if these girls, and even boys, with high I.Q.s, never left the technical classes? What if they refused to go to the universities? What if they left school at the same time as ordinary people? Then they would be trusted. They would be technicians at heart, if élite in brain. Their high intelligence at the service of their fellows, they would give the leadership that men like Bevin and Citrine once gave to the old trade unions. A new socialist movement would be built up from the grass roots, new meaning given to the old slogans of equality. It was a dazzling prospect.

But when it came to practical proposals, all the planners could suggest was that a proportion of the more able children in each generation should leave school at the minimum age and become technicians themselves. But how would they be chosen? By ballot? Some of them played with this idea, even suggesting that every tenth person among the over 125s, a tithe of the intelligence in every generation, should be allocated to technical work. This was obvious nonsense, and was never pressed. But if not by ballot, then how? The reformers ended by proposing that teachers should stop bringing pressure on parents and children who were not keen on higher education. They wanted the Parent–Teachers Associations abolished, so that parents would be less influenced by the teachers. They actually wanted schools to close the evening and weekend classes for parents. They wanted all sorts of things that were clearly no longer practicable. The plain fact was (and is) that most clever people want to get on in the world. There was little need for the schools to encourage. The children agreed with teacher before she spoke.

In their dilemma the dissidents then turned back to an old idea much in vogue in the century before 1944—the idea that manual work was as valuable as mental. For a long time indeed, though never in any Communist country, the adherents of Karl Marx's labour theory of value professed to believe that manual work was actually *more* valuable than any other sort. (A strange idea, it seems to us, yet the historian can have no doubt it was once widely accepted.) And the theorists went on to urge a revival of these old notions. They really had no alternative. They had to admit that most clever children wanted to become brain–workers. They also thought the children wrong. Since they wanted the children to become manual workers of their own voluntary choice, they had to argue that the children *should* be satisfied to do manual work. In other words, the very system of values had to change! They could reach no other conclusion. They said that the carpenter was as important as the crystallographer, ignoring the awkward fact that none of the theorists was a carpenter.

The agitators of twenty–five years ago were led on to ask more and more questions about society. From these discussions derive the modern theories of equality with which we are grappling today. Why, they asked, is one man regarded as superior to another? It is, they said, because we put up with such narrowness in the paramount values, or criteria, by which men judge one another's worth. When Britain was governed by warriors who depended for their power on their ability to kill, the great fighter was the great man; and thinkers, poets, and painters were treated with scorn. When Britain was governed by landowners, men who made their living by trade or preaching or singing were all lesser breeds. When Britain was governed by manufacturers, all other men were regarded as inferior. But, they say, there has never been such gross over–simplification as in modern Britain. Since the country is dedicated to the one overriding purpose of economic expansion, people are judged according to the single test of how much they increase production, or the knowledge that will, directly or indirectly, lead to that consummation. If they do as little as the ordinary manual worker, they are of no account. If they do as much as the scientist whose invention does the work of ten thousand, or the administrator who organizes whole clutches of technicians, then they are among the great. The ability to raise production, directly or indirectly, is known as 'intelligence': this iron measure is the judgement of society upon its members.[2] 'Intelligence' is as much qualification for power in the modern state as 'breeding' was in the old. The stress on this sort of ability was produced by a century of wars and threats of war, in which the kind of occupational achievement which raised the national war–potential was lauded above all else; but, say the theorists, now that the threat is no longer so immediate, can we not encourage a diversity of values?

In 2009 a local group of the Technicians Party issued the 'Chelsea Manifesto'. Although it attracted little public attention at the time, it has had a considerable influence, especially within the movement, during the last decade. It is a long and turgid document which begins by claiming (in an interpretation which no historian could accept) that the primary aim of the group, as of all their socialist predecessors and of the Church before them, is to cultivate variety. Their goal is the classless society. They oppose inequality because it reflects a narrowness of values. They deny that one man is in any fundamental way the superior of another. They seek the equality of man in the sense that they want every man to be respected for the good that is in him. Every man is a genius at something, even every woman, they say: it is the function of society to discover and honour it, whether it is genius at making pots, growing daisies, ringing bells, caring for babies, or even (to show their tolerance) genius at inventing radio telescopes. It is perhaps worth quoting the last paragraph of the Manifesto; this summarizes the writers' odd views on what a classless society would be like.

> The classless society would be one which both possessed and acted upon plural values. Were we to evaluate people, not only according to their intelligence and their education, their occupation, and their power, but according to their kindliness and their

courage, their imagination and sensitivity, their sympathy and generosity, there could be no classes. Who would be able to say that the scientist was superior to the porter with admirable qualities as a father, the civil servant with unusual skill at gaining prizes superior to the lorry–driver with unusual skill at growing roses? The classless society would also be the tolerant society, in which individual differences were actively encouraged as well as passively tolerated, in which full meaning was at last given to the dignity of man. Every human being would then have equal opportunity, not to rise up in the world in the light of any mathematical measure, but to develop his own special capacities for leading a rich life.

The Manifesto reveals its archaism most quaintly in the supporter whom it rustles forth from his grave—not one of the modern scientific 'divines' but, of all people, the almost–forgotten Matthew Arnold. It actually italicizes the absurd notion of 'culture' in his *Culture and Anarchy*—which 'does not try to teach down to the level of inferior classes; it does not try to win them for this or that sect of its own, with ready–made judgements and watchwords. It seeks to do away with classes; to make the best that has been thought and known in the world current everywhere; to make all men live in an atmosphere of sweetness and light, where they may use ideas, as it uses them itself, freely—nourished and not bound by them.' Oh God, oh Galton!

In the light of this approach the authors of the Manifesto sought to give a new meaning to equality of opportunity. This, they said, should not mean equal opportunity to rise up in the social scale, but equal opportunity for all people, irrespective of their 'intelligence', to develop the virtues and talents with which they are endowed, all their capacities for appreciating the beauty and depth of human experience, all their potential for living to the full. The child, every child, is a precious individual, not just a potential functionary of society. The schools should not be tied to the occupational structure, bent on turning out people for the jobs at any particular moment considered important, but should be devoted to encouraging all human talents, whether or not these are of the kind needed in a scientific world. The arts and manual skills should be given as much prominence as science and technology. The Manifesto urged that the hierarchy of schools should be abolished and common schools at last established. These schools should have enough good teachers so that all children should have individual care and stimulus. They could then develop at their own pace to their own particular fulfillment. The schools would not segregate the like but mingle the unlike; by promoting diversity within unity, they would teach respect for the infinite human differences which are not the least of mankind's virtues. The schools would not regard children as shaped once and for all by Nature, but as a combination of potentials which can be cultivated by Nurture.

These first phases of reformism are important to us today because they saw the formulation of the ideas which have since become so notorious. In point of organization there has been little continuity. That generation of malcontents returned home and many of them are now the respected wives of some of our leading scientists. But not all; some did not marry, some kept their rebellious spirit alive in the nursery. They have been joined by further recruits from some of the best homes in the country, culminating in the rush of the last three years. Why so many women[3] up in arms? It is not altogether easy to explain. I would, however, be no aspirant to sociology were I to allow any role to accident. That would, I believe, be a serious misinterpretation. It is worth noting, what is sometimes forgotten, that there were several excellent studies made of female psychology towards the end of last century before the resurgence in politics. The gist of them was that society seemed to many women, especially the able ones, in mind men if at heart women, to have been constructed expressly for the convenience of the opposite sex. Are there not, the indignant asked, as many intelligent girls born every year as there are boys? They get much the same education as any male cadet for the meritocracy. But what happens then? They take the post for which they have been trained only until they marry. From that moment they are expected, for a few years at any rate, to devote themselves to their children. The sheer drudgery of their lives has been much relieved by the revival of domestic service and the help of husbands. But they cannot, if they take any notice of the teaching of psychology, entrust the entire care of their offspring to a person of low intelligence. Infants need the love of a mother; they also need her intellectual stimulation, her tender introduction to a high culture, her diligent preparation for a dedicated life. She will neglect her motherly duties only at the peril of her children, not to speak of the displeasure of her husband.

What these early studies showed were that this dual role—in her chosen profession and in her biological vocation—often gave rise to mental tension in all those women who could not feel that child–rearing is (as it is in fact) one of the noblest occupations of them all, especially when it is part–time. The problem has never been an easy one to solve. Some women have taken their own way out by limiting the size of their families so that they can return to paid work as soon as possible—with the unfortunate result that the stock of intelligence has been endangered. Others have denounced the traditional family as an anachronism and transferred their motherly role entirely to servants. Others have signed the pledge that they would send their children only to the London School of Arts and Crafts, where science is not taught at all! Yet others, a small but significant minority, have been lured by the old mystique of equality. The early striving for social equality was greatly strengthened by its association with the movement for emancipation of women. Equality irrespective of sex or class—it was a good slogan, only it lost much of its appeal when hereditary classes, though not hereditary sexes, were gradually abolished. But for some women the appeal remained as bright as ever. As they saw it, the sexes were treated as 'unequal'. They wanted sex equality, but since this is obviously unobtainable, they displaced their antagonism from men in general on to the 'ruling classes', the scapegoat whom they imagined to be in some way responsible for the dictatorship of biology. It was all the easier to vent their antagonism because many of them had time on their hands, once their children entered nursery school, which they could devote to discussions in their women's circles. Most of them did not react by going to the extreme of refusing to make use of domestic service. The determination of so many of the present leaders of the movement to do all their own household work is unusual and in some ways welcome since it means the married ones have little time left over for political organization.

Through the women's circles, the activists have been able to assert their influence and show their menfolk, who perhaps show too little humility about the wonders with which they have furnished our estate, that they are a force to be reckoned with. In so doing they are making a protest against the standards, those of achievement, by which men assess each other. Women have always been judged more by what they *are* than by what they *do*, more for other personal qualities than for their intelligence; more for their warmth of heart, their vivacity, and their charm than for their worldly success. It is therefore understandable that they should wish to stress their own virtues, only regrettable that in this the quality have joined with women of no more than ordinary ability.

Astringency has been added to the debate, first, by the 'impoverishment' of women, and second, by the eugenic campaign. The impoverishment is the result of the reform of remuneration. Men are paid as business assets, and housewives cannot ordinarily pretend to be only that. Élite wives benefit indirectly from the new conception of home as just a branch office. Their servants are on the employer's expenditure roll. But they do not benefit as much as men. They do not attend so many stylish business dinners at the employer's expense; they do not need to travel abroad so often; they do not have two bars, one at work as well as one at home. Naturally they sometimes resent the privileged standard of living which their husbands, as business assets, have to enjoy whether they like it or not. This is one reason why the sex war has embraced politics.

Then there has been the eugenic campaign. This was founded on ordinary common sense. Professor Eagle and his collaborators were really saying, to begin with, that before choosing their marriage partners people should consult the intelligence register. This was obviously in the national interest; it was also in the interest of happy marriage. No man with a high I.Q. could in the long run be as proud of a child destined for a secondary modern school as of one destined for Oxford; yet the chance of such an unhappy issue was obviously greater, the lower the intelligence of the woman he married. A high–I.Q. man who mates with a low–I.Q. woman is simply wasting his genes and it is therefore common prudence for him to examine the records of her father and grandfather as well. Hence the success story of the pretty young mother who discovers she is going to be all right after all, the Registry has wrongly docketed her grandfather—it has become a favourite theme of popular fiction. Altogether this was, one would think, sensible advice. At any rate many men but not all—for what age is not an age of lust?—have thought so. It is now rare for a sober senior civil servant to consider marriage with any girl who cannot produce an I.Q. of over 130 at some point in her intelligence genealogy. For one thing, if he married beneath him there would be too great a danger of the news spreading through his department, and nothing would more surely give him the reputation of unreliability.

But women—and for once I am bound to confess I do not understand why—have not taken so kindly to this advice. Where, they ask, is the romance in an intelligenic marriage? And to underline their question they have echoed the lower classes who esteem bodily prowess and give a heightened value, a sort of symbolic value, to a superficial quality not at all related to intelligence, that is, to appearance. Beauty has become their flag. The more energetically Professor Eagle campaigns against men who choose women for their appearance—he has been most ably assisted by his wife—the more do the Populists decry his efforts, and the more often do the chic cadres attend their own meetings clad in the most extravagant clothes, with Salpanas on their shoulders, and sandals on their feet, their faces decorated in the most beguiling way and their hair styled according to the latest decrees from the fashion committee. One of their favourite slogans is the ridiculous 'Beauty is achievable by all'.

The remarkable appearance of the women members of the 'flying seminar' cannot be denied. They are not the sort of people who wear wool next to their skin.

Without the events to which I will now turn, this women's movement would have been no more than a high–spirited charade. It has been rendered a threat to the State by the sudden crystallization of an issue which has long remained submerged. I refer, of course, to the enunciation of the new revolutionary doctrine on the right wing of the Conservative Party. Lord Cecil and his followers have done what no one has dared to do within living memory: they have actually urged—not in so many words but that is their regrettable tenor—that the hereditary principle should be openly restored to its former pride of place. The shock has been profound. Extremism on the right has always led to extremism on the left.

Their plea cannot be ignored, for they claim that they are only seeking the stamp of public approval for a trend which has been evident for at least twenty-five years. The fact is that every advance towards equality of opportunity creates resistance to going any further. A century ago educational reform was vital to reduce the waste of ability in the lower classes. But every time intelligence was skimmed off and transferred to the upper classes, the reasons for continuing the process were correspondingly weakened. By 1990 or thereabouts all adults with I.Q.s of more than 125 belonged to the meritocracy. A high proportion of the children with I.Q.s over 125 were the children of these same adults. The top of today are breeding the top of tomorrow to a greater extent than at any time in the past. The élite is on the way to becoming hereditary; the principles of heredity and merit are coming together. The vital transformation which has taken more than two centuries to accomplish is almost complete.

The meritocracy is undoubtedly more brilliant as a result. Fifty years ago many members of the élite were first–generation, and for that very reason suffered in comparison with their fellows. They came from homes in which there was no tradition of culture.[4] Their parents, without a good education themselves, were not able to augment the influence exercised by the teacher. These clever people were in a sense only half–educated, in school but not home. When they graduated they had not the same self–assurance as those who had the support and stimulus of their families from the beginning. They were often driven by this lack of self–confidence to compulsive conformity, thus weakening the power of innovation which it is one of the chief functions of the élite to wield. They were often intolerant, even more competitive in their striving for ascent than was necessary, and yet too cautious to succeed. Now that so many of the élite are second–generation or better, these faults are no longer so evident, and society is no longer courting the risk of degenerating into a stratified mob. No longer is it so necessary to debase standards by attempting to extend a higher civilization to the children of the lower classes. This is what the new Conservatives allege. They claim that the advantages of the new disposition should be frankly recognized—even to the extent of allowing to the élite not only the privileges which are their accepted right but also, and this is the moot point, the guarantee of a privileged education for their children.

The shock administered by this demand has in a way been aggravated by some of the recent advances in the social sciences, whose consequences seem, quite independently, to threaten some of our most cherished beliefs. The fact is that the accumulation of knowledge in psychology has made it possible to identify the intelligence and aptitudes of the individual at ever earlier ages. Up to the turn of the century, there was still such a margin of error about the tests as they were applied, even at fourteen, that if people had had their last chance at that age much ability would have been lost to the nation. The late developers could not be neglected if full meaning was to be given to equality of opportunity. Hence modern adult education. Hence the regional centres. Hence the opportunity for anyone to have himself re–tested at any stage of life. But step by step the rapid advances in their discipline have given the educational psychologists the means to identify intelligence during childhood, even though it is so far latent that the untrained observer cannot detect it, and to forecast the age in adult life at which it *will* develop. These discoveries weakened the rationale of the adult education movement. If on the basis of tests at the age of fifteen, the experts could predict the future, what purpose was any longer served by the Regional Centres? The experts merely had to tag the late developer and, at the appropriate age, confirm that their prediction was correct. Provided they made generous allowance for borderline cases, they could not go wrong. The organizers of adult education have fought against this iconoclasm (as it seems to them) and, quite apart from disputing the validity of the new findings, have argued that their movement should continue if only to maintain the morale of low–I.Q. subjects who would otherwise be without hope.

The test–ages at which highly reliable predictions could be made have become steadily lower. In 2000, the reliable age was nine; in 2015, the reliable age was four; in 2020 it was three. This was as severe a blow to many teachers as the earlier discoveries had been to the adult educators. The real justification for a common education in primary schools for everyone up to eleven was that no one could be quite sure of the ultimate value of any young boy or girl. It was only fair that they should not be segregated until their I.Q.s were finally known. But when ability could once be tested and identified at the age of three, there was really no point at all in the brighter children going to the same co–intellectual school as others who would almost inevitably retard their development. It was much more sensible to segregate outstanding children from the ruck in separate kindergartens and primary schools, just in the same way as at the top the outstanding young people sent to Oxford and Cambridge were divided off from the others who could not rank any higher than the provincial universities. The late developers could remain with the *hoi polloi* until their time came, or be sent to experimental schools where the processes of nature would be hurried forward.

Faced with these facts, some teachers reacted in the same way as the adult educators and said, granted that the reliable age is three, it is still necessary to pretend that it is not. Children cannot be condemned so early: they will cease to strive when they know that no effort will prove the psychologist wrong, except within a small margin of error. They must be given the stimulus of hope; so must the teachers, and so also, above all, must their parents. Any sociologist must admit the strength of the argument. Equality of opportunity has for so long been the ethos of education that it will not do to abandon it overnight. So important is social cohesion that we shall have to make haste slowly.

But science does not move slowly. Three was not the limit. The reliable age was in effect pushed back into the womb. Dr. Charles, the Nobel Prizewinner who has taught us so much about the mode of transmission of intellectual ability, has recently shown that the intelligence of children could at last be safely predicted from the intelligence of their forbears. His early and remarkable experiments on progeny testing were with rats. His X–hypothesis was later confirmed by the wide–scale census tests of all three–year–old babies in 2016. In Britain, at any rate, Eugenics House already has records for four generations, from the 1950s onwards, as well as a large number of retrospective estimates compiled as the result of the most painstaking research, particularly since the study of obituaries became a recognized branch of sociology. By using these records, and making all necessary allowances, the ability of the offspring of any couple can be forecast with remarkable accuracy; and indeed, on various assumptions about marriage habits, and inward and outward migration, intelligence trends and distributions have actually been calculated for the next 1,000 years.

Dr. Charles's work has undoubtedly helped to alter the attitudes of intelligent parents. They no longer need to send their children to an ordinary primary school, and if the State will not provide special ones, they are already in a few districts establishing private schools, where their children will mix only with their own special class. They no longer need to look questioningly into their cots, not knowing what kind of education the occupants will eventually deserve. Their children are, in their eyes, not just children but rulers born to a high destiny. All this has led to hardening of class sentiment. Once the need for common treatment of all children up to a minimum age was questioned, once the foundations of society were shaken in this way, some intelligent parents were stimulated to go further and ask whether equality of opportunity is not a wholly outdated idea.

If the argument ended there, we defenders of the existing social order would not rest too uneasy. The flaw in the reasoning thus far is obvious, and all but the most bigoted and family–loving of the Conservatives, who have not even read Charles, heard of Galton, or paid attention to the most elementary genetics, are aware of it. The flaw is that intelligent people tend, on the whole, to have less intelligent children than themselves; the tendency is for there to be a continuous regression[5] towards the mean—stupid people bearing slightly more clever children as surely as clever people have slightly less. If it were not so, a ruling élite, once established, would rightly be hereditary. As it is, this brute fact makes some degree of social mobility essential, even though it need not be as great as a century ago.

As I say, most of the Conservative leaders are fully apprised of the tendency towards regression and have tried to take account of it in their schemes. Their proposals differ, in emphasis if not in kind. The most extreme right–wing asks, what does it matter? A few stupid children of clever parents may receive higher education—and most of them will not be all that less intelligent than their parents; but the polish given them in their homes will fit them to succeed to the élite, which they will man with no disgrace, if not adorn. Any loss of effectiveness in the meritocracy will be more than outweighed by the benefits of making it hereditary. Parents will be easier in their minds and their children will not have to go through all the psychological stresses of having to prove themselves in competition with children from the lower classes. Nor will ambitions have to be aroused in the minds of all parents, however stupid, lest their children escape the attentions of education; and if their ardours can be left cool, the body politic will gain in stability. A further wave of social mobility may be necessary later on, they say, if the distribution of intelligence gets too much out of line with the distribution of power; but let it wait; give us a half–century of peace from the pandemonium of social mobility.

Such professions have no chance of acceptance, they represent too sharp a break with our ethos. A more subtle school urges that the distribution of intelligence should be adjusted to the existing distribution of power; although the approach is the opposite of what the educational system aims at doing, the goal is the same. Some encouragement has been given to this group by the experiments carried out by Academician Donikey at Ulan–Bator, which cap a long sequence in many other countries, including our own. If the reports are to be believed, the biophysicists there have shown how, in the lower animals at any rate, controlled mutations in the genetic constitutions of the unborn can be induced by means of radiation so as to raise the level of intelligence above that which would otherwise be yielded. Were anything really practical to come of this, the crucial question would be, whose children are to have their intelligence artifically raised in this manner? The Conservative leaders claim that those who already have should have more, as the surrounding environment which the parents could provide would then be as favourable as possible to the nurturing of capacity; and that it would be absurd to tinker with ordinary have–nots since they already have quite as much ability as they need for their allotted functions. Obviously the decision must rest with the meritocracy, not the democracy who have no means of weighing the gravity of the issue. I recognize that any increase in knowledge must be welcomed for its own sake, but all the same I am bound to say that, speaking from the standpoint of sociology, the application of such knowledge, rather than its acquisition, cannot proceed too slowly. The rumours that have circulated about the tampering with the wives of leading civil servants at the Volunteer Maternity Centre on South Uist have already caused much alarm.

Meanwhile, it has been proposed that the Ministry of Education should at once make its Adoption of Children scheme mandatory upon all local authorities. Adoption of children is as old as man. Always, in all societies, would–be parents, unfortunate enough to have had no children themselves, or not as many as they would have liked, have sought out the kind of infants most approved—bonny–looking and chubby, fair with blue eyes, dark with grey eyes, boys or girls, small or big. The difference between us and other people in other times and other places is that we value intelligence more, and that the psychologists and biologists have given us the means of estimation even in the cradle. A genius without parents automatically becomes a ward of state. An intelligent orphan is now a prize for any family, especially for wives who are not prepared to seduce leading professors or seek artificial insemination from the few highly intelligent men attested by the Ministry as I.Q.–donors. The normal demand upon the Adoption Societies has been multiplied in recent years by members of the élite who wish to fill their quiver. The supply is grossly deficient; hence the disturbing growth in the black–market baby traffic, stupid babies from élite homes being sent, sometimes with princely dowries,[6] in exchange for clever ones from the lower classes. Desperate parents have even descended to baby–snatching after keeping a watch on pregnant mothers of the lower classes whose intelligence genealogies are promising. Private detectives and geneticists have worked together in a scandalous compact. Better, plead the culprits, to adopt the élite into their future class when they are tiny than to do it much later and in a much more cumbersome way through the 'foster parents' of grammar school and university. After a very full government inquiry the Welfare of Children Act was passed in 2030. It provided that private adoptions should henceforth be void unless the local authority in the area where the adopting parents lived had introduced the model scheme, and conformed to the safeguards, laid down by the Ministry of Education. The Cheltenham, Bournemouth, Harrogate, and Bognor Education Committees immediately took advantage of this permissive Act, but their lead has so far been followed by very few other local education authorities. The demand of many Conservatives is that all local authorities should now be obliged to comply, and it is this, on top of everything else, which precipitated the crisis of last May.

The sociologist, with his trained insight, can perhaps understand even more clearly than others why these events, and the discussions surrounding them, have caused such a profound revulsion. Any hint, let alone the assertion in influential quarters, that the hereditary principle should be restored, after the struggles of two centuries to destroy it, is tantamount to an attack on the core and centre of our value system, and one all the more disquieting because events have moved so swiftly. Even the upholders of the lower classes, the Owenites, the Chartists, and the Socialists, were not as shocking as this to their social superiors two centuries ago. Those rebels could at least profess their affinity with the Christian religion. These other rebels, of the right as they are, cannot claim any such respectable descent: the doctrine of equal opportunity has won a complete ascendancy in the realm of practical ethics. The Conservatives want two luxuries at once—the luxury of inheritance and the luxury of efficiency. But they cannot have them both. They have to choose, and they have chosen wrongly. Could we tolerate men as Directors of Eugenics House, of the Centre at South Uist, even as Prime Ministers, although that admittedly does not matter so much, who enjoyed power merely because they had clever fathers? Could we tolerate the clever sons of stupid fathers wasting their lives in some dingy Union office in Manchester? We could not. The sanction for such folly would be sharp. China and Africa would draw ahead in productivity. British and European influence would fade as our science became clumbered up by the second-rate. We should once again be 'over-matched in the competition of the world.' Does one need to say more? So obvious is it, that the Populists can now parade as protectors of what is best in our established society. A phantasmagoria indeed!

Public opinion surveys have shown that the disturbances have been fired more by a sentiment of opposition to the Conservatives than by a sentiment of loyalty to the Populists. Whatever the combination of motives, there is no doubt about what happened. Every little dispute, which would ordinarily have been quietly smoothed out in the course of conciliation, has instead been charged with a bitterness without parallel in modern times. The events at Stevenage, Kirkcaldy, and South Shields, the action of the domestic servants, the deputations sent to the Ministry of Education and the Trades Union Congress—all overflowed their nominal purpose in a very flood of rebellion. A thousand petty grievances became one.

Many of those who demonstrated were, of course, quite inarticulate about their aims, being reduced to incoherent murmuring when asked, in Court, to express themselves. They looked for upper-class leadership, and found it in the only one bizarre quarters where it existed. The women's circles, and their leaders, Urania O'Connor, Lady Avocet, and the Countess of Perth, did not create the movement, the movement created them, and if the study of social history had not (until the last few years) been so neglected, it would have been obvious to all that such is the custom of politics. The women merely had to seize their historic opportunity, which they have done to the best of their considerable ability. They sailed when the wind blew. Bonds have been formed between the women's circles and dissident technicians of very different levels of intelligence, indeed with dissidents from every walk of life. Long moribund branches of the Technicians Party have been suddenly visited with hundreds of applicants for membership. The commotion came to a head in the Leicester Convention, where the Populists issued their now celebrated charter.

What a strange document this is! With its echoes from the past in the quotations from the now long-forgotten Tawney and Cole, William Morris and John Ball, the authors dress out their claim to be the 'heirs' (this word was surely a mistake?) of one of the great streams in British history. But they dare not vouchsafe more than a few trite words about domestic service lest their intelligent ladies desert them. They dare not espouse equality too openly, lest their upper-class supporters take fright, though they came perilously close to it in the section of the peroration which starts 'Oh, sisters'. When stripped of its decoration the charter contains few concrete demands apart from the banning of adoptions; the preservation of primary schools and adult education centres; more allowance for age and experience in industrial promotion; giving the technicians a share in increasing productivity; and, most revolutionary and perhaps most meaningful, even a trifle nostalgic, to a historian, the raising of the school–leaving age to eighteen, and the creation of 'common secondary schools for all'. On their face–value these demands do not constitute a political programme of more than the crudest sort, but the authors could not go further to concentrate the loyalties of their very diverse followers without antagonizing some of those upon whose support they lean.

It was not my purpose in this essay to predict the course of events next May, but rather to show that the movement of protest had deep roots in our history. If my view be accepted, opposition even to the greatest institutions of modern society is inevitable. The hostility now manifest has long been latent. For more than half a century, the lower classes have been harbouring resentments which they could not make articulate, until the present day.

If I have succeeded in adding at all to understanding of this complex story and persuaded any of my fellows not to take present discontents *too* lightly, my purpose has been well achieved. But I am mindful that I may be expected to say a word about what is likely to happen. It can, of course, be no more than a personal opinion on which any reader of these pages is as well–tutored as myself. Nevertheless, I hold firmly to the belief that May 2034 will be at best an 1848, on the English model at that. There will be stir enough. The universities may shake. There will be other disturbances later on as long as the Populists survive. But on this occasion anything more serious than a few days' strike and a week's disturbance, which it will be well within the capacity of the police (with their new weapons) to quell, I do not for one moment envisage.

The reason I have already referred to. The charter is too vague. The demands are, with one exception, not in any way a fundamental challenge to the government. This is no revolutionary movement but a caucus of disparate groups held together only by a few charismatic personalities and an atmosphere of crisis. There is no tradition of political organization on which to draw. There are, indeed, already signs of dissension within the camp, as the result of the wise concessions which have been made. Since I began to write this essay a fortnight ago, the Chairman of the Social Science Research Council has proffered his weighty recommendations to the government. The Prime Minister quickly acted on these counsels of moderation, instructed Weather Control to bring on autumn a month early and announced, in his speech on 25 September at Kirkcaldy itself, that his party was going to expel half a dozen of its right–wing members, that the adoption scheme would not be made mandatory for the present, that equality of opportunity would be maintained as official policy, and that there was no intention at present of tampering with the primary schools or with adult education. His speech has, as *The Times* put it, 'stolen the girls thunder'.

Behind the shift and turn of current politics is the underlying fact with which I opened my essay. The last century has witnessed a far–reaching redistribution of ability between the classes in society, and the consequence is that the lower classes no longer have the power to make revolt effective. For a short moment they may prosper through an alliance with the odd and passing disillusion of a section of the upper classes. But such *déclassé* people can never be more than an eccentric minority—the Populists have never been more than that as a serious political force—because the élite is treated with all the wise distinction that any heart can desire. Without intelligence in their heads, the lower classes are never more menacing than a rabble, even if they are sometimes sullen, sometimes mercurial, not yet completely predictable. If the hopes of some earlier dissidents had been realized and the brilliant children from the lower classes remained there, to teach, to inspire, and to organize the masses, then I should have had a different story to tell. The few who now propose such a radical step are a hundred years too late. This is the prediction I shall expect to verify when I stand next May listening to the speeches from the great rostrum at Peterloo.[7]

REFERENCES

1. These were composed of young intellectuals who on return from universities abroad decided, under the influence of Bakunin, Kropotkin, and Stepniak, to go to the people for inspiration, dressed themselves as peasants, lived in the villages, and tried to promote revolution. When the peasants merely gaped at them, they were driven to terrorism. Fortunately there were no Sophie Perovskayas in England; it is not easy to imagine British women with a bomb, hydrogen or any other kind.

2. They have, of course, no use for the orthodox view that it is the very complication of modern society which demands the sort of basic intelligence which can speedily relate one part of a complex whole to another.

3. Dr. Puffin (of York University in an unpublished M.Sc. thesis) has pointed out how difficult it is to get reliable figures for membership, and asserts that, on a count he made at the Populist Convention at Leicester, women only numbered sixty–two percent of the delegates, the rest being men, with the old predominating.

4. One of the signs of the times is that T. S. Eliot is much read again—that is, his *Notes towards the Definition of Culture*. Particularly his words 'An élite, if it is a governing élite, so far as the natural impulse to pass on to one's offspring both power and prestige is not artificially checked, will tend to establish itself as a class.' Less often quoted are the words that follow 'But an élite which thus transforms itself tends to lose its function as an élite, for the qualities by which the original members won their position will not all be transmitted equally to their descendants.'

5. The phenomenon of regression was well understood even in my special period of history—that just as children of tall parents tended to be tall, though not so tall as their parents, so with intelligence. As Professor Eysenck said, 'The average I.Q. of members of the higher professional and administrative classes is in the neighbourhood of 150; that of their children is slightly in excess of 120. The lower professional and technical executive groups have I.Q.s in the neighbourhood of 130; their children tend to be in the 115 region on the average.' *Uses and Abuses of Psychology*, 1953.

6. In *Rook v. Stork* (4 QB, 2028) it was alleged that Mr. and Mrs. Rook had promised £150,000 in exchange for an I.Q. of 140, and a sum of £50,000 to Dr. Finch who arranged the deal. Mr. Justice Gosling's animadversions in his summing up led to the setting up of the Salmon Committee on the Adoption of Children.

7. Since the author of this essay was himself killed at Peterloo, the publishers regret they were not able to submit to him the proofs of his manuscript, for the corrections he might have wished to make before publication. The text, even this last section, has been left exactly as he wrote it. The failings of sociology are as illuminating as its successes.

4

The Need for an Open University

> The author was not content just to make forecasts; he endeavoured to make some of them come true. For example, in this paper published in 1962, he predicted an increase in the demand for university places and proposed that an Open University should be established as one way of meeting this extra demand. When the government of the day would not set up a National Extension College as a step towards this end, the author, not long after the paper appeared, himself created the new College as a prototype for the sort of university which would teach through broadcasting, correspondence and face–to–face methods. The Extension College, which now has some 10,000 students, showed that such teaching could be effective. The creation of the Open University followed.

Children born in the war have had comparative peace at school. Children born in the early years of peace, after their fathers came out of the Forces, have had to struggle through schools packed out with others of the same age. It should not need great foresight to plan ahead for yesterday's births, but the authorities were caught out when the bulge arrived in the infant schools, the primary schools, and the secondary schools. This year they have been trying to cope with all the extra school–leavers from the unlucky generation of 1947.

Will the last scene be the same as the others? In 1965 children who stay on at school will be besieging the universities. The number of 18–year–olds at school is expected to jump more than a third in the single year between 1964 and 1965. Are the universities ready to meet the crisis? They have, after all, had much more warning than the schools.

'Bulge' is no longer quite the right word. It would have been if birth–rates had fallen off in the early 1950s as sharply as they rose in the late 1940s. But they did not. The task is not how to ascend a steep peak and go down again but how to get on to a plateau and stay there until 1971. After that year demand is expected to start climbing sharply again.

This fact largely rules out the kind of action taken in two previous emergencies. The first was after the war when ex–Servicemen, instead of (or as well as) begetting future schoolchildren, flooded into the universities; the second when National Service was ended, and men who had been through the Forces competed for entry with others straight from school. On both occasions the universities were able to spread out the temporarily increased demand. This expedient will no longer be open to the same extent. To promise university places to people who reach 18 in 1965 if they wait until they are 19 or 20 would merely make things that much worse for those who become 18 in 1966 or 1967.

What can be done? Expansion of permanent university places needs to be stepped up—Lord Robbins' Committee on higher education is surely bound to make this its principal recommendation when it reports to the Prime Minister in 1963. Many of the old arguments against growth no longer apply to this new situation. University expansion has often been opposed on the grounds that if a higher proportion of each age group is admitted, the extra people are bound to have less 'ability'. Although I don't agree with this view, at least it is arguable. But the same thing cannot be said about the bulge. Unless the universities grow much faster than they are doing, the proportion of each age group going to them will be smaller in the late than in the early sixties, and people of greater ability than those admitted now will be squeezed out. Futher expansion is the only way of giving children born in 1947 the same chance as children of the same ability born in 1945.

The case for expansion is therefore very strong. Many university people admit that, but still argue it is not practical to do more than we are doing. There are not enough potential university teachers, they say, to expand much faster without lowering standards, and not enough resources of other kinds as well. Obviously a powerful argument, but one that is far too pessimistic for me. In the rest of this article I shall, by way of illustration, suggest three steps which could be taken in the emergency to make more economical and effective use of potential teachers and other resources.

1) Build on Research Stations

The first step would be to create further new universities more cheaply than in the past by bringing colleges to teachers rather than teachers to colleges. It is easy enough to understand the location of the new universities decided on so far. As the Empire shrinks, the country has been dozy with nostalgia, and mid–century universities have therefore been placed in towns associated with Roman and pre–industrial Britain—York and Lancaster, Canterbury and Colchester, Norwich and Brighton. It has been very costly. Everything has had to be built from scratch. Sir Nevill Mott and Dr. Bowden have urged that some of the new universities should have been started close to a supply of part–time teachers highly qualified in science subjects, Atomic Energy at Harwell, the National Physical Laboratory at Teddington, the Royal Aircraft Establishment at Farnborough and the Royal Radar Establishment at Malvern. This is surely what should now be done. Some teachers would have to be imported, especially in Arts subjects; some new buildings put up for students and for teaching purposes, but much less than when all the teachers have to be found and supplied with houses, libraries and laboratories. To create new universities of this kind would be the best thing that could be done. But what gives special point to the other two proposals is that such new universities will certainly not be established in time for 1965. No decision will be taken by the Government until the Robbins Report has been considered, probably not before 1964. A University of Malvern decided on then could hardly open much before 1968.

2) University Double Shift

The second step would be to make fuller use of existing universities. Sir Geoffrey Crowther has pointed out that their capital equipment is under–employed. Full terms do not ordinarily last for much more than half a year—less at Oxford and Cambridge, and during vacations the hostels, laboratories, libraries and lecture rooms are either empty or not used fully. If the same were true of the teaching staff—if they were also largely idle during the vacations—a second shift of undergraduates would be easy to introduce. But this is, of course, not so. The vacations are the time when the staff do their own research, prepare their lecture courses and select students.

So if there is to be a second shift of students there will have to be a second shift of teachers. Where from? They will have to come from qualified people doing other things—mainly from scientists and others working in industry, given part–time release and paid their ordinary salaries. In doing this we should be following good overseas practice—in Holland, for instance, staff from the Philips Research Laboratories act as special professors at the new Technical University of Eindhoven—and in England, too, there are precedents in the Royal College of Art and in Technical Colleges. Women graduates whose children are at school, and active dons prepared to continue beyond the ordinary age of retirement, could also be employed. Some of the ordinary university staff would, of course, have to act as Professors for the second shift.

I suppose it is difficult to imagine Oxford or even Cambridge taking notice of the bulge, but if they did, one way for them to take on a thousand or two additional students would be by establishing a second university using part of their premises in the vacations. For universities in larger cities, where the extra students could live at home or find their own lodgings, another arrangement would be to run an evening course during the ordinary terms, as the London School of Economics has done for many years. Birkbeck is another College of London University which has for many years given education to evening students. Additional teachers would be required for an evening shift, but not so many as for a 'vacation university', since some of the ordinary staff would presumably be ready to repeat their lectures and tutor too in the early evenings, if salaries were increased (as they should be) for those who worked longer.

What would be best in one place would not be in another. The immediate need is for different universities, and different faculties within each, to plan experiments to suit their own circumstances which they would be ready to try out in 1965, or, on a pilot scale, earlier. An evening shift could also help Teacher Training Colleges and Colleges of Advanced Technology to admit more students who would otherwise be deprived of full–time higher education.

3) Open University

The third step, not as far as I know suggested before, would be to establish an 'open university' to prepare people for External Degrees of London University. All the civic universities in England and Wales, as well as the University Colleges of Africa and the West Indies, at one time entered their students for this Degree, and it has also given an opportunity to many thousands of people in Britain unable to gain admission to a university. Although most of the universities at home and abroad now award their own degrees, 13,000 students qualified for university entrance were still registered for an External Degree in 1961. The number will certainly increase in the middle of this decade, due to the birth–rate at home and the demand from overseas. The External Registrar of London University is responsible for thousands of people who will one day be amongst the rulers of Africa, Asia and the West Indies.

Since London University has strangely failed to provide teaching for its own beneficent Degree, the quality of teaching these students get is far from being as good as it should be. The more fortunate ones are enrolled as full–time students in Naval, Military and other specialized Colleges, and, above all, in Technical Colleges and Colleges of Commerce. The real problem is the majority of external students who are not full–time anywhere. Most of them rely on private Correspondence Colleges. The inadequacy of the teaching of these Colleges is partly responsible for poor results in the External examinations.

The failure of orthodox higher education to adapt to the 'revolution of rising expectations' has given the Correspondence Colleges their chance to expand. They have an estimated enrollment of about 250,000 'pupils', mainly adults but including some children. Nothing much is known about how they work, and an official enquiry is badly needed. But we know enough to be sure that most Correspondence Colleges will have to be reformed if the extra students starting on the External Degree in the mid–sixties are to get a decent education. On how to do this a few suggestions can be drawn from the experience of the U.S.S.R.; and on the use of television, from the U.S.A.

In many other countries correspondence courses are run by, or in conjunction with, universities or other official bodies. In France, for instance, they have a part in the 'Promotion supérieur du travail' which allows industrial workers to become qualified at universities and the 'grandes écoles'. The Sorbonne, with its 100,000 students, can be thought of (though no doubt it would not care to think of itself) as mainly a vast correspondence college, though the notes of the lectures (course polycopiés) are usually distributed by the student organizations rather than by the university authorities. But it is Russia which has developed higher education more rapidly than anywhere else—the number of students in higher education has grown from 105,000 in 1914 (somewhere near the present British level) to 2,396,000 in 1960—and taken correspondence colleges more seriously than anywhere else. In 1960/61 the majority of all entrants to higher education were, for the first time, in correspondence colleges; and 40 percent of all graduations from higher education were from correspondence colleges. 'They reason that persons who hold jobs are more mature, responsible and experienced and that they can reconcile theoretical learning with work experience.'[1]

What makes the colleges different from the British ones is that they have premises all over the country which the students are encouraged to attend in order to discuss their reading with resident tutors, that students can make use of library and laboratory facilities in any local institution of higher education, and that students are not only given several weeks of additional leave from their employment each year to attend special 'summer schools' and prepare for preliminary exams but several months' leave before the final exams. Since a recent reorganization students who have got through their first two years in a Correspondence College have their written work supervised by the full–time academic staff of a university or other institution. These are supposed to have a complement of correspondence students in addition to their regular full–time ones.

The U.S.A. offers a different lesson—about the effectiveness of educational television for the teaching of adults. Many universities have their own closed–circuit television stations for full–time students and open broadcasts for 'external' students. Famous scientists and other experts broadcast early–morning courses to large audiences. Students remember just as much of a T.V. lecture (according to checks made) as of a lecture attended in person. Where pictures have special advantages, as in surgery or geography, the T.V. lecture may leave a more lasting impression—not only on the students either, for lecturers can, on a replay, see themselves in action for the first time![2] This does not mean that the traditional methods of university teaching, as practised in Britain, are about to be superseded—far from it—but it does suggest that if T.V. and radio courses were arranged to tie in with their written work and reading, Correspondence College students would be a great deal better off than they are now.

To make use of such overseas experience a new centre is needed— a National Extension College—to act as the nucleus of an 'open university' and to work closely with London's External Registrar. With a special Government grant, the College would have the following main functions.

To organize new and better correspondence courses for the External Degree. This would mean persuading more university teachers and other qualified people to prepare and supervise the courses. The Commerce Degree Bureau of London University already runs correspondence courses for external students taking the BSc (Economics) degree. The Bureau could be the model for similar courses in other subjects.

To promote lectures and residential schools. The College would work through the Extra–Mural Departments of London and other Universities. They would run special lectures for external students related to their correspondence courses and supply tutors for personal discussion and supervision. All students should have the opportunity to attend a two–month 'summer school' at a university during its vacation before they sit for their final exams. Employers would be pressed to grant leave of absence for this period, as they do now for day–release. External students should get maintenance grants while attending their final 'summer schools'.

To teach by means of television. The National College would work with the B.B.C. and Independent Television to secure programmes for its students.

Such a National Extension College would only be a second–best. Full–time study at a university will always be preferred, except by the hardy minority who feel they must earn their living as soon as they leave school. But though a second–best, it would be a great deal better than what happens at present. It would cost money—very properly so. Most people admitted to universities are doubly fortunate: they get a good education and a large gift from the taxpayer as well. People not admitted who try to pay their own way to a degree get little or nothing. It would be more just if they received some financial help.

These three illustrations—new universities, second shifts, a National Extension College—show the kind of thing that could be done about the coming crisis. Nothing will be if the Government continues to cut down expenditure on higher education. But if there is a change of mood in the Government, and if the Robbins Committee brings home the need for expansion, the sort of proposals made here could yet be adopted. There are still two or three years left before we have to meet the last post–war problem, face to face.

REFERENCES

1. Nicholas de Witt, *Education and Professional Employment in the U.S.S.R.*, U.S. National Science Foundation 1961

2. Wilbur Schramm (ed.), *The Impact of Educational Television*, University of Illinois Press, 1960

Postscript: Ten Years Later

Ten years after the National Extension College the Open University was established in Britain, the concept has since been copied in 30 other countries. The author welcomed it in the London *Times* in January 1972, on the day before the first O.U. broadcast, and pointed to the value of the new institution for the Third World.

Tomorrow morning anyone in Britain who wants to turn on a television set will be able to attend the first lecture of the first university in the world without walls. That is its strength as well as its weakness—its strength because hundreds of thousands of people not themselves registered as students of the Open University will be able to get a flavour of what this kind of higher education is about, and perhaps some of them may be led to try themselves out later on as full students; its weakness because its critics, who will be vociferous anyway, will be able to claim that they have seen the product, and do not like it.

Perhaps the fact that the new university is an experiment unique in the world will do more to inflame than appease the critics. Why should taxpayers' money be spent on an experiment? For supporters this is, of course, the point. This is an experiment on the grand scale and one which is about the central problem of world education.

There is no end in sight to the increase in the demand, or the need, for education. On top of the insatiable needs of children will be piled the need for adults to re-equip themselves in middle life for new roles and new interests. The rate of obsolescence of childhood education will grow; the need for continuous education will become more and more insistent.

The resources devoted to education cannot possibly grow in step. One half of the nation cannot be fully engaged in teaching the other half. So the need for new ways of economizing on these resources is urgent, and will become more so. The Open University is a device for economy. If it succeeds, it will do so by showing that its methods squeeze a little more out of the pint pot.

There have been so many gimmicks in education that Mrs. Thatcher and others can be excused for regarding the three–way teaching which is the speciality of the Open University—a combination of correspondence, broadcasting and face-to-face teaching—as just another.

At the National Extension College we would perhaps say the same had we not personal experience to the contrary. The college was started in Cambridge in 1963. For seven years we and our colleagues have been conducting a small–scale experiment before the large one to come; we are now convinced that three–way teaching of home students can work. It is cheap and effective, especially if the three vital ingredients are combined instead of doled out separately.

It began with the Dawn University (names to describe this new animal have never been easy to find) at Cambridge University. It has continued with 20 other three–way projects run in conjuction with Independent Television companies and with the B.B.C. Without the steady support of the B.B.C. for this new development in education neither the National Extension College nor the Open University would have been able to establish themselves. During these seven years 35,000 students have passed through the N.E.C. After this small success, success on the large scale of the Open University could add a new kind of institution to British education, which could be reproduced in new open schools and in technical colleges, also without walls.

Much more important is the value that three–way teaching could have in the developing countries. Their need is greater still than Britain's. The Open University at the university level and the N.E.C. at the pre–university will continue to be second–chance institutions for people who have had a first chance and for one reason or another failed to take advantage of it. In the developing countries there are countless millions of people who have not even had a first chance. In the 1920s Professor Tawney wrote a famous pamphlet, *Secondary Education for All*. In most African and Asian countries primary education for all is still a fairly distant goal; secondary education is mostly for the few who are victors in an equivalent of the 11 plus exam which makes the British one look gentleness itself; higher and vocational education is for the fewer still. If Nigeria, to take one example, built a new school every week from now until the year 2000 she would still not have a network of schools as ample as that which William Forster inherited in Britain in 1870.

If these countries are so poor how can they afford more for education? They are straining their budgets already for the sake of schools and teachers. Hence the importance of new methods which could make their scarce resources go further; and hence the significance for them of the work that is being broached tomorrow morning. It would almost be justified for the whole cost of the Open University to be borne on the overseas development funds of the government.

The university's task for the next few years is to test, change and develop the new approach and to begin to recruit as students more and more British working–class students whose first chance was nominal. The time for it to open its student body wider still, to the people of the poor south of the world, will come later. Ahead of that time there is more advance work to be done, which is why in this same week the International Extension College has been launched as a sister body to the National Extension College. It will act as an international resource centre for three–way teaching materials—above all correspondence courses—and supply them to non–profit-making educational institutions in Africa and other countries. We shall help to start new correspondence colleges and the like wherever countries do not already have them. We are just about to start a round of consultations with governments and universities abroad about the ways in which this new international venture can best help them.

People who can rouse themselves by 10:30 tomorrow may or may not like what they see. If they do not, they might still recognise that they are observing an experiment which could change the lives of children yet to be born in Nigeria or Tanzania, Burma or Guyana. It is the world spin–off from Milton Keynes that will matter in the end.

5

Third World Alternative to Schools

The author started the International Extension College at the same time as the Open University went on the air in order to promote distance learning in the third world of Africa, Asia and Latin America, and for the poor majority who will get no education at all in the future, if things go on as they are. Since then I.E.C. has started a chain of indigenous colleges in Africa. This essay is taken from the 1980 book, *Distance Teaching for the Third World,* written in conjunction with three colleagues. It is a plea for radio colleges in place of the standard schools. There is no requirement of history which forces the poorer countries to reproduce the West in their schools. The poorer countries could do something different, and if they did they might find themselves not at the rear of the long column headed by the industrial countries but at its head, moving in a different direction and themselves giving the lead to the rest of the world.

Even a few years ago it did not seem too optimistic to believe it was only a matter of time before most of the poor countries possessed the rudiments of a school system. No doubt they would remain, for as far ahead as anyone could see, behind the rich countries, with the gap between them at worst widening, at best staying the same. The poor countries would only be able to do better if they managed to attain faster rates of educational expansion than the rich countries and this seemed highly unlikely. But it was expected that they would in the foreseeable future have primary schools for the great majority of their children, and secondary for many. As a result, before too long the schools, with the aid of adult education, would at least have eliminated illiteracy.

Now that guarded optimism has been destroyed by the population explosion. Every poor country has strained to put more of its budget into education, regarded as the gateway to modernization by the one great alliance of parents and governments which has, on this issue, stood firm almost everywhere. More schools have been built. More teachers have been trained. More children have been enrolled. But not enough for these countries to do much more than hold their own.

Illiteracy figures are bound to be suspect, especially when the counts made on many different bases by governments who all have an interest in underestimating run into hundreds of millions. Given the bias of the arithmeticians, the real situation is likely to be worse than that displayed by UNESCO; and that is bad enough. The Office of Statistics contributed its conclusions to the UNESCO report, *Learning to Be*.[1] The absolute number of illiterate adults rose between 1950 and 1970 from 700 to 783 million. Though the proportion of people who could not read had decreased, world population was rising too fast for the teachers to keep up with the demand. Looking forward from 1972, the report was more gloomy about the decade to come. It said that[2]

> The effect of the huge increase in the adult population in the seventies of 536 million—as against 418 million in the sixties—will continue to undermine all the efforts made by Member States to undermine illiteracy.

This has become an ever more common refrain. It is almost conventional to say, as the World Bank did later on, that 'there is a prospect not only of stagnation in progress toward universal education, but even of a retrogression which would leave larger numbers and proportions of the populations of many countries without even a minimum education.'[3]

To pick up one of those figures, if for no more than illustration, what is to happen to those 783,000,000, to the still larger numbers there may be to come who have never been to school, or to the great numbers who have been to school but then dropped out?

It is not just a question of numbers. We need an approach which will not only make it possible to reverse the trend towards growing illiteracy, but will do so by giving students a chance to learn how to improve the quality of their lives and of their societies. This cannot be done by setting up for adults and adolescents who have not been to school something which is a poor image of what goes on in it. The 'banking' system, where students are led to store the pearls of wisdom which their teachers give them (and which they themselves learnt by heart from the teachers who went before them), produces submissiveness, not the search for new ways of doing things. If people are to learn to control and change the world in which they live, they need to learn through dialogue and participation. Can the techniques of distance teaching be used to this end?

Development of non–formal education on more systematic lines might reduce the frightening number of illiterates; in their place might emerge more people educated to help themselves. The purpose of this essay is to show how this new model might work in practice.

We recognise, of course, that what might be in one place could not be in another. There can be no one blueprint for the future of non–formal education in the third world, or any other world for that matter. The differences between countries, and districts within countries, are far too great for that.

But if there has in effect been a single blueprint for schools, both primary and secondary, why not for adult colleges as well? The third world has taken over many of its notions about education from Paris, London, Moscow, Washington, which are themselves sufficiently similar to make it quite sensible to take about 'the school' as though it were one animal. But this clearly will not do for adult education. Adults cannot or do not want to go to school. Learning for them only makes sense if it springs from issues in their own lives which matter to them. These issues differ immensely from one country or one district to another.

Yet there is, we assert, some value in generalising; not in order to lay down what should be done in any one place, nor even in some dream–house of education, but in order to suggest the agenda, a list of checkpoints, to anyone who wants to change the existing provision for adult education or add to it. An agenda is always a kind of generalisation, until it is known who is going to propose exactly what, on each item. We know now what the agenda is for. It is for a system of radio colleges which could be an alternative or complement to the schools which so many people have never been inside.

We use the term radio colleges because we know that the majority of the 800,000,000 people who have never been to school, as well as those who have started but have dropped out, live in villages and homesteads. They have been deprived of education because of their remoteness from schools, or even extension services. There is not enough money to build the new schools or to train and pay additional teachers or extension officers. An alternative system must reach them in spite of these constraints. We believe that distance teaching might do so. Distance teaching, that is, which rests on the three–legged stool of broadcasting, print and study group meetings. And from the examples we have looked at we draw the conclusion that radio is the focus around which the study groups should meet.

What, then, are the questions on the agenda? There are, we think, three main ones:

1. Who will the students be?
2. What will the organisation be?
3. What will they learn?

1. Who Will the Students Be?

We have been concerned throughout the book with people deprived of education. The first target of an alternative must therefore be the millions who have never been to school at all. But in some societies now, and in many in the future, where universal primary education has or will have been achieved, the educationally underprivileged are those who have been to primary school but dropped out, or 'failed' the primary school-leaving exams. Our system must also be able to offer them a chance to build on what they have learned, or to re–learn what they have mislearned or forgotten. These two groups, the wholly unschooled and the school–leavers or dropouts, have at least one major difference. The latter will have acquired the basic skills of education; they will have learned to read, write and count, whereas the former will not.

The system must therefore provide a chance for some to acquire these essential skills of learning from scratch, while allowing those who have them already to practise and improve them. The Freirean concept of dialogue between teacher/learner and learner/teacher, and the Laubach 'Each One Teach One' literacy method, might consummate a marriage. Those with some schooling, while continuing to be students for part of the time, could become the monitors and group leaders, and even the literacy and numeracy tutors, for those who are just starting. As in the radio schools of Colombia, their role would be to guide and tutor rather than to teach. Their own lack of expertise should be more than counterbalanced by the printed and broadcast lessons. Literacy and numeracy apart, these two groups of potential students would have very similar learning needs. They share the same village societies, they struggle with the same economic necessities, they bring up families in the same conditions of life, whether or not they have been to school. The really important differences will reflect the differences between their economic and social roles. The majority, both men and women, will presumably be farmers. But the skills and knowledge needed by farmers vary enormously from one ecological district to another. There will also be carpenters and carvers, builders and technicians, housewives and mothers, traders and businessmen. Our colleges must offer each of them the chance to master the skills which they need to build a better life for themselves and for their families, including educational skills.

Most of the students in the radio colleges we propose will be adults, or at least adolescents who are beyond the normal school–leaving age. For it is highly doubtful whether distance teaching can provide children with sufficiently structured learning: it has not done so yet. Strong personal motivation is a condition of successful learning with these techniques, and such motivation requires maturity; it is for adults who have been persuaded by life (rather than by teachers) that it will be of advantage to them to have some education. This is not to say that young children could not benefit from a radio college as long as there were adults in it. This seems to have worked well on occasion in the Latin American radiophonic schools. But we expect that the radio colleges will be mainly for adults.

2. What Will the Organisation Be?

The study group will be essential to the system—or any variation of it—which we are proposing. The radio programme and the correspondence pamphlets are, by their very nature, likely to be centrally produced—although it would be a great advantage if they could be adapted regionally and, if necessary, to each main ecological environment. Even so they are bound to be generalised, whereas the problems to be solved, and the circumstances in which they must be defined, are local. The study group, in which families, neighbours or members of local communities meet as colleagues for the purpose of learning together, is a local institution, built and dependent on local resources, and in which the information and ideas received from a distance are related to local development and local realities. It is there that new knowledge and new skills from outside can be synthesised with local understanding and experience. The study group would, for the non–formal system, become the organisational equivalent of the school. But a study group does not need a separate building, trained teachers or extension officers, the main constraints upon orthodox expansion. It is these characteristics which make expansion by study groups economically attractive.

Such groups cannot, of course, be entirely self–sustaining. They need stimulation and organisational support. These can most conveniently be provided by the existing educational and extension officers—the primary school teachers and the health, community development, cooperative and agricultural officers. The value to them is that they can reach larger numbers and a wider cross-section of their potential clientele than they can ever hope to reach by individual visits. They can be relieved of the task of being the primary transmitters of information, and can concentrate on the human support and interpretation which they are best able to provide.

We have looked at the study group in several different forms. There are very attractive features to all four variants. An alternative system should attempt to retain all these features, the permanence of the forums, the consultation of the clubs, the mass mobilisation of the campaigns and the clearly-defined role of the monitors in the radiophonic schools. But on one point there is a basic choice between the radio forums and the radio clubs on the one hand, which are new and separate groups, and the campaigns and the radio schools on the other, which graft study groups onto existing organisations. We believe that the latter approach is generally preferable. The campaigns in Tanzania were directed at groups set up by the political party, local government and educational organisations. Existing groups became the vehicles for the campaign. In this way they reached out to large proportions of the total adult audience. Some radio schools used the family as the only appropriate base on which to build study groups in the most remote areas, others the farmers' cooperatives and federations. Both relied on the Catholic Church for distribution of materials and local support.

Attaching study groups for particular courses on campaigns to existing social organisations—youth clubs, sports clubs, women's clubs, church groups, adult education classes, cooperatives, trade unions and local party branches—takes people where they are, and approaches them where their involvement and loyalty are already present. (It can present problems where only the most prosperous belong to such groups.) But it is then possible to operate on a much larger scale than new and separate groups can, if, like the clubs and forums, they are entirely dependent on a single central institution, whether or not it is attached to the broadcasting organisation.

One point to make about study groups is that their members should be given the fullest possible opportunity to plan for themselves. All too often the political élites of third world countries, and the first- or second-world experts who run the development programmes of international agencies, determine the sort of change they think best for the rural areas where other people live. This is not too likely to be what the others really want. There is a much better chance of providing what ordinary people want if they are involved in making the plans.

Despite the difficulties of involving learners in the production of centrally made broadcasts and correspondence lessons, there are three ways in which study group members can and should participate. The first is by expressing their needs and becoming aware of their own ability. We have seen how in Senegal radio clubs led peasant farmers to define for themselves the reasons why they were kept poor. They realised that they could make the authorities listen to what they said. This in turn gave them the confidence to consider and use the advice they were offered, instead of reluctantly submitting to orders from above. In Tanzania likewise: the radio campaigns mobilised millions of people to discuss their own health and food habits critically. They then decided, community by community, what they could and should do to change them. These examples show that distance media allied with local study groups can help people with little or no schooling to a 'deepened consciousness of their situation' which, as Freire says in a different context, 'leads men to apprehend that situation as an historical reality susceptible of transformation'.[4]

In two other countries we have also seen how study group members can say what they want to learn. In Botswana one of the objectives set for the radio learning group campaign on the Tribal Grazing Lands policy was to find out from group members what topics they would like to know more about. Enormous numbers of questions were sent in which were the basis of a further radio series of 'Answer Programmes'. It should be possible to analyse listeners' questions so as to plan follow–up courses to meet what is a proven large–scale interest. In Mauritius in 1973 a small–scale campaign was run on population called 'Ma Vie Demain' (My Life Tomorrow). It contained basic information on the social, economic and biological aspects of family planning and was aimed at adult and adolescent men, two vital groups largely ignored by family planning agencies. One important purpose was to reveal in the discussions the particular interests as well as the fears, prejudices and ignorance of these groups. The campaign was too short to bring about any marked change in attitudes. But the correspondence which it stimulated was enough to guide several courses on human biology, sex education, sociology and economics. Had they been offered, these would have been in direct response to a demand by large numbers for more information on particular topics. Study group campaigns can stimulate members to define what they want to learn so that future courses can become 'organised, systematised and developed "representation" . . . of the things about which they want to know more.'[5]

The second way to ensure participation is for study groups to be self–help affairs. All their members, usually including the group leaders, are students: there is no 'teacher' to impose or maintain an unequal relationship. The group's chairman and secretary are usually elected by the members. The leaders are taught that their role is to facilitate learning by discussion rather than to teach. This partly because they are rarely that much more knowledgeable than their fellow group members, if at all. Learning has to be by sharing information brought to the group by radio or in print, and adapting it to the local situation. The groups' very existence as organisations depends largely on their members' will and skill. So in a way that can rarely be rivalled in a formal classroom, filled with the traditional authority of the teacher, a study group encourages, in fact depends on, its members' participation. The learning that takes place in their own responsibility.

Third, as we have seen in the farm forums of Canada, India and Ghana, in the campaigns of Tanzania and in the correspondence course forums of INADES in West Africa, great emphasis has been laid in many places on linking study and action. The kind of action has varied, as has the learning which led to it. But where it has worked best the group has had a chance to put learning to a practical purpose.

3. What Will They Learn?

One of the strengths of non–formal education is that it tackles people's immediate practical problems. If as a result they can get better jobs, or earn more money by doing their job more efficiently, or bring about other improvements in their conditions of life, education will seem worthwhile.

Since the jobs are in agriculture, so will the content often need to be predominantly agricultural. At the same time most of the students are raising families, building homes and running small–scale businesses, whether in villages or urban ghettoes. This suggests that several different practical courses at a very basic level will be needed to serve as entry points for the various groups according to their interests. The decision as to the number of basic courses to be included will obviously depend on local circumstances—the degree of economic and social variety amongst the students, and the production and organisational resources which can be mustered. The advantages of a simple core curriculum on the one hand and of flexibility and breadth of appeal on the other will always have to be weighed against each other.

But it will not be enough to provide one–off courses which offer unconnected training in particular skills. One of the great attractions of the formal system of education, and a feature common to all its varieties in the first, the second or the third world, is its sequential curriculum. Each year pupils are supposed to progress from stage to stage, to higher levels of competence and to increasing depths of understanding. In each year there is the hope of going on to more advanced stages in the following year. They can look forward to an end, whenever that is and for the few who reach it, when they will graduate with a wider knowledge of the world in which they live and work, and some ability to cope with the demands which will be made on them. Our alternative system will also need a sequential element to it.

The value of the sequential curriculum is not just that students always have an end in sight. Rather, as Bruner has argued,[6] it helps us learn to approach repeatedly familiar subject matter at deeper levels of understanding and analysis, always working from the familiar to the unfamiliar. In England pupils in some primary schools used to study English history right through from Roman times to the present day in a superficial way. They would go through the whole cycle again in greater depth in secondary school, and yet again but even more so at university, if they should chance to get there and to read history for their degree. The strength of this repetition was that it could steadily increase intellectual power. The curriculum should lead students to grasp generative concepts—concepts which enable them to solve not only the old problems in the classroom, but also the new ones met outside. As they work through a school curriculum they should find that they are increasingly working out principles for themselves and thereby increasing their ability to understand and change their own environment. A good, structured curriculum does not just enable us to memorise discrete items of information but gives us intellectual tools of general value.

In non–formal education a similar structure is needed for students, so that they can progress from a simple understanding of a particular vocational skill to a more complex and deeper study of the same thing. On the way they must have the opportunity to learn whatever related knowledge and skills are needed at the more advanced stage. The challenge is to work out a curriculum that is more than a series of instructions about better health or better agriculture—a curriculum that will be as intellectually powerful and rewarding as a good school syllabus. To do so, we need to adapt the schools' cyclical pattern of learning to non–formal education. Here are some obvious examples of how this might be done.

First is to link with the agricultural cycle. Farmers joining classes or groups, which would anyway have to be concentrated into the agricultural slack seasons, would in the first year be introduced to the most elementary scientific information that forms the basis of the agriculture that are already practising. Aims would of course include the encouragement of better agricultural practice, where there is scope for this. But, beyond that, the intention would be to lay the groundwork both for understanding the reasons behind better practice and for future learning at a deeper level in another year. The same annual cycle would be followed in succeeding years, but the skills and information would become increasingly sophisticated. Child–bearing and child–rearing with their own cycles could also be used as the basis for a curriculum of human biology. Business could lend itself to the same approach. A beginning might be made with the most straightforward activities involved in running a newly–formed cooperative through its first harvest and marketing season. The knowledge and skills for somewhat more sophisticated business management would be provided as experience grew from year to year. Or a mechanics course might start with the maintenance of the simplest machine such as a bicycle or flour mill, and progress from there to the motor bike and on to the tractor.

Thus the basic, and not–so–basic, facts of elementary science, of arithmetic and mechanics, of language, economics, commerce and civics, could all be taught through a study of the agricultural, mechanical, social and human concerns of everyday life. Essential skills such as literacy and numeracy would need to be included within such a framework both for their immediate practical value and because they enable various subjects to be studied further.

On this also we can learn from the various traditions we have been trying to bring together. The short, intensive and widely publicised courses which make up the campaigns are good at mobilising and motivating adults. If that initial stimulus is to be turned into something more long–term, the most highly motivated will have to be able to go on learning long after the campaign itself is over and before the next campaign has begun. INADES in francophone Africa and ACPO in Colombia have both shown what can be done with a carefully constructed series of courses including campaigns but in the context of a sequential curriculum.

The obvious fact is that people will never find liberation from one–off courses which teach them how and why to dig latrines. The power to alter their conditions of life in any more fundamental way depends on understanding their causes and having the skills and ability to change them.

We will try to sketch two examples from very different settings.

The first has been happening, in Honduras. The other is more hypothetical: set in Tanzania, where the need for radical answers to educational problems is recognised.

We have already described some of the work of the radio schools programme of Acción Cultural Popular Hondureña (ACPH). We stressed there the growing conviction of ACPH's leaders that education for liberation must be centred round an increase in peasant awareness of the forces which promote poverty and dependency, and the power of cooperative organisation as the only countervailing means. The normal content of education—literacy, numeracy and social and scientific knowledge—is presented in ACPH's courses in a way that promotes not only educational skills but, equally, political consciousness and economic, social and organisational skills.[7]

> Material is arranged around four main subject areas: 'work' (agriculture, use of resources, commercialisation, crafts); 'health and family' (personal and environmental hygiene, nutrition); 'communication' (written documents, letters, telegrams, means of social communication (written, spoken and mass), transport, migration, art, folklore, geography); and 'organisation' (social and civic—unions, leagues, political organisation, forms of government, national symbols, laws, workers' laws, and human rights, and social stratification). In addition 'numeracy' is developed in a functional way in conjunction with these themes.

All the subjects are included at each level and in each section of the courses. In the first stage for example, key words, such as 'plough', 'harvest', 'child', 'bathing', 'school', 'forests', are used as the basis for literacy training, as the themes of discusison of vital social and economic concerns, and as the source of numeracy exercises. In the second stage the discussions move on: under the heading WORK there is an investigation of the most important agricultural activities of village life, natural resources and how they are used, marketing of village produce and local employment. Common village illnesses, village hygiene, educational opportunities for *campesino* families and nutrition are the topics related to HEALTH AND FAMILY. Under COMMUNICATION transport and road construction, telephone, radio and the press are discussed, and the use and construction of simple sentences are practised. At the same time, questions of population distribution, the local situation of peasant federations, the local land tenure system, and the local problems and set–up of workers' unions are raised as the ORGANISATION topic. Parallel and related NUMERACY exercises are introduced in measurement.

In a later stage a similar approach is used, but again at a higher level of sophistication. The productive activities of the *campesino* are analysed, and improved techniques for the cultivation of basic grains are taught as part of the WORK syllabus. More scientific knowledge of the common diseases, details of the local health services and how to use them, and the role of the family in education, are examined under HEALTH AND THE FAMILY. The national communications system, and the use and usefulness of letters, telegrams and telephones for *campesinos*, and dialogue as a means of promoting understanding, are themes in the COMMUNICATIONS syllabus. And an analysis of the principal characteristics of Honduran society, more detailed information about peasant organisations and workers' unions and how to participate in them, the system of government and opportunities for *campesinos* to participate, and the role of women figure prominently under the heading of ORGANISATION. NUMERACY continues to concentrate on the development of the basic skills of arithmetic.

The government of Honduras agreed to recognise the successful completion of a four–level ACPH course as the academic equivalent of the government's own seven-year primary school programme. More important than government equivalency recognition, however, was the linking of the radio schools to peasant organisations and unions, and the integration of academic content with social, economic and political concerns. ACPH's curriculum and its organisation both attempted to demonstrate in practical ways the relationships between education, development, political organisation and liberation.

Two vital themes have run through Tanzania's attempts to reorganise society. The first has been the need to apply socialist principles to development in a country where more than 90 percent of the people live in villages. This requires the diversion of resources from urban to rural areas and from industry to agriculture. In order to achieve a better balance between the quality of life in towns and villages it has been necessary to build up rural welfare facilities. To do so it has also proved necessary to persuade people to move from their traditionally scattered homesteads into much larger planned villages. These are the *ujamaa* (or socialist) villages.

Only to *ujamaa* villages is it possible to supply the schools and clinics, the piped water supplies, roads and markets on which so much of their economic and material quality of life depends. And only in village communities of a reasonable size does it make sense to talk about village government and popular political participation. The concept of education for self–reliance has been part and parcel of a general philosophy. It has in part grown from recognition of the irrelevance to Tanzanian villages of an exam–oriented system of education based on imported curricula. In contrast, it stresses the potential of a reoriented system which will promote the attitudes, the relationships and the skills which are prerequisites for village socialism to succeed. The new system must also be as accessible to adults as to children. Both the change of emphasis in the curricula of schools and the creation of widespread facilities for adult education have been characteristics of education in Tanzania during the last decade. Another, the natural result of the promises inherent in the *ujamaa* village drive, has been the demand for, and rapid moves towards, universal primary education, and the consequent recognition that for the forseeable future there will be no resources for any significant expansion of secondary and higher education. But, whatever happens in the future, many older people will not have been to primary school and their educational rightly remains a high priority.

Tanzania has already experimented with various forms of distance teaching. Two other programmes, both run by the Correspondence Education Department of the Institute of Adult Education, offer alternatives to traditional patterns of formal education. First is the production of a range of correspondence courses leading to the national public examinations for secondary schools. These courses are taken by very large numbers of young people and adults who have not been to secondary school. The syllabuses and subjects are identical to those studied in schools. The second programme is for the in–service training of tens of thousands of untrained teachers recruited in order to make possible universal primary education.

Tanzania offers fertile ground for an alternative non–informal system. The organisational base exists as a result of these experiences. Some of her senior educational officials have recognised the need for some such alternative for the many primary school graduates in the middle 1980s for whom there will be no places in secondary schools. The following suggestions for a network of radio colleges are, however, purely ours. They are put forward only to illustrate the potential of such a system, not in any way as a prescription for Tanzania. They are an illustration of what might be done; what should actually be done must be decided by people on the spot who have far more knowledge than we do.

The prime target of such a system would be the people in *ujamaa* villages. The base on which it would be built would be the radio study groups which have been used in the mass campaigns run periodically over the last ten years. Such campaigns would be used to focus attention on subjects of vital everyday importance, on what can be learned about them and on what can be gained from that learning. The difference from the past would be that people would be encouraged to continue to learn by the same means after the campaign was over. Continuation courses for study groups would be offered in practical skills—mechanical, craft, agricultural, social and organisational—which had been shown to be necessary during the campaigns.

These two sketches (and we recognise that of course they are no more than that) of a real and a hypothetical programme seek to show how a more systematic development of non–formal education could occur. We believe it is worth trying. It could be a way of holding out hope of education to some of the many millions of people who, unless something unusual is done, are going to be deprived of it. Each of the two is set in a different national tradition. What they would have in common, however, is to our minds more significant than the differences between them. They would both be concerned to help people learn about their own lives and apply the knowledge and skills which make an improvement possible. They recognise the close relationship between education, home and work which is often missing from formal schools.

It will no doubt be obvious from the tone adopted in this essay where our sympathies lie—with the kind of alternative which has just been outlined. We would dearly like to see some radio colleges established in other continents than Latin America. If this were done, blending intercontinental experience in a new amalgam, distance teaching would emerge as something more than a supplement to schools. As things are, distance teaching ordinarily supports the work that is done in them, or enables people outside them to follow the same syllabus and pass the same examinations as internal students. In the absence of a radical alternative as a complement to the school, it will remain the master, and distance teaching merely one of its lesser handmaidens. But if things were turned round and the kind of alternative we have been discussing were built up, it would be done around the core of distance teaching, and made possible only by these relatively new methods. The fact that within distance teaching we have given primacy to the human element does not mean that in our new model that element could operate on its own. Radio and print are also of the essence, one so much so that it has produced the name we have chosen.

It is easy enough for us to declare our hopes in this way. What chances are there of them ever being realised in practice? The circumstances would clearly have to be very favourable for governments to be interested. They are for the most part much more likely to tread the well–trodden path and go on augmenting the formal system when any more money becomes available, in the way they have always done, with more teachers and more buildings. Well–trodden paths do not provoke questions about the direction in which people are walking, especially when trying to run gives them little time for thought.

What then should the argument be? The practical problems for any government advanced enough to consider distance teaching are real enough. They are about its multiple uses and about the best balance to strike between them. Which to go for? If more than one, how should they fit together? Such questions cannot, of course, be decided by reference to distance teaching so much as by reference to educational principle, and always in a particular context.

If the paramount purpose of an educational system, in practice if not admitted in the rhetoric, is to produce an efficient elite for running the government, the army and the economy of a country, then there is no place for distance teaching.

Were this goal to be paramount it would be best to damp down expansion as much as politically possible, avoid the loss of quality which expansion usually entails and concentrate on the best education that can be given for a small minority at primary, secondary and tertiary levels. If all that were wanted were a well-taught and well-prepared aristocracy or meritocracy there would be no need to bother with the new-fangled armoury of broadcasting, correspondence and study groups. The image of education in an elitist society is a classroom with rows of neatly dressed children filling their exercise books with the algebra of education. The other image, which we have been calling forth, is of a group of men and women sitting in the shade of a tree or in a hut lit by a hurricane lamp and learning not only about fertilisers and nutrition but also about the means by which the poor can become less so.

The usual purpose, as expressed, is not to produce an elite. If it is accepted that all people, whatever the power or position of their parents, have an equal right to respect for what they have in them, they must have an equal right to education. If that be so, it follows that distance teaching has to be considered: it offers a means of speeding up the extension of the privilege of education from the few to the many, or, if one has got that far, from the many to the all.

The first question that has to be asked by any government so minded is how far they are prepared to put right the injustices of the past. In all the poorer countries educational expansion has left in its wake successive waves of people who have missed out on the benefits accruing to people born later in the century. There are the adults who have never been to school at all. In many countries these constitute the majority. Are they to get any consideration? There are the adults and teenagers who have been to primary school for a year or two and then dropped out. Are they to be left out because they have not been able to grasp the opportunity when it was first presented to them? Of like kind are the adults and teenagers who finished primary school but for whom there was no place in secondary. The cumulative backlog is in most countries a very large one and will remain so for generations to come.

Recognising the existence of the backlog does not settle the issue of what distance teaching should be used for. We have shown in this book that multi-media education is also multi-purpose. The combination of media can be employed for acceleration in teacher training, for support for teachers in the classroom, for imparting a formal education at the secondary level to people not at school, or for doing the same with something much less formal. Distance teaching is the shadow of ordinary teaching. If its powers are not to be deployed on all educational problems at once, how is the choice of priorities to be made?

It is very difficult to deny the strength of the argument for building up primary schools, and certainly we would not wish to do so. Wherever the quality of teaching allows, these schools can provide a basic education better than any alternative. Primary schools can excite some interest in further learning and produce the literacy and numeracy which are the conditions of full citizenship as well as of further learning. They are therefore the first and most indispensable element in any educational system. It follows that distance teaching should be employed to support them, and this can be done in no better way than by joining in the crucial task of training and retraining their teachers. Primary schools are unlikely to be of higher quality than the teachers in them. Distance teaching can raise that quality, and should be used to that end. Otherwise, at this level its purpose should be to provide some out-of-school equivalent for people who have never been to primary school or left it before their course was run. This would, rightly, be seen only as a stop-gap measure, even though the gap were a very wide one which might not be filled for decades.

One long-term priority should therefore be the training of teachers for primary schools. When it comes to secondary education the case for distance teaching out of school is that much stronger, because the case for 100 percent coverage is much weaker than it is for primary schools. The two are in competition for resources, and, if primary is to have priority, the expansion of secondary cannot proceed at the same rate, especially in view of the fact that secondary is so much more expensive per head. In no developing country is it yet possible for all qualified primary leavers to enter secondary school, let alone to stay there till the end of the course; and in relatively few countries will it have come about even by the end of the century.

Despite the way schools have expanded, then, there will long be a huge backlog of adults whose life chances are limited because they were born too early to go to school or too poor to afford to stay there. Behind the generations who missed primary school march the continuing ranks of those who missed, and will miss, secondary school. Some will continue to demand formal education out of school, leading to the same examinations as those taken by the more fortunate in school. Every country should offer that kind of second chance. But there is a different kind of second chance: while adolescents outside as well as in school may see the examination route as the all–important one, there is a better hope of capturing the interests of adults on topics more clearly related to what they are doing in the rest of their lives.

We have been talking of stop–gaps or second–best alternatives for those who cannot get into school. Primary equivalence would be in that category in any country which was still making progress towards the goal of universal literacy, and secondary equivalence would have that cast to it as well. But, to underline one of the crucial points, it need not be so. The radio college need not remain a second-best if as much imagination is embodied in the new institution as in the old. It has not been tried anywhere on the sort of scale that we would hope for, not even in Latin America; and, until it has been, no one will know how bounded ambition must be.

For our part we are, as we have shown, rather optimistic. Judged by purely academic criteria we would not expect that a radio college would compare well for most people with an ordinary secondary school. From that point of view we willingly accept the superiority of a daily seven–hour grind in a classroom. But academic criteria are not the only ones. A college not governed by the scramble for diplomas could in one way be at a great advantage. Almost everyone in an ordinary school who recognises the deadening effect of exams would also recognise that an institution not dominated by them would be in one respect enviable. It would be free to develop new curricula linked to life rather than textbooks.

The planners of radio colleges would have no choice on one matter. Their timetable and curriculum would have to be oriented to work, because that is where most of their students would be. The times set aside for study would have to be compatible with working hours, and the subjects taken up would have to be relevant to that work and such leisure as there was from it, if the interest of the students were to be maintained. As we have already argued, it follows from this, and from the fact that in developing countries the majority of people live in rural areas, that the curriculum would need to be about rural work, health, housing and leisure, though always set in the context of the broader national and international society of which each village is perforce a part. These are necessities of a rural radio college; they could as well be styled advantages.

Another necessity is that the college should be open to students of different ages. This is partly because people of different ages will be keen to try themselves out as its students, especially if, as we think should happen, the distinction made in the formal system between primary and secondary is blurred instead of being perpetuated. There will be youngsters who cannot get to secondary school and older people who were not able to, who dropped out from primary school or never went. They will all be entitled to consideration. The mixing of ages has been a phenomenon in third world schools for a very long time. It is still not impossible to find a person in his twenties sitting alongside someone under ten. The segregation of people by age has not, in other words, been so marked in poorer countries as it has become in the richer. That same phenomenon would almost inevitably be present also in a radio college and could be put to advantage. The older students, some of whom could even be grandmothers and grandfathers, would have a lot to add to their own to the collective experience of the practical subjects which would be the core of the curriculum. A mixed–age college would in its basic constitution recognise that education needs to be permanent.

This is not to say that we envisage that, in the ordinary way, a radio college would contain children of primary age, though it would have adults who had not been to primary school. The first priority for any country will, as we say, remain the creation of primary schools for all young children. But beyond that we do envisage that radio colleges will serve some adolescents who cannot get to ordinary secondary schools because there are not enough places for them, and that they will mix there with people older than themselves. This happens already in the radiophonic schools of Latin America.

To urge all this is at the same time (despite all the manifest difficulties) to urge educators in the developing countries to do something different from what has been done so far in the other countries which have been their exemplars. Long after the colonial powers have ceased to be masters, their former subject peoples are still striving all they can to copy their educational system. It is almost as though the same gene were reproducing itself in society after society; or in other words that the education system were reproducing itself on the same template. The growth unfolds itself according to the same pattern, with primary schools being started first, teachers being painfully trained to work in them, secondary schools being gradually developed and then tertiary, with the first dribble of students at each stage being followed by great masses. As long as it is this example which is being followed it is only too easy to forecast what will happen at various points in the future, after colossal expenditure of resources. In half a century some poorer countries will be as far advanced as, say, Britain was twenty years ago; in others it will take a century to get as far as that, both in quantitative and qualitative terms.

The present plight of these same countries is in itself enough to discourage too much faith in the rightness of the goal. Dore may have been somewhat harsh in his judgment on the contemporary state of affairs, but surely not so that the picture is quite unrecognisable, when he described education in developing countries in the following terms:[8]

> Primary schools which serve chiefly to give the majority of their pupils the label 'failed drop–out'; secondary schools and universities which seem designed to squeeze every ounce of curiosity and imagination out of a man before he is discharged into the bureaucracy to take responsibility for his country's destinies; growing armies of secondary and university graduates for whom no slots can be found in the bureaucracy, and—despite these growing numbers of educated unemployed—relentless and growing pressure for more secondary schools and universities in order to 'widen opportunity': such, in the developing countries of the Third World, are the consequences of using schools as the chief means of sifting each generation into those who get the prize jobs and those who don't, and of letting that sifting function dominate—even it seems, obliterate—the schools' ancient function of providing education.

But there is no requirement of history which forces the poorer countries to follow my leader in this way. They could do something different, and if they did they might find themselves not at the rear of the long column headed by the industrial countries but at its head, moving in a different direction and themselves giving the lead to the rest of the world. Our own belief is that the radio college which embodies more of the technology of the West than of its social and educational ideas could be one of the instruments whereby this new and distinctive sort of education could be brought into existence.

The head of the column? A new excellence? Is it not a cranky bit of intellectual arrogance to suggest that we can produce something better than the English primary school, MIT or Oxbridge? Or, at best, a piece of inverse intellectual snobbery? We believe it is more than that, and we would sum up the case for the radio college by reemphasising its three advantages over a system where education in school is the only sort of education that really counts.

The first advantage comes in playing the numbers game. Tomorrow's children, like yesterday's children, will not all get to school. If it is possible, as it should be, to create a system of radio colleges more cheaply than we could create schools, then they offer the chance of redressing the dangerous imbalance between the educated haves and the uneducated have–nots. The building of schools will not solve the problem of equity in education for generations to come; a different sort of institution has a chance of doing so by providing education for adults who missed the chance of going to school when they were children.

The second advantage has to do with the diploma disease. The radio college's curriculum would be based on the concerns of its members' everyday lives, not on those of a remote and external body of examiners. Of course, with any educational body there is a danger of academic drift, of seeking academic respectability at the expense of the interests of underprivileged students. But our radio colleges would have a chance of resisting the process so long as their objective remained that of educating the majority outside school rather than the minority within. The diploma disease is most serious where education becomes principally a filtering process, separating out the educated, or educable, few from the uneducated many. The radio college's vision is of a quite different sort of education.

The third advantage is that the radio college offers an alternative method to the scholastic one in which pupils quietly sit down to learn what the teacher tells them. Forty years ago A.N. Whitehead argued that the educational tradition from classical times on[9]

> is warped by the vicious assumption that each generation will substantially live amid the conditions governing the lives of its fathers and will transmit these conditions to mould with equal force the lives of its children. We are now living in the first period of human history for which this assumption is false.

And yet, as we saw, under–equipped teachers can only teach what, and as, they were themselves taught. The methods we are advocating can short–cut, bringing to radio college or to school new resources, recently produced: education need no longer be limited to the stale facts which a teacher remembers from his own education, and from his regular annual recital of them. By changing the function of the teacher, and supporting him with resources from outside, the radio college could offer a better sort of education.

It is this set of advantages which would enable a network of radio colleges, or something like them, to offer a different kind of education—not an inadequate copy of traditional schooling but something qualitatively different.

One fundamental objection to any such proposal is that it runs counter to all the prevailing notions of modernity. The way modern societies are organised, anything with a rural bias is liable to be attacked just on those very grounds as inevitably second–best. Village life, so it is alleged, is inevitably thin, and a life down on the farm a thinner one. The only good life is in the cities, as witness the mass migration that has gone on and is still going on apace from the countryside to the towns. This exodus, our critics would say, could not be stemmed by a modern Virgil, let alone by lauding the virtues of a college with rural life at its heart. People are trying to escape from agriculture; if you ever suggest they should stay in it your fate will be that of all those well–intentioned colonial administrators who tried to organise schools by the plough instead of the Oxford University Press.

Harsh words, yes, but even so we doubt whether they have as much force as they once had. In rich and poor countries alike, our cities are facing problems to which we have not yet found solutions. If we can do anything to reduce the educational inequalities between town and country, there will be social as well as educational benefits. And, looking beyond our present problems, there is the new recognition of the limits placed upon further pell–mell urban expansion by the exhaustion of natural resources. Centuries of effort have gone into digging great holes in the rural areas of the world, extracting the minerals and re–fabricating them into cities; or pumping out oil from other depths for the sake of vital transport. It is not only in rich countries that people are becoming aware they cannot go on indefinitely consuming ever more scarce fossil fuels, adding more waste products to an environment whose capacity to absorb them is limited. When the oil finally runs out, it may force upon the world a reversal of the long–term trend whereby the city has gained people at the expense of the countryside. To survive, more of the world's growing population will have to grow more food from the limited land available to mankind. It is still a question whether they will be able to. If they cannot ensure that the expansion of food production keeps pace with the expansion of population there may be no long–term survival for anyone.

Seen in this light, an education which embodies the view that food production is the most vital work of all could be one of the keys to human survival. We would accept, of course, that production is not, and never will be, all that matters. The countryside needs enough food for the people who live there, and enough to export some to the city; it also needs a higher quality of life, adorned with rural industry and with many of the amenities so far exclusive to the city, if people are not only to survive but find it worthwhile doing so. Gandhi may yet come into his own.

There is another way of looking at the material presented in this essay. Although there can (and of course will) be disagreements about what should be done in the future, there is less room for them on what has been happening up to date. There is not much doubt that distance teaching has been on a growth path, and also that the form it can most usefully take has become more sharply defined.

As we would now see it, many innovators have in the past put more faith in the mass media than they can bear. The mass media, and in the richer countries television in particular, have transformed the entertainment industry. They have gone some way towards transforming the home too, especially for children who cannot be dragged away from the screen. If a revolution in one sphere, why not in another? Could not education be transformed in the same way, and the best teachers the world can produce be put straight into communication with their pupils? The questions have long been obvious and pointed, and there was only one way of answering them—by practical trial.

There have now been many such trials. The conclusion we have drawn is that the big technology of television, above all when it is used on its own, has not justified the hopes once placed in it. The early enthusiasts of television seemed to think that you could replace the teacher with the glittering screen as easily as soap opera has replaced ballads round the piano. It did not work out quite like that. Of course broadcasting can distribute information more rapidly than ever before. But practice has confirmed what theory predicted:[10] broadcasts can seldom replace the teacher, though they can change his role from one of providing information to one of helping learning. Even if we could easily distribute books, radios, radio repair shops and batteries throughout the whole world, we would still need group leaders and teachers to stimulate discussion about broadcasts, to see how they related to ordinary people's lives, and to tell the broadcasters when their programmes were on the right lines or on the wrong ones.

Technology, meaning far more the little technology of radio than the big technology of television, can be of great value, but usually only when it is used in support of live teachers interacting with other people. If you have the technology without the face–to–face groups, then in educational terms nothing much may happen. If you have the groups without the technology something will happen, but it will often happen better with the support of broadcasting. For there is technical knowledge available—about better methods of agriculture, about health, about birth control—which can raise the quality of life for millions of people, and increase the control they have over their own lives, if the knowledge is made more freely available. The mass media do not have a solo part in this, but they can have a very worthwhile supporting one.

On this there has been a remarkable convergence in many different countries. It has been the experience of the Open University in Britain, and this even though it has made more use of broadcasting in conjunction with correspondence courses than almost any other of the institutions we have referred to. The lesson drawn from the developing countries has been even more emphatic. For people who are illiterate or not far from being so, the face–to–face element is even more crucial, with radio being relatively more important than print, at any rate in the early stages of any learning process. The special feature of the many institutions we have reviewed is the way in which radio is employed. That is their distinguishing mark. Hence the name we are suggesting, radio college. But this does not mean that radio has been as important as the face–to–face element. This much has been learnt from the ordinary school which we sometimes decry. The outcome has been the same in Latin America as in Africa or Asia, and as much in teacher training as in adult education.

This trend has belonged to an even more fundamental convergence. In what has been called the post–industrial society, new attitudes to technology have replaced the old. The emphasis is on humanising the machine, which means reducing its size to a human scale in education as in industry, in agriculture as in consumption. The new distance learning belongs to a worldwide movement. The barefoot technologist of education is partner to the barefoot manager and the barefoot doctor.

REFERENCES

1. International Commission on the Development of Education, *Learning to Be*, UNESCO, 1972
2. Ibid., p. 297
3. World Bank, Education Sector Working Paper, Washington, D.C., 1974
4. P. Freire, *Pedagogy of the Oppressed*, Herder, 1968
5. Ibid., p. 83
6. J. Bruner, *The Process of Education*, Cambridge, MA: Harvard University Press, 1960

7. M. Young, 'Note on the Honduras Radio Schools', International Extension College, 1977

8. R. Dore, *The Diploma Disease*, Allen and Unwin, 1976

9. A. N. Whitehead, *Adventures of Ideas*, Penguin, 1942

10. Compare E. Katz and P. F. Lazarsfeld, *Personal Influence*, Free Press, 1955

PART III
Family and Social Policy

6

Conservation of Family Life

The argument is still about the future in these excerpts from *Family and Kinship in East London,* written jointly with Peter Willmott and published in 1957. This was the first of a series of sociological studies made in the working–class district of Bethnal Green in East London. The book has sold about one million copies but had very little influence upon the planners. The greatest regret of the author's work life is that he did not follow the book by launching a determined campaign against tower blocks and the demolition of old houses. The plea of the book was for conservation of the community and extended families of Bethnal Green and of other places like it. But his training in politics had been inside a political party which was committed to 'slum clearance'. He had not yet learnt how to build up pressure groups against government. The clear conclusion was that Bethnal Greeners did not like the shape of the future at it was unfolding.

Since family life is so embracing in Bethnal Green, one might perhaps expect it would be all–embracing. The attachment to relatives would then be at the expense of attachment to others. But in practice this is not what seems to happen. Far from the family excluding ties to outsiders, it acts as an important means of promoting them. When a person has relatives in the borough, as most people do, each of these relatives is a go–between with other people in the district. His brother's friends are his acquaintances, if not his friends; his grandmother's neighbours so well known as almost to be his own. The kindred are, if we understand their function aright, a bridge between the individual and the community.

The function of the kindred can be understood only when it is realized that long-standing residence is the usual thing. Fifty–three percent of the people in the general sample were born in Bethnal Green, and over half those not born locally had lived in the borough for more than fifteen years. Most people have therefore had time to get to know plenty of other local inhabitants. They share the same background. The people they see when they go out for a walk are people they played with as children. 'I've always known Frank and Barney,' said Mr. Sykes. 'We was kids together. We knew each other from so high. We were all in the same street.' They are the people they went to school with. 'It's friendly here,' according to Mrs. Warner. 'You can't hardly ever go out without meeting someone you know. Often it's someone you were at school with.' They are the people they knew at the youth club, fellow–members of a teenage gang, or boxing opponents. They have the associations of a lifetime in common. If they are brought up from childhood with someone, they may not necessarily like him, they certainly 'know' him. If they live in the same street for long they cannot help getting to know people whom they see every day, talk to and hear about in endless conversation. Long residence by itself does something to create a sense of community with other people in the district. Even an unmarried orphan would have local acquaintants if he were established in this way. But, unmarried orphans being rare, as a rule a person has relatives also living in the district, and as a result his own range of contacts is greatly enlarged. His relatives are also established. Their playmates and their schoolfriends, their workmates and their pub–companions, are people whom he knows as well. Likewise, his friends and acquaintances also have their families in the district, so that when he gets to know any individual person, he is also likely to know at least some of his relatives.

The Bethnal Greener is therefore surrounded not only by his own relatives and their acquaintances, but also by his own acquaintances and their relatives. To show what this means in practice, let us accompany one of our informants on an ordinary morning's shopping trip. It lasted about half an hour. As she went along the street, nodding and chatting to this person and that, Mrs. Landon commented on the people whom she saw.

1. *Mary Collins.* 'She's a sister of Sally who I worked with at the button place before I got married. My Mum knew her Mum, but I sort of lost touch until one day I found myself sitting next to her in Meath Gardens. We both had the babies with us and so we got talking again. I see quite a lot of Mary now.'

2. *Arthur Jansen.* 'Yes, I knew him before I was married. He worked at our place with his sister and mother. He's married now.'

3. *Mavis Boot.* 'That lady there, I know her. She lives down our turning,' said Mrs. Landon, as she caught sight in the butcher's

Conservation of Family Life 101

of a back view of a large woman carrying the usual flat cloth bag. 'She's the daughter of one of Mum's old friends. When she died Mum promised to keep an eye on Mavis. She pops in at Mum's every day.'

4. *Joan Bates* is serving behind the counter at the baker's. 'She used to be a Simpson. She lives in the same street as my sister. My Mum knows her better than me.'

5. *Sybil Cook.* 'That's a girl I knew at school called Sybil.'

6. *Katie Simmons.* 'She's from the turning. Mum nursed her Mum when she was having Katie.'

7. *Betty Salmon and her mother.* 'They live in the next turning to ours. Betty says she's had nothing but trouble with her daughter since she went to school.'

8. *Richard Fienburgh.* 'That man over there at the corner. He's a sort of relative. He's a brother of my sister's husband. He lives near them.'

9. *Patrick Collis.* This was a man in an old car parked by the shops. 'His mother lives in the turning.'

10. *Amy Jacobs* is an old and bent woman who turns out to be Mrs. Landon's godmother. 'Usually it's only when I'm with Mum that we talk.'

11. *Sadie Little.* This time there was not even a nod. The two women walked straight past each other. 'She's quarrelled with my sister so we don't talk to each other.'

12. *Alfred Crosland.* He is the father of the Katie seen a few minutes before.

13. *Violet Belcher*, a tall, thin lady talking to another at the street corner, is an 'acquaintance of Mum's. She's got trouble with her inside.'

14. *Emma France.* This was an elderly, very jolly woman, with grey hair and a loud laugh. She engaged Mrs. Landon in conversation.
    'How's that other sister of yours?'
    'Lily?'
    'Yes, your Mum told me. She's gone to live in Bow, hasn't she?'
    'She's got a place with her mother–in–law there.'
    'She don't like it? No! It never did work and I don't suppose it ever will.'

They both collapsed into laughter at this. Afterwards Mrs. Landon explained that Mrs. France had been her landlady in the first rooms her Mum had got for her.

That was just one unexceptional shopping trip. 'Some days', says Mrs. Landon, 'you see so many you don't know which to talk to.' She kept a record over a week of all the people she saw in the street and whom she considered herself to 'know'. There were sixty–three people in all, some seen many times and thirty–eight of them relatives of at least one other person out of the sixty–three. Her story showed how she had built up a series of connexions with people she had known in school, work, or street, and, even more forcefully, how her mother and other kin acted as a means of communication between herself and the other people in her social world.

We should make it clear that we are talking mainly about what happens *outside* the home. Most people meet their acquaintances in the street, at the market, at the pub, or at work. They do not usually invite them into their own houses. We asked people whether they visited, or were visited by, friends in one or other home at least once a month. 'Friend' was here defined as anyone other than a relative. Out of the ninety men and women in the marriage sample, eighty–four exchanged visits with relatives, and only thirty–two with friends. Those exchanging the most visits with relatives also did so with friends; those most sociable inside the family were also the most sociable outside. But the majority neither had, nor were, guests.

Several people said they had possessed many more friends when they were single. Marriage and children made the difference.

> 'Since we've had the children I've got no more friends—outside the family I mean.'
>
> 'I don't see my best friend much. She's married too, and she's always round *her* Mum's like I'm always round mine.'
>
> 'Since we've had the baby, I've got no men friends—outside the family, that is.'

The general attitude was summed up by Mr. Jeffreys.

> 'I've got plenty of friends around here. I've always got on well with people, but I don't invite anyone here. I've got friends at work and friends at sport and friends I have a drink with. I know all the people around here, and I'm not invited into anyone else's home either. It doesn't seem right somehow. Your home's your own.'

Where every front door opens on to street or staircase, and houses are crowded on top of one another, such an attitude helps to preserve some privacy against the press of people.

This exclusiveness in the home runs alongside an attitude of friendliness to other people living in the same street. Quite often people have themselves lived there for a long time—one out of every ten women and one out of every twenty men in the general sample still live in the street where they were born—and consequently know many of the other residents well. Quite often, too, either they or their neighbours also have relatives in the street who add to the spread of social contacts. If a person gets on bad terms with another person in the street—like Mrs. Shipway whose neighbour 'started spreading stories about me and told me off for sending my children to Mum's when I go out to work'—she is also on bad terms with her family. 'They're all related in this street,' said Mr. Lamb. 'It's awful, you can't talk to anyone in the street about any of the others, but you find it's a relation. You have to be very careful.' But if he is careful and keeps on good terms with his neighbours, he is also on good terms with their relatives, and can nod to them in the street, knowing that he will get a response. He only has to stand at his front door to find someone out of his past who is also in his present.

> 'I suppose people who come here from outside think it's an awful place, but us established ones like it. Here you can just open the door and say hello to everybody.'

The streets are known as 'turnings', and adjoining ones as 'back-doubles'. Surrounded by their human associations, the words had a glow to them. 'In our turning *we*', they would say, 'do this, that, or the other.' 'I've lived in this turning for fifty years', said one old man proudly, 'and here I intend to stay.' The residents of the turning, who usually make up a sort of 'village' of 100 to 200 people, have their own places to meet, where few outsiders ever come—practically every turning has its one or two pubs, its two or three shops, and its 'bookie's runner'. They organize their own parties: nearly every turning had its committee and celebration (and several built wooden stages for the display of local talent) for the Coronation of 1953. Some turnings have little war memorials built onto walls of houses with inscriptions like the following:

R.I.P.
IN LOVING MEMORY OF THE MEN OF CYPRUS
STREET WHO MADE THE GREAT SACRIFICE
1914–1918
J. AMOS, E. AGOMBAR, A. BOARDMAN, A. H. COLE . . .

—there follow the names of the other twenty–two soldiers from Cyprus Street. Above it is a smaller plaque to the men killed in 1939–45: 'They are marching with their comrades somewhere on the road ahead.' Pots and vases of flowers are fixed in a half–circle to the wall; they are renewed regularly by the women of the turning, who make a street collection every Armistice Day.

There is the same kind of feeling in the few small courts still standing where a few houses face each other across a common front yard. In one of these the houses are covered from top to bottom with green trellis–work, tiers of window boxes stand out from the trellis, and on one wall is a proliferation of flowers around a war memorial, a Union Jack, and some faded pictures of the Queen. One of the residents told us, with evident satisfaction, that she was born in the same courtyard house that she had lived in for sixty–two years and spoke with slight disparagement of her neighbours: 'They're new here—they've only been here eighteen years.' She had been shocked to hear that the authorities might be labelling her beloved court a 'slum', and was now terrifed lest they pull it down.

Sometimes a person's relatives are in the same turning, more often in another nearby turning, and this helps to account for the attachment which people feel to the precinct, as distinct from the street, in which they live. A previous observer remarked:

> There is further localism within the borough. People are apt to look for their friends and their club within a close range. The social settlements draw nearly all their members from within a third of a mile, while tradition dictates which way borderline streets face for their social life. The main streets are very real social barriers, and to some residents the Cambridge Heath Road resembles the Grand Canyon.[1]

In Bethnal Green the one–time villages which have as elsewhere been physically submerged and their boundaries usually obliterated—Mumford talks of London as a 'federation of historic communities'[2]—live on in people's minds. Bow is one, Cambridge Heath another, Old Bethnal Green Road another, the Brick Lane area, once just outside the environs of the City, another. 'I reckon it's nice—this part of Bethnal Green I'm talking about,' remarked Mr. Townsend. 'I'm not talking of Brick Lane or that end. Here we're by Victoria Park.' 'It's all right on this side of the canal,' said Mrs. Gould, who lives in Bow. 'I wouldn't like to live on the other side of the canal. It's different there.' Another man, in a letter asking for help in getting another home, wrote, 'I am not particular where you send me, the farther the better. I do not mind if it is as far as Old Ford as I have left my wife and wish to keep as far away as possible.' Old Ford is five minutes' walk from his wife. Other researchers have reported how difficult it was to get people to move even in the war.

> Many stories were told of families who would rather camp in the kitchens of their uninhabitable blitzed houses or sleep in public shelters than accept accommodation in another area of the borough.[3]

When people have to move away from one part of the borough to another, they can appreciate the difference. Mr. Gould, when he married, moved away from his parents and went about ten minutes' walk away to live near his wife's parents elsewhere in the borough, in this case in Bow. 'I'd like to be back in Bethnal Green,' he said, 'I would really. In Bethnal Green we have good neighbours, better than those in Bow I can tell you.' Mrs. Tawney had moved as unwillingly in the other direction.

> 'We're both from Bow. We're not very well known around here. We've only lived here since we got married, you see. In Bow you knew everybody, grew up with everybody, everybody recognized you. Over here they're a bit on the snobbish side— they know you're a stranger and treat you like one. They cater for you more in Bow. You like the place where you're mostly born, don't you?'

People who have moved know that their own old neighbours would still stand by them if necessary. Mrs. Jeffreys told us that in Ramsgate Street, where she had lived all her life until she was bombed out in 1944, even now, over ten years later, 'They all know Edith Jeffreys. Any of them'll give me a character.'

When there is such localism within the borough it is not surprising that for a few people places beyond Bethnal Green are another world. One woman had never been outside the borough except for an odd visit to the 'Other End', as the West End of London[4] is known locally. Another never left the borough except for the usual day–trip once a year to Southend. Yet another said, 'I only went out once when we went to Canvey just before the war. I felt very strange and lonely when I went there. I've never been out of Bethnal Green since except once to go to Southend for the day.' Many of the most rooted people do not talk about fares but about 'riding fares', and while we do not know the origin of the term, in context it sometimes suggested that to pay a fare to travel anywhere was something outlandish and even a little daring. One man said his aged mother was in an Old People's

Home 'over the water'. 'Over the water' meant over the Thames, a mile or two away in Southwark.

In Bethnal Green the person who says he 'knows everyone' is, of course, exaggerating, but pardonably so. He does, with various degrees of intimacy, know many people outside (but often through) his family, and it is this which makes it, in the view of many informants, a 'friendly place'. Bethnal Green, or at any rate the precinct, is, it appears, a community which has some sense of being one. There is a sense of community, that is, a feeling of solidarity between people who occupy the common territory, which springs from the fact that people and their families have lived there a long time. We cannot do better than put it in our informants' own words.

> 'Well, you're born into it, aren't you? You grow up here. I don't think I'd like to live anywhere else. Both my husband and me were born here and have lived here all our lives.
>
> 'You asking me what I think of Bethnal Green is like asking a countryman what he thinks of the country. You understand what I mean? Well, I've always live here, I'm contented. I suppose when you've always lived here you like it.'

The family contributes in another way to this sense of community, by giving people a very personal link with its past. People's parents and sometimes even their grandparents were born in Bethnal Green.

> 'I was bred and born in Bethnal Green and my parents and their parents before them: no, I wouldn't leave Bethnal Green, I wouldn't take a threepenny bus ride outside Bethnal Green.'

In such families local history does not have to be learnt from books: it is passed on by word of mouth from parents to children. Mr. Firth probably had not read that Pepys once came to Bethnal House and had 'a fine merry walk with the ladies alone after dinner in the garden'. But he related with a certain satisfaction that:

> 'My father used to tell me about the old days when sheep were grazing where Victoria Park Gardens are now laid out and Cambridge Heath Road was still fields. At weekends my father was a keeper at the Burial Ground. It's in Defoe; there's a book on it, father knew all about it.'

The past lives on most tellingly in the families of French descent. Almost everyone in Bethnal Green knows about the Huguenots. The economy stems from the early silk weavers. The love of birds, animals, and flowers, which to this day makes some backyards a glory of bright colour, is said to be due to their influence. The Society for Protestant Refugees from High and Low Normany still flourishes and serves many local people who could not claim French blood. But in the Huguenot families—and especially those with the French names which still stand out on the electoral rolls—the connexion is a source of special pride.

They rarely have documentary evidence of their ancestry. One local informant not in the sample was exceptional: he brought out an old paper written in somewhat strange French in the year of the Revolution, which as far as could be made out was a petition from a man who was his ancestor beseeching the Governors of the French Hospital in Hackney to employ, and at the same time treat, his granddaughter. Others did not know the details of their genealogies, nor were they even sure of their relationship to other local people of the same name. Mr. Michaud thought that some other people were the offspring of his paternal great-uncle, but they were 'not quite up to Mum's and Dad's standard'. Mr. Berthot told us that he had once by accident met a girl who was probably a relative. 'Once a girl came up to me at work and said, "You look like my Dad, what's your name?" It turned out that her name too was Berthot.' But though the details were hazy, they did claim to come of Huguenot stock—as one man put it, 'My people came over from Lyon with the weavers.' For them, and to a lesser extent for other local residents, the fact that their 'people' as well as themselves were born in Bethnal Green helps to keep alive a very personal sense of history, and this sense of history reinforces the feeling of attachment (just as it does in a regiment, a university, a trade union, or a political party) to the community and to its inhabitants.

We did not ask in our interviews as closely or systematically about non-relatives as about relatives. But we were left with the impression that the kindred, far from being a barrier, are in fact a doorway to the community. Some people do, no doubt, enclose themselves completely within the family; many do not willingly admit any but family to the privacy of their homes; most have no friend who takes pride of place over close relatives. But in general, it seems, relatives do not compete with friends, rather act as intermediaries with them. We said earlier that each of the relatives in a person's family of origin is a link with yet another family, and so on in a widening network, 'each family of marriage being knitted to each family of origin and each family of origin to each family of marriage by a member that they have in common'. Our present proposition is that each of the relatives in the families of origin, and indeed in the network as a whole, is a link not only with other families but with people outside the family as well.

In itself this is only a formal proposition, just as the original proposition was formal. To say that there is a 'link' (a clumsy metaphorical term, we admit) is not to say anything about its character. We have to inquire what actually happens between the family and the outside world, that is, into the nature of the 'links', just as we have to inquire what actually animates the formal structure of the family. Our belief is that in Bethnal Green the links, with a mother who lives in the next street and hence with her friends, acquaintances, and enemies, are more continuously effective because of the proximity to her and of the length of time for which proximity has existed.

The interaction between length of residence and kinship is therefore the crux of our interpretation. Neither is by itself a sufficient explanation. People in their families of marriage, let us suppose, live for a long period in one district without being related to others. They will establish many common associations through having children at the same schools, through meeting in the same shops, and through travelling on the same trains. But since there are no related families in the locality they will not be able to make use of the kind of social connexion which we have described. People could also, let us suppose, migrate in a caravan of related families. They would then have relatives around them, but these relatives would not be able to introduce them to so many outside the family precisely because none of them would be rooted in the district. Either length of residence or localized kinship does something to create a network of local attachment, but when they are combined, as they are in Bethnal Green, they constitute a much more powerful force than when one exists without the other. Then people have a number of links, or ways of orienting themselves, to the same person: he was at school, he is a relative by marriage, he lives in a well-known neighbourhood. Then people can make use of one or other of their possible approaches to establish a relationship with almost anyone. We only make these distinctions in order to clarify the interpretation. In practice it must be very rare to find long residence without local kinship or local kinship without long residence.

In this old–established district the relatives are a vital means of connecting people with their community. We do not suggest that family is the only doorway to friendship; by taking account of the associations of school and work we have tried to keep a balance between kinship and the rest. Certainly, many friends of whom informants spoke were made by them quite independently, at school, at work, or in the army. But here the family does more than anything else to make the local society a familiar society, filled with people who are not strangers. This has its disadvantages. If you know other people's business, they know yours. Feuds may be all the more bitter for being contained in such small space. But there are advantages too. For many people, familiarity breeds content. Bethnal Greeners are not lonely people: whenever they go for a walk in the street, for a drink in the pub, or for a row on the lake in Victoria Park, they know the faces in the crowd.

If we are to pick out one conclusion, it is the importance of residence. The Bethnal Greeners whom we have been describing did not change their residence just because they got married. They have remained in their district, and consequently in their families, of origin. The wife stays close to her mother because she already shares so many common interests and associations, and since she stays nearby, she keeps them alive and renews them. The wife's relationship, most of all with her mother, but also with her other female relatives, is firmer than the husband's relationship with his men relatives, unless indeed he works with them. But the husband, while he may move towards his wife's home, does not usually move far from his own parents; he maintains his connection with them at the same time as he does in the ordinary way succeed in resolving the tension between himself and his in–laws.

A special cast is given to all these adjustments and readjustments by the fact that they are played out within a limited physical space. Relatives in a double sense close cannot easily avoid each other: they either quarrel or merge at least part of their lives. Where mother and daughter are also neighbours they are almost bound to share with each other the tasks which fall to women, and this despite the many changes in housing, in the child welfare services, in the birth–rate, and, above all, in the relationship between man and wife.

The view we have formed and tested more or less daily for three years is that very few people wish to leave a district like this. They are attached to Mum and Dad, to the markets, to the pubs and settlements, to Club Row and the London Hospital. There are, of course, exceptions. Some people have secured a job, or wish for one, in another part of the country, and where job calls, family must usually follow. If there are so few people in Bethnal Green under this necessity to move, it is because the local economy, far from being tied to one industry, offers such a variety of manual work. Social ascent (as it is called) has also been quite rare. The people are manual workers, and, compared to other social classes, these are not nowadays the most on the move.

Some wives also wish to leave because they have fallen out with their own relatives, and more husbands because they cannot get on with their in–laws. When kinship relations go wrong, they can become intolerable. To prevent such people from starting an independent life elsewhere would be even less defensible than to prevail upon the majority to move away from relatives against their will. People should obviously have as much choice of residence as possible: given choice, they will be able to meet best the individual needs of which they, and they only, should be the judge.

We suggest that the majority wish to stay in their district. If this opinion is to carry any weight, we must try to say why. The first point—one we have made before but will repeat—is that they are tied to the district by time. In some places people divide their lives into two, in one home while they are growing up, and another, far off, when they marry. In Bethnal Green there is no sharp division. People do not, after marriage, throw off the past which contains their former family and friends. They combine past and present. They continue to belong to the same community, and, since the sense of belonging which comes from knowing and being known by so many of their fellow residents is something which most Bethnal Greeners prize, this alone goes some way to explain their attachment.

But their sense of belonging cannot be explained simply by long residence. It is so deep because it is rooted in a lasting attachment to their families. In this, Bethnal Green may be unlike other districts and other classes in which children appear, from superficial observation, to draw away from their parents when they grow up. If this be true—only further research can show—the difference may be related not only to the occupations they follow, but also to the different length of 'childhood'. In the middle classes children are usually dependent on parents until they are adult; their delay in reaching economic independence may make the break all the more complete when at last it does come. On the other hand, in Bethnal Green, as in other working–class districts, nearly all the people left school at fourteen or fifteen and were earning their living not long after puberty, at an age when their fellows in other classes were still sitting at school–desks. Some of them did (and certainly do) use that independence to assert their own personalities by making at least a partial break from their families while still adolescent. Having previously experienced some freedom from parental influence, the women at least seem ready, by the time of marriage, to re–form their ties with their families of origin.

The local kinship system, as we have said again and again, stresses the tie between mother and daughter; and, if we are to understand the disinclination to move, it is the strength of this tie that we should say a word about, even if we cannot hope to explain it at all fully within the small ambit of this study. The initial group is everywhere parents and children, not just mother and daughters. Sons too are in the cradle. Why then should a closer tie between mother and daughter than between the son and either of his parents crystallize out of the initial situation?

It was probably not always like this. Before Britain was industrialized the bond between father and son was probably no less enduring. After a long apprenticeship on the parental holding, at least one of the sons knew enough of the vagaries of soil and stream, animal and crop, and was, by dint of long indoctrination, attached enough to the family's plot of earth to become devoted to husbandry and to live on in his father's house.[5] Father and son, as well as mother and daughter, were linked not only by family but by their common property rights and by their common occupation, this being also true of the handicraft industries which survived for so long as part of the British economy. In modern times, although the practice has no more entirely disappeared from Bethnal Green than from anywhere else, sons more rarely follow in their father's footsteps. They more often get different jobs, and, when they do, they no longer share the same associations. But the woman's economy has not become so diverse as the man's. Despite the arrival of the doctor and the teacher, child-rearing cannot, by its nature, be subjected to the same division of labour, the same specialization, as the work that men do. Daughters, since they still follow their mothers and inherit the same occupation, continue to have a host of interests in common.

These bonds, important still, probably counted even more in the earlier days of factory industry, when the mother–centred kinship system served to give working–class women some security in a life beset by its opposite. The insecurity of men was translated into an even greater lack of security for women, who needed it more, then as always. In a district like Bethnal Green, wives could not rely upon their husbands to stand by them while they reared their children. Death too often removed the prop. Nor were they assured of support from husbands whose lives were spared. In an unstable economy, nearly all men were at some time unemployed and at all times frightened of it; and even when they were in work, they frequently kept their families short of money. So the wife had to cling to the family into which she was born, and in particular to her mother, as the only other means of ensuring herself against isolation. One or other member of her family would, if need be, relieve her distress, lend her money, or share to some degree in the responsibility for her children. The extended family was her trade union, organized in the main by women and for women, its solidarity her protection against being alone. It is, to judge by anthropology, almost a universal rule that when married life is insecure, the wife turns for support to her family of origin, so that a weak marriage tie produces a strong blood tie.[6] East London does not seem to have been an exception.

Such defensive action might, ironically, produce the very result it was designed to guard against. Aware that the wife's overriding attachment was to her family of origin, excluded from the warmth and intimacy of the female circle, resentful husbands were only too likely to react by withdrawing themselves to their own consolations outside the home, in the pub and in *their* families of origin. The process was a circular one, the husband's withdrawal making her cling to her mother, and her action making the husband withdraw: insecurity bred insecurity.[7] In Bethnal Green, even today, social workers still lay the blame for some desertions and divorces upon Mum's sometimes far from benign influence. The two–way repercussion of insecurity upon kinship cannot be documented from historical investigation. It is rare to find a mention like Lady Bell's: 'The affectionate relation between the young married daughter and her own home, indeed, sometimes causes an additional difficulty, as there are cases where the young wife neglects her own house to go to her mother's.'[8] But though we cannot document the process, the witness of our informants in Bethnal Green leaves no doubt that, here at any rate, insecurity and kinship were inextricably bound together. The conditions of the past have, we believe, given a certain cast to the kinship system which can still be observed, in some families, to the present day, and whose influence is still felt in the moral code with which that system is surrounded.

The daughter's attachment to her mother is no longer such a compelling necessity now that the economy is more stable, broken homes fewer, the birth–rate lower, and the husband's role in the home different. But she still stands to gain a great deal from the person with whom she can share the mysteries as well as the tribulations, the burdens as well as the satisfactions, of child–birth and motherhood. Child–rearing is arduous, it is puzzling, it is monotonous, and the person on whom the primary responsibility falls, if usually on her own when her husband is out at work, may be hard put to avoid the loneliness and exasperation of being confined, day in, day out, in her one–person workplace. She may, if she cannot get any respite, find the five or ten years' hard labour of bringing up her children too exacting and continuous to bear with patience; and if she suffers, so will her children. But with a companion—and who more obvious for her to claim than the woman with whom she has shared her previous life?—her work can be less arduous because it is shared; her life less lonely because she has someone to talk to; the behaviour of her children less perplexing because she has someone whose experience she can draw on; and her lot less monotonous because she can, for the occasional evening or day, leave her children in someone else's care. Whenever the harmony between them exceeds the strife, the wife has something to gain from the help of her mother.

The two women can cooperate so effectively because the younger has not only the same work, but has learnt how to do it from the older woman. Sons, as we have said, usually earn their living at something so different from their fathers that they cannot so often be their pupils as they were in the past. Even when sons follow the same trade, the change in technique from one generation to another may be so great that they have, in their apprenticeship, to attend to other masters. Not that the women's world is static. Techniques of housekeeping and fashions in child care also change, and the faster the rate, the quicker the obsolescence of the mother's skill. The improvement in the technical equipment of the home may yet change the mother–daughter relationship, for instance, by making the daughter her mother's teacher as well as pupil, as much as the improvement in the technical equipment of the farm has, we are told, weakened the authority of the farmer over his son.[9] But changes in the home are less revolutionary, and easier to assimilate, than changes in industry. Technical progress has removed only part of education from the home; long after either she or her husband has ceased to be one for their son, the mother is for her daughter a teacher who accustoms her to a particular way of doing things in the home, and the daughter, since her ways are also her mother's, is likely to feel that she can trust the good sense of her helper.

The benefit is not all one–sided. For the grandmothers and grandfathers the gain is even more obvious. They too, as old age draws on, are even more likely to be lonely than their daughters, and oppressed by their uselessness. If they have children and grandchildren around them, they can not only be of some value to youth, they can also enjoy the reward of being appreciated; and, as they watch over their grandchildren, they can perhaps find some comfort in this evidence of the continuity of life. In their declining years they can call on their descendants to complete the circle of care by easing the strain of infirmity, illness, and bereavement. In a three-generation family the old as well as the young both receive and give services; the aid is reciprocal.[10]

We are certainly not suggesting that the family can be self–sufficient. Although three generations can muster more resources than two, there are still many essential services which no family can possibly provide for itself. Few grandmothers can perform operations or teach algebra. Few grandfathers can, on their own, maintain children stricken by illness or unemployment. Children, unaided, cannot support their parents through the years of retirement. The family is not a society on its own, merely part of the wider society, and, if it is to perform its proper function within its own sphere, the family needs the support which only the wider society can give. This vital support the social services in some measure already supply. The health services have made a great and obvious difference to the well–being of the family, especially to mothers and children. Old age pensions, inadequate though they often are, have enabled children to care for their parents all the more effectively. Anthropologists have reported how much even the old non–contributory pension sweetened relations between the generations in Ireland, and what is true there is just as much true in East London. The social services have in many ways already made the family of three generations or two not less, but more, viable, and perhaps the administrators will be in a position to do even more as knowledge accumulates of the structure and needs of family life.

Nor are we suggesting that the three–generation family has advantages for all women, let alone for all men. Some people favour the extended family, others the isolated household. It all depends on the individual. We do not know which kind of personality, in woman or man, old or young, flourishes in the one rather than the other. Personality, far from being an independent variable, is probably related to family structure. But we can at present hardly even guess which kind of family produces which kind of person. In what way, if at all, are children reared by one mother on her own different from children reared by mothers intimately assisted by grandmothers? This is the kind of question which psychology should in time be able to illuminate, and thus add another, and vital, dimension to our understanding of kinship. For the moment, all we can say for certain is that, for one reason or another, whether rightly or wrongly, most of the women we have interviewed think they get advantages from their attachment to their mothers.

Though they both derive benefit from the relationship, it is far more than a mere arrangement for mutual convenience. The attachment between them is supported by a powerful moral code. This moral code which surrounds kinship is sometimes harsh, imprisoning the human spirit and stunting growth and self–expression, and sometimes observed only in its outward forms. But it need not be so. In most of these families (and Bethnal Green is obviously unexceptional in this) duty and affection seem to coexist and, indeed, reinforce each other, duty fostering affection as much as affection fosters duty. Parents do not choose their children, nor children their parents; the relationship exists whether or not either has the qualities which might arouse affection. Both are usually accepted despite their faults, the dutiful parent not discarding the child born mentally defective nor the dutiful child the parent who has committed what is a crime in the eyes of the greater world; and what applies to parents and children applies in some measure to other relatives as well. Secure in the knowledge that they are valued because they are members of the family, not because they have this or that quality or achievement to their credit, they respond with affection which then becomes as reciprocal as duty. Affection, for its part, helps to make duty not so much the nicely balanced correlative of rights as a more or less unlimited liability beyond the bounds of self–interest and rational calculation. The mother does not inquire whether she will be repaid before she does the washing for her sick daughter, the daughter whether she can afford the time to nurse her mother through a long illness.

We set out to say why most people are attached to the district, and this has led us to consider some of the advantages, for wives in particular, of the local kinship system. The reason they do not want to leave the borough is that its effectiveness depends a good deal upon the geographical proximity of the key figures. During the stages of their lives when they are most in need of support, neither wives nor their mothers can easily move about. If they have babies and young children to look after, the wives cannot readily make longer journeys than they can easily navigate with a pram. Nor can aged parents easily travel far. The mobility of both is often small. This is all the more severe a limitation if they have little money to pay for transport, and little of the time–sense and organizing power which enable some people to maintain a kind of cohesion in a widely scattered circle of friends and relatives. Migration by young couples interposes a barrier of distance which impedes the reciprocal flow of services between the generations. Hence the significance of the move of only a few miles to Greenleigh.

It seems that when the balance of a three–generation family is disturbed, the task of caring for dependents at both ends of life, always one of the great and indispensable functions of any society, becomes less manageable. Dr. Sheldon has underlined the consequences for the old of such a disturbance.

> The enormous building developments in this country since the war have been devoted in the main to the needs of the immediate family of parents and children and are not necessarily so well suited to the care of three generations. One way in which many families used to cope with this problem has unintentionally been made more difficult by the shift, mainly of the younger generation, out to the new dwellings. Both the old people and their younger relatives are agreed on the layout most suitable for

many families which can be summed up as one of independent propinquity—i.e., separate establishments sited reasonably close to each other, so combining the advantages of independence and ready mutual aid. The movement away of the younger generation inevitably leaves more old people who can no longer depend on the ready accessibility of their children; but it is essential to recognize this aspect of the natural history of old age and to assist a desire of the two generations to live closer to each other, for otherwise we are depriving ourselves of what has hitherto been one of the principal methods by which so many families have elected to care for their old people.[11]

In a three–generation family the burden of caring for the young as well, though bound to fall primarily on the mothers, can be lightened by being shared with the grandmothers. The three generations complement each other. Once prise out two of them, and the wives are left without the help of grandmothers, the old without the comfort of children and grandchildren.

The question for the authorities is whether they should do more than they are at present doing to meet the preference of people who would not willingly forgo these advantages, rather than insisting that more thousands should migrate beyond the city. To supply good houses for families with young children as well as flats for others is not a simple operation in a congested town; we do not pretend that it is. It would mean sacrificing some of the many projected open spaces, earmarked in the plans for future public gardens and parks, for the only reason which could justify so grave a step, that on balance people would much rather have houses than spaces. It would mean putting some factories rather than residences in high flatted buildings. It might mean gradually moving out to the country some of the vast railway yards, the unwelcome inheritance of another transport age, which at present sprawl smokily across the face of the city—and using the sites for houses instead. It would certainly mean saving as many as possible of the existing houses, where these are structurally sound, by installing within the old fabric new bathrooms, lavatories, and kitchens. The problems are formidable, but if the purpose of rehousing is to meet human needs, not as they are judged by others but as people themselves assess their own, it is doubtful whether anything short of such a programme will suffice.

Not everyone could, under this or any other plan, hope to stay where he is. People will have to move about within their own district, if not outside it, as the slums beyond salvage are cleared and replaced. But reshuffling the residents could be accomplished by moving as a block the social groups, above all the wider families, to which people wish to belong. Movement of street and kinship groupings as a whole, members being transferred together to a new setting, would enable the city to be rebuilt without squandering the fruits of social cohesion.

The physical size of reconstruction is so great that the authorities have been understandably intent upon bricks and mortar. Their negative task is to demolish slums which fall below the most elementary standards of hygiene, their positive one to build new houses and new towns cleaner and more spacious than the old. Yet even when the town planners have set themselves to create communities anew as well as houses, they have still put their faith in buildings, sometimes speaking as though all that was necessary for neighbourliness was a neighbourhood unit, for community spirit a community centre. If this were so, then there would be no harm in shifting people about the country, for what is lost could soon be regained by skillful architecture and design. But there is surely more to a community than that. The sense of loyalty to each other amongst the inhabitants of a place like Bethnal Green is not due to buildings. It is due far more to ties of kinship and friendship which connect the *people* of one household to the *people* of another. In such a district community spirit does not have to be fostered, it is already there. If the authorities regard that spirit as a social asset worth preserving, they will not uproot more people, but build the new houses around the social groups to which they already belong.

REFERENCES

1. P. J. O. Self, 'Voluntary Organizations in Bethnal Green', in A. E. C. Bourdillon, (Ed.), *Voluntary Social Services*

2. L. Mumford, *City Development,* Secker and Warburg, 1946

3. R. Glass and M. Frenkel, 'How They Live at Bethnal Green', in *Contact: Britain Between East and West,* Contact Publications Ltd

4. Some people regard the West End as an immoral place which good East Londoners should not frequent. In some parts of the East End the last bus at night from the West End was ironically known not so long ago as the 'virgin's bus'. See W. Matthews, *Cockney Past and Present,* Routledge, 1938

5. Some hints are given in other studies about the persisting importance of the father–son tie in rural areas of the British Isles. See A. D. Rees, *Life in a Welsh Countryside,* University of Wales Press, 1951, and C. M. Arensberg and S. T. Kimball, *Family and Community in Ireland* (Cambridge, MA: Harvard University Press, 1948)

6. Some extreme examples of mother–centred extended families are to be found in the West Indies and the southern states of America, where 'husbands' at one time drifted out as easily as they drifted in. See F. M. Henriques, *Family and Colour in Jamaica,* Eyre and Spottiswoode, 1953, and

E. F. Frazier, *The Negro Family in the United States* (Chicago: University of Chicago Press, 1939)

7. Of another place an anthropologist has written that, 'Time and again the instability of Hausa marriage and the high incidence of divorce is seen to be closely linked with the attachment of wives to their kin, an attachment which usually overrides any fondness they may feel for their husbands when they conflict, which frequently happens at the instigation of kinswomen of a senior generation.' M. G. Smith, *Baba of Karo: A Woman of the Muslim Hausa*, Faber and Faber, 1954

8. Lady Bell, *At the Works*, Edward Arnold, 1907

9. W. M. Williams, *The Sociology of an English Village: Gosforth*, Routledge, 1956

10. The meaning of kinship for the old is explored in P. Townsend, *The Family Life of Old People*, Routledge, 1957

11. J. H. Sheldon, 'The Social Philosophy of Old Age', *Old Age in the Modern World*, Livingstone, 1955

7

The Old World to Redress the Balance of the New

The Bethnal Green studies, and a succeeding one made in the London suburb of Woodford, both brought out the continuing importance of kinship networks. But were these networks bound to disappear in the course of time? One way of suggesting an answer was to consult American experience, on however small a scale. As America is today, so may Britain be tomorrow. This small study in Menlo Park, near San Francisco, made with Hildred Geertz, suggests, however, that kinship ties are of great importance there as well, with more of the Californians knowing about their pedigrees.

To what extent do older people in modern society become isolated from their families, and which family ties remain strongest? The small-scale study described here, by comparing the family relationships of older people in two suburbs—one outside London, the other near San Francisco—attempts to give some preliminary answers to this question.[1]

In brief, we found the two groups similar in two ways, and different in one. (1) Parents in their old age maintain close ties with their adult children, ties 'close' both in geography and in frequency of contact. Older people are by no means deserted by their families. (2) Of the adult children, daughters play consistently more important parts in their parents' lives than sons. The difference was that a larger proportion of the American group have knowledge of and pride in their pedigree, while the English group have relatively little knowledge of ancestry. This finding seemed to be of sufficient interest to investigate on a countrywide basis, and this was done in a limited way with a sample of 3,964 for U.S.A. and one of 900 for Britain.

In both districts the ties of kinship play a much more significant part in the lives of old people than is often assumed. An expression of a common point of view that the family has 'withered away', especially for older people, is found in Max Lerner's *America as a Civilization*.

> The two–generation nuclear American family, usually constricted in living space, has little room for the old people, nor does it allow them any participating role. In a society of rapid change the gap in outlook between the generations is too great to leave the older people any sense of their function in transmitting the mores of their culture. They retire from business or are arbitrarily retired from their jobs. Absorbed as they have been with making money, making a living, or running a household, they are unprepared for the burden of leisure, and helpless when the family web has been broken.[2]

Is such a statement justified? In many studies the overemphasis on the geographic dispersal of the wider family and on the way in which the family has lost economic functions has obscured the fact that its central role in Western society is not economic but psychological—the provision of emotional security and expression for the individual personality[3]—and this is true for those who visit each other frequently, as well as for those sharing a common domicile. Stress on the relationships among members of the immediate family who live together, and disregard of the wider network of kinsmen, naturally enough support the assumption on which many studies have been based, that the immediate family is 'isolated'. Such an argument begs the question.

Woodford is a low–density suburb[4], about 11 miles from the centre of London, with a population in 1958 of about 60,000, with a majority of the people living in owner–occupied separate homes. The American suburb, with a population of about 22,000 in 1957, is also of low density, rather farther from the centre of San Francisco, with a smaller population likewise living primarily in owner–occupied separate homes. Most residents of both places have non–manual jobs, and travel to work outside their communities. Woodford expanded fastest between the two world wars; Menlo Park, explosively, after the second one.

There are, however, many differences between the two. One of these is due to the automobile. While both suburbs have railways for daily commuting to the city, almost all local transportation in Menlo Park is by car. In Menlo Park a pedestrian blinking into the headlights at night is an extremely rare and therefore suspect sight. Even amongst these old people, 71 percent of our sample had automobiles in Menlo

Park; in Woodford it was 11 percent. In Menlo Park, people who have had their driving licences taken away owing to age or infirmity have lost a vital link with society. They can no longer ride down El Camino to the supermarkets, drive–ins and restaurants, nor visit relatives or friends.

The houses, although alike erected by speculative builders, do not look the same. In one place they are mostly one–story ranch houses, made of white–painted wood or untreated redwood, with picture windows opening on to paved patios. In the other, they are brick, two–story, semi–detached, displaying that hint of the past in the leaded panes, that touch of medieval in the rough cast, with which every suburban English builder makes his bid for respectability.

Inside the Californian houses the furniture was more often contemporary than in the older established Woodford. On the walls were pictures of San Francisco cable cars instead of deer by Loch Lomond or cows outside an Essex cottage. But the photographs were the same: in Menlo Park as in Woodford children and other young relatives had pride of place on the mantelpiece or television set. In Menlo Park many front lawns merge, fenceless, on to the 'sidewalk' whose edges are smoothed so that cars *can* rise on to them. In Woodford the hedges and fences around every carefully tended flower garden mark more clearly the frontier between public and private.

Woodford people have been written about at some length in a book about them, and their description will therefore be omitted here. Our account of the Menlo Park sample will be brief, limited to three aspects: migration, class, and church. First, where did our informants come from? 17 out of the 98 had the proud distinction of being born in California, and 19 were born in Europe. Of the others, the great majority came from the Middle West. As for social class, we made no attempt to establish class membership by objective criteria. Our informants placed themselves; we asked only 'what social class do you belong to?' without providing the subject with ready–made categories in which to place themselves. Only three people styled themselves 'upper class' or 'aristocratic'. Mrs. Lyons,[5] a lady from Georgia, said for example, 'We are aristocrats. My mother wouldn't even let me go to a public school.' At the other extreme, there were ten who considered themselves 'working–class'—such as Mr. McCaul, who said, 'I belong to the working class. When I want something I pay cash for it.' The others who were ready to ascribe a class to themselves at all were mostly doggedly middle–class, subscribing to the view expressed by one of their number that 'I never feel superior until I'm around someone who does.' 55 of the subjects belonged to Protestant churches (Episcopalian, Presbyterian, Methodist, Congregational, Unitarian, Lutheran); 24 to the Roman Catholic Church; 13 to other churches (Christian Science, Christian Church, Quaker, Jewish, Seventh Day Adventist, Mormon); and 6 to none.

In comparing family relationships of people in Menlo Park and Woodford, we shall, of course, be speaking of generalities, which conceal variations between one individual and another. These variations were very striking in both places. We can, for Menlo Park, illustrate what we mean by two extreme examples. Mrs. Mishkin and Mrs. Knight lived almost next door to one another in a shady avenue near the main shopping centre. They could hardly be less alike. Mrs. Mishkin was a thin woman in a faded yellow cardigan who all through the interview hopped bird–like about her bare bedroom. She was almost completely alone in the world. Born near Lake Baikal, she married in 1910 an attaché at the Imperial Russian Legation at Peking, and, after the Revolution, lived with him in Tientsin for 20 years until he died in 1938. She spent a long time selecting a photograph of him to show the interviewer, rejecting those of him as an older man, as not doing justice to him, until she found what she wanted, a picture taken in 1910 of a handsome young officer with a long, straight back and long, waxed moustaches. The last ten years she had spent being shunted about from one refugee camp to another, in Shanghai, the Philippines and Australia, until eventually a relative of hers, a daughter of her mother's cousin, signed the necessary affidavits for her to come to the United States. This person was her last remaining relative—all the others had either disappeared or been executed—and such friends as she had left alive were scattered over four continents. In one way Mrs. Mishkin was like many of the pensioners of Woodford: she travelled by the infrequent buses to her ill–paid job as a waitress. It was a great treat for her to be taken out in a car two or three times a year.

Her neighbour, Mrs. Knight, was the opposite in every way. Large and calm, she was born 65 years ago in Menlo Park itself. She said her health was very good, 'except for some trouble with arthritis, which is a hazard of middle age', and she was very active both as a full–time nurse and in her family. At the time of the interview she was looking after two of her daughter's children. Mrs. Knight lived with an unmarried daughter; next door lived her widowed sister, an unmarried sister and an unmarried brother; one married daughter is in the next street and another is ten miles down the Bay. When she was asked about frequency of family gatherings she said: 'All the time—we're always having a family gathering. I also do a great deal of visiting over the telephone.'

In terms of formal structure, the framework of explicit and enforced rights and duties between kinsmen, the kinship systems of Britain and the United States seem to be identical. Both have bilateral (or 'multi–lineal') descent and inheritance customs, serial monogamy, and free choice of marriage partner and of place of residence after marriage. In both countries, hard–and–fast legal obligations between kinsmen, such as requirements for economic support, apply only to conjugal couples and to parents and their immature children. As far as explicit norms go, the immediate family of married couple and their offspring is indeed 'isolated' from the rest of their relatives, from their adult children, their siblings, aunts, uncles, cousins and so on.[6] Our aim was to find out to what extent the immediate family is also 'isolated' in terms of actual relationships. We had, of course, expected to find structural similarities. What we did not expect was that, in so far as it could be inquired into in a brief interview, behaviour, as distinct from the formal kinship structure, would be so much the same.

Consider, for instance, the residence of the children. We had expected that almost anywhere in a country so vast and with a population so migratory, married children would in general be farther away from their parents than on an island much smaller and more stay–at–home. What we found is compared with Woodford in Table 1.[7]

The proportion of children living in the same house as their parents was the same in Menlo Park, and also the proportion beyond 50 miles. The differences were in the intermediate categories, fewer children living within 5 miles, and more between 5 and 50. There is no indication from this table of any great difference between the two places.

Attitudes about residence seemed to be much the same too. Of the old people not actually living with their children none thought it was right to do so.

> 'I'd rather take in stairs to mop than move in with my children,' said Mrs. Ferriera.
>
> 'I figure that Sunday morning is the only time that a husband and wife can see each other, and if they want to run around the

Table 1. Distance of Married Children from Parents

	Menlo Park	Woodford
	%	%
Living in same house	15	14
Less than 5 miles away	28	45
Between 5 and 50 miles	21	9
Elsewhere	36	32
Total percentage	100	100
Number of married children	151	363

house in their underwear they should. But to have the mother-in-law watching them . . .'

Mrs. Kepler left it to the imagination to complete the terrifying picture.

The ones that did, despite this strongly held belief, share a house with their children were mostly widowed people; either they had nowhere else to go or they were glad to stop 'rattling about in a large house with rising taxes and termites to worry about'. The general view was that you should live not with, but near, your children. In this Menlo Park was echoing Woodford.

We have already said that most of the old people originated outside California. How was it, then, that so many of them had children close by? They must either have come with or to their children. They did, of course, do both. Many of the people who migrated to California before the age of 60 came with their children and, what is more striking, many of those who made the journey after 60 did so in order to be near their families. Out of a total of 24 subjects who moved to California after they were 60 years old, as many as 20 moved in order to be with children, 16 of them to be with daughters. The daughter moved first, typically for the sake of the son-in-law's job in California, and the parents came later. Widowhood was one of the chief reasons for this second move; 12 of the parents who followed their children were widowed, and nine of them moved into the same house as their offspring. One son was exceptional; he sent for his mother to look after his children, not when her home broke up, but when his did, owing to divorce. Here are a few examples of elderly people whose motive for migration was clear enough. . . . . . .

> Mrs. Silberman: Even before Mr. Silberman died, they both lived with her married son, Joseph, in St. Louis. As Joseph had bad health, he lived rent-free with his parents and continued to be with his mother after his father died. Mrs. Silberman came to Menlo Park to live with her daughter when Joseph too died, bringing with her Joseph's widow, her granddaughter and four great-grandchildren. She has three grandsons, too, in the San Francisco area. Two of their wives take it in turns to set Mrs. Silberman's hair. She thought her grandsons more attractive than her husband had been. 'I used to tell him he was as homely as a mud fence.'
>
> Mrs. Blake: When her husband died, Mrs. Blake left Des Moines and came to live not with her daughter but her daughter's daughter Jean. She lived there for 10 years until Jean got married, left work, and had a child Tessa. Mrs. Blake still sees her

granddaughter and great–granddaughter every couple of days. 'Tessa always cuddles up to her Nana[8] and watches the television with me.' When she was ill recently, with influenza, Mrs. Blake immediately called up Jean. Jean came round with the car and took her grandmother home with her until she was better.

Mr. Boyd: Mr. Boyd joined his only child, a son, a few years after his wife died. So did his daughter–in–law's parents and sister. They built a large house for everyone. Mr. Boyd bought his room from his son; it has a private door onto the patio, and does not connect with the rest of the house. Until a serious illness Mr. Boyd cooked his meals himself, but now he eats in one large dining room with his assortment of relatives.

These are only three examples. Like most other old people who came to California in order to join their children, they saw a great deal of them. People who had been in the State for longer were more on their own. The frequency with which all informants saw their married children, in Menlo Park and Woodford, is shown in Table 2.

If Mrs. Silberman and the other two parents described above had been typical, there would have been far more extended families[9] in Menlo Park than in Woodford. As it was, there was once again no great difference between the two places.

So far we have said that older people in Menlo Park as well as Woodford maintain close relationships with their adult children. We shall now distinguish the children according to sex. But before doing so we should explain that the importance of the mother–daughter tie was one of the main findings of a third comparative study which has been referred to in the previous essay. In Bethnal Green older people, particularly old women, commonly belonged to what were called 'three–generation extended families', clusters of several households living within the same block, consisting of the old person, her children and grandchildren. They represented a tight network of

Table 2. Frequency of Contact between Parents and Children in Menlo Park and Woodford

	Menlo Park	*Woodford*
	%	%
At least once a day	30	20
Between once a day and once a week	25	21
Between once a week and once a month	19	24
Less often	26	25
Total percentage	100	100
Numbers	151	363

kinsmen seeing, working and relaxing together almost daily. Mothers and daughters were the core of these extended families. In Bethnal Green the married woman is unusual, who cannot say, 'If anything goes wrong and I'm in any trouble I always go running round to Mum's.'

We tried to find out whether there was the same tie between mothers and daughters in Woodford and Menlo Park, and discovered that it did exist, although in a rather attenuated form. Menlo Park daughters were just as prominent as in Woodford, although less so than in Bethnal Green.

The child living nearest in Menlo Park was much more often a daughter than a son, and parents also saw more of their daughters. Table 3 compares the proportions of sons and daughters (single as well as married) seen every day in the three places.

What people said about the content of the relationship was also similar. Menlo Park mothers who had daughters living with them described what each did in the house, and explained how much easier it all was than being with a daughter–in–law. 'You know the proverb,' said Mrs. Burdick, ' "A daughter's a daughter all her life, A son's a son until he gets him a wife."[10] I think it's true. A daughter gets a different reaction about going home; she goes into a familiar kitchen, into familiar cupboards, familiar linens and serves familiar food. A daughter–in–law comes in and she hasn't ever lived there and doesn't feel at home. A father sees his daughter moving around as a familiar picture, while to him the daughter–in–law is an alien.'

Mrs. Liversidge expressed the view of Woodford. She and her husband had bought a large Edwardian house with the express purpose of sharing it with their son. 'I did think it was going to be so nice,' said Mrs. Liversidge sadly. 'I never had a daughter and I thought I was going to have companionship in the daytime when my husband and son were at work. But it hasn't worked out like that. My husband and I don't really agree with the modern way of bringing up children, and it's all very well, but you have to speak out sometimes and one evening I did speak out and lost my temper and my daughter–in–

Table 3. Proportions of Sons and Daughters Seen at Least Once a Day in Menlo Park, Woodford and Bethnal Green

	Daughters		Sons	
	Percentage seen at least once a day	Total Number 100%	Percentage seen at least once a day	Total Number 100%
Menlo Park	42	92	22	81
Woodford	41	197	19	224
Bethnal Green	45	312	26	314

law lost *hers*. We decided after that that the best thing would be for us to live apart. Now we've got two gas stoves out in the kitchen, mine and hers.'

Mothers who lived near their daughters frequently spent much of their time with them, helping them to look after their young children. With the grandchildren, especially the daughter's children, they had the same bond of affection as was noticed by us in London and, before that, by anthropologists in many more primitive societies.[11] Mrs. Lockwood of Menlo Park told us how she ate most of her meals at her daughter's house and helped to bring up her grandchildren during the years when her daughter went out to work. A few nights ago she had been over there as usual with her granddaughter aged 15.

> 'The other night Nancy was going to her first big ball at the high school. She looked so pretty. I said, "I never expected to live to see a grandchild going to a party." "Oh, Grandma," Nancy said, "you'll live to see me married." I said, "I hope not. You'd be too young." '

In both Woodford and Menlo Park, too, the old people reported that in illness and infirmity they had received care more from their daughters than their sons. This of course varied in extent. Mrs. Krogh was blind and, although she was not helpless and could sew, dress herself and tidy up the house, she spent most of the day listening to the sound on the television, and for care relied very much on her daughter. The daughter had stayed for the last ten years in the same small house she had had when she was first married, although she and her family had much outgrown it since. She did this for the sake of her mother.

> 'If we had moved to a new house I would be falling down and hurting myself because I didn't know my way around.'

Mrs. Chick, from North Dakota, was better able to fend for herself. But her daughter came fairly regularly to see her and perform small services, to cut her toenails for instance. Since she was confined to her home she had been helped more by her neighbours as well as by her daughter. 'Since then my neighbours have all been acting like North Dakota people.'

These findings in Menlo Park, following hard upon similar ones in Woodford, bid us look again at one of the conclusions of the first report on Bethnal Green. We presented there our reasons for thinking that a 'closer tie between mother and daughter than between the son and either of his parents crystallises out of the initial situation'. In brief, they were that father and son are no longer joined, as they were in an agricultural society, by a common occupation. Different occupations direct the interests of men outside the family.

Mothers and daughters have the same job, and the younger woman usually learns the way of it from the older woman.

For these reasons, we said, 'we would expect the stressing of the mother–daughter tie to be a widespread, perhaps universal, phenomenon in the urban areas of all industrial countries, *at any rate in the families of manual workers*'.[12] We inserted, and have here italicized, the qualification because we knew that non–manual workers often have to move from one part of the country to another for the sake of their work, and thought that their wives would consequently often be separated by the barrier of distance from their mothers. Woodford raised the first doubt about this idea, and now Menlo Park, by producing the same witness, has suggested that in making the qualification we under–estimated the extent to which people, particularly old people no longer bound to an occupation, migrate specifically for the purpose of being close to children and other kindred. The needs of male occupations are, as we now see it, very often reconciled with the needs of female occupations. One of the conclusions of the Woodford study was that occupational mobility produced a barrier between fathers and sons but not between women. We attributed this to the fact that women retain the same principal occupations even when their husbands have occupations of quite different status.[13]

To generalize from three small local inquiries in only two industrial countries is, no doubt, rash. But at least we would now express the hypothesis more firmly, and remove the qualification. We expect further research to show that in all industrial countries, because of the similarities in their occupational structures, the tie between mothers and daughters is more strongly stressed than that between mothers and sons or between fathers and either sons or daughters, the strength or significance of the tie varying for social groups, such as class. If we are right, daughters and mothers are the organizers of the wider family and the repositories of information about it, and form the central nerves of the loose but still highly important kinship network which is characteristic of modern society.

Kinship in this California suburb has, to judge from the accounts of the old people interviewed, very much the same meaning as in the London suburb with which we have been comparing it. The two places are, as far as family structure goes, very similar. Now, to end this short account, we come to the only sharp difference that we found. This was that in Menlo Park far more people were aware of remote ancestors[14] than in either of the English districts in which research has been carried out by the Institute of Community Studies. In England it is comparatively rare for anybody outside the aristocracy to know anything about their pedigrees. But in the Menlo Park sample 43 people out of the 98 claimed knowledge of more distant ancestors than grandparents. Five of them claimed that ancestors came to America on the *Mayflower*, 10 that they arrived at some other time in the seventeenth century, 14 during the eighteenth century, and 14 in the first half of the nineteenth century. England and Scotland were the most common countries of origin, although France, Germany, Switzerland, Spain and particularly Holland were also mentioned.

The degree of genealogical knowledge shown varied a great deal. Our 43 informants can be roughly divided into two groups, about a third having documents on their family history and the other two-thirds having information which they had picked up by word of mouth from parents and other relatives. In the first group were people like Mrs. Hilmer and Mrs. McMillan. Mrs. Hilmer was able to trace her descent to no less than three of the families on the *Mayflower*, that is to the Brewsters, the Fullers and the Bradfords. She produced manuscripts giving the dates of births and deaths of her ancestors through ten generations going back to William Brewster, and she knew something too about the great man himself. 'He spent his youth on the great estate of the Archbishop of York at Scrooby where his father was bailiff. At age 15 he was a student at Cambridge. He left Cambridge at the age of 17 to enter the service of Sir William Davidson. He was committed to the Tower of London with Davidson for two years etc., etc.' Mrs. McMillan also showed us a number of documents which testified to her descent from one of the early secretaries of the Massachusetts Bay Colony. The documents named 1,462 other descendants of his in the United States, and traced his own pedigree back to an English squire in the reign of Richard II. Mrs. McMillan had in her possession a book written by her aunt for members of the family to read; this was about the more recent past of her family in the South. Old letters[15] and records were there preserved.

These were two people who knew a great deal. In the second 'hearsay' group were the people like Mr. Arcangeli and Mrs. Peck. Mr. Arcangeli had been told by his mother that her grandfather fought in the war of 1812, and by his father that way back he was related to the Cunard steamship people in England. Mrs. Peck remembered listening to her mother talking by the hour about all her ancestors and relatives in Tennessee, and what this man and that man did in the Civil War—'just like "Gone with the Wind" it was'. 'The woods,' she said, 'are full of Pecks.' But she did not know anything very precise about more than a very few of them.

These few examples give some idea of the variation in the knowledge displayed. Why are some people nearer the Hilmers and others nearer the Pecks? The first thing to say is that a good deal seemed to depend upon accident, that is the accident of whether there was an amateur genealogist in the family. Of the people with family documents, few were like Miss Michaels. She thought of herself as the 'family historian', wrote letters to libraries and other sources in Washington, New York and England seeking information about ancestors, and was in her turn written to by her living relatives on family matters. It was our impression that many of the self–appointed 'family historians' were bachelors and spinsters or other people who had been deprived of normal family life. Usually the 'family historian' was not our informant; one of his relatives, a female aunt or cousin or a lawyer uncle who was used to records performed Miss Michael's function. Some of them had paid for the services of one of the many firms who trace genealogies professionally; the 'genealogy industry' does, indeed, seem to be a growing one.

In a few families there is a more formal system than this. These are the ones in which there is something close to a 'clan–organization'.[16] Mr. Clark's relatives on his father's side, for instance, have a formal family association in Ohio, with a secretary and chairman and family reunions every year in the hometown attended by 50 or 60 people from all over the United States. The association publishes a book containing detailed genealogies and accounts of illustrious ancestors.

Another less formal affair had grown up because of the action of a railroad company. Mrs. Price's great–grandmother was one of the first Mormon pioneers.

> 'Her name was Rebecca Darvel and she died in a prairie schooner on the way over. After she died they put up a wagon wheel to mark the site of the grave with her name carved on it. Later when they were building the railroad they came across this wheel and somehow got in touch with Rebecca's descendants, and the company told them that they would like to put up a tombstone in place of the wagon wheel, which they did and they fenced her grave around, and planted it with beautiful flowers and the trains stop there and water that grave.'

Mrs. Price has a copy of a book on Rebecca's life and her ancestry, and so do a large number of Mrs. Price's living relatives.

Mr. Kellinger belongs to the most formal of any of the family associations we came across—the Kellinger Family Association Inc. Mr. Kellinger used to live in San Diego before he moved to Menlo Park. One day he was called up by a man who said he had seen his name in the telephone directory—whenever he went to a new town he looked up to see if there were any Kellingers in the directory—and thought he would be interested to know of the existence of the Association. Any descendants of John and Sarah Kellinger who farmed in Connecticut in 1641 are eligible to join. Mr. Kellinger did join and in return for an annual subscription receives a quarterly magazine. The Association owns and maintains the original farm in Connecticut as a memorial to their seventeenth-century founders. A recent issue of the magazine reports on the annual meeting at the farm.

> 'The group moved from there to the cemetery to find a good number of cousins waiting at the boulder. Then the group formed a circle around the boulder and joined in a brief ceremony honouring those members of the family who had departed during the past year. Honorary President Alfred Kellinger led the service.'

This Association has appointed a genealogist who has at her disposal a fund of several thousand dollars for research on the Kellinger family tree. It is not surprising that our informants' documentation was impressively ample.

There was not much doubt that more of the old people of Menlo Park were aware of their ancestors than in Woodford. But were these two places at all representative of their countries? The contrast seemed sufficiently unexpected to make further inquiry worthwhile. On the two other questions discussed—the relationship of old people to their children and the mother–daughter tie—there is a certain amount of evidence from other inquiries besides those drawn on in this paper. But as far as we know there is no evidence which would enable this further transatlantic comparison to be made, and for that reason we asked two survey organizations, Elmo Roper and Associates in the U.S.A. and the Gallup Poll in Britain, to help us. We had no funds for the research reported here, and so all that we could do was ask the organizations to add one question on the subject in which we were interested to a survey mainly concerned with other topics.[17] There was a danger that the obvious question about the number of generations for which the family can be traced back would prove too complicated in a survey of this kind. So a less pointed but more simple question was put to informants, asking them whether any of their ancestors had fought in various wars or been connected with other historic events. The samples were in each survey representative of the population at large, the U.S. sample being of people over 15 years of age and the British of people over 16.

The results for the U.S.A. are given in Table 4, and presented in this form because the most striking difference found was that older people know a good deal more of their ancestors than young people. There were also some differences between regions—people in the southern states, for instance, claimed more ancestors who fought in the Civil War and people in the Pacific states (California, Oregon and Washington) claimed more ancestors from the *Mayflower* than any other region except New England—but these were less striking than the differences between age groups.

The comparable results are given for Britain in Table 5, and the numbers claiming ancestry of the kind mentioned are so slight, except for the recent Boer War, that it is not worth distinguishing by age. The two tables are not strictly comparable: the proportions of the populations of the two countries engaged in the wars (even when they came as close together in time as the Crimean and the Civil wars) were not the same, nor is the rate of increase of population since these historic events, nor the rate of immigration. But even when this kind of allowance is made, the difference between the two countries is striking. The most significant comparison is between the proportions on each side of the Atlantic who *don't know* whether or not their ancestors participated in the ways shown. If anything, these

Table 4. Knowledge of Ancestors in the U.S.A.

	Age			
	15–34	35–49	50 and Over	All Ages
	%	%	%	%
Came to America on the *Mayflower*	4	3	5	4
Fought in the Revolutionary War	6	10	13	10
Fought Indians during the pioneering days	6	9	8	7
Fought in the Civil War	16	24	32	24
Took out a homestead	12	16	15	14
Went to California in the Gold Rush	2	3	4	3
None of the above	38	36	36	37
Don't know or—no answer	34	25	21	27
Total numbers	1146	1146	1352	3964

Numbers in each age group total more than 100 percent as some respondents knew of ancestors who had participated in more than one of the historical events listed.

Table 5. Knowledge of Ancestors in Britain

	%
Fought in Napoleonic Wars	1
Fought in Crimean War	4
Fought in Boer War	22
Fought in none of these	10
Don't know	63
Total percentage	100
Number	900

results strengthen the impression we gained from our miniature inquiry, that knowledge of pedigrees is greater in the U.S.A. than in Britain, interest in the past greater in the newer than it is in the older country.

These national inquiries, slim as they are, led us to ask ourselves why there should be so much difference between the countries. Although we are even less qualified to talk about this than about many other aspects of our subject, it seems that part of the answer lies in American history. For hundreds of years (although the reason is not altogether clear) earlier arrivals in America have enjoyed greater prestige than later ones. People of English descent, especially original settlers in New England and Virginia, have considered themselves superior to those of German or even Dutch descent; Germans superior to Irish, Irish to Italian, and so forth. But unless you could in fact trace your ancestry to one of these earlier arrivals, you could make no claim to prestige of this sort. There was therefore a very particular point in working out genealogies. The same motive fostered the growth of patriotic associations—the Society of *Mayflower* Descendants, the Daughters of 1812, the Daughters, Sons and Children of the American Revolution, the Society of the Cincinnati and hundreds of others. They include even such esoteric affairs as the Baronial Order of Runnemede, which is composed of the offspring of the barons who forced Magna Carta from King John, and the Societé de Guillaume le Conquérant, limited to the progeny of the Normans who won the day at Hastings.[18]

This kind of prestige has been accessible to a comparatively large number of people, and will in time presumably become so diffused as to be worthless, because the bilateral reckoning of descent—through parents of either sex—rapidly multiplies the number of ancestors to whom one can legitimately make claim.[19] This is not true of all American patriotic associations. Membership in the still flourishing Society of the Cincinnati is restricted to the male descendants of officers who fought in the Revolutionary Armies, reckoned according to the rules of primogeniture, that is, restricted to the eldest male descendant in each generation. But much more common is the looser specification of the D.A.R. that membership shall be open to any woman descended from 'a patriot of the Revolutionary period who aided the cause of American Independence.' Our informants followed the D.A.R. rather than the Cincinnati pattern.

They (or at any rate the 'family historians' on whose knowledge they draw, if sometimes a little shamefacedly) were certainly aware of the 'status' to be obtained by claiming ancient ancestry. Some of them went far back in time and, like the Mrs. Hilmer quoted above, claimed a connection with the *Mayflower*. Or, on occasion, they mentioned other ancestors as illustrious. Here were some of the forbears claimed by our Menlo Park group:

William Tell	The Dutch Minister of War
Mary Queen of Scots	A.D.C. to General Washington
The teacher of James Fenimore Cooper	General Custer
Robert Bruce, King of Scotland	Charlemagne

After saying that much more is known about ancestry in Menlo Park than in the English districts, we have suggested one of the reasons: that claims of this kind are more effective as claims to status in a country populated by successive waves of immigrants. That is not all there is to it. Another clue is given by what people have often said to us in England. Here we have noticed that the minority of people who do show interest in and knowledge of their more distant ancestors are mostly people whose forbears have moved from one part of England to another, or from another country. In Bethnal Green the people who were so concerned were the people with French names who knew their ancestors had come to England with the Huguenots; in Woodford they were people whose families had moved from Lincolnshire, Gloucestershire or Kent. In this there is something in common between the two countries. Forbears who moved even a hundred miles from a little village in Lincoln left a mark, created a tiny legend, handed on a story about a drastic change in their lives. In this respect almost everyone in America has a family history more dramatic than can be produced by any but the most exceptional people in England. This would often be remembered for its own sake—and all the more so when memory has given a claim to status, which still holds good for many people today even if this kind of status is no longer so much prized as it once was. Another way of putting our hypothetical explanation would be to say that the more disrupted the family, the firmer its historical reconstruction; and the people who are most prone to perform this reconstruction are the old, the widowed and the single who feel most cut off from an ongoing family in the present. The past is invoked to make up for the shortcomings of the present.

In any full explanation of this difference between the two countries, an important place would also have to be given to differences in their class structure. In England pedigree has been to some extent the prerogative of the aristocracy and landed gentry and bounds have been set to those who can convincingly claim ancient descent by *Debrett, Burke* and similar authorities. Pedigrees have been as it were institutionalized, and, this being so, it has not been easy for many members of other classes, even if they wished, to claim distinguished ancestry. But in the United States aspirations and pretensions to 'nobility' and to long pedigrees are in no way discouraged; there is no bar to anyone asserting his connection with one of the great names of the Old World or one of the greater pioneers or founders of the New. Paradoxically enough, the aristocratic pedigrees of England can be drawn on more freely by Americans than by Englishmen. The more 'closed' society of the Old World aids the diffusion of status in the New.

REFERENCES

1. Interviews in the American community were conducted from November, 1958, to February, 1959, while Michael Young was a Fellow of the Center for Advanced Study in the Behavioral Sciences, at Palo Alto, California. The English study was carried out by Peter Willmott and Michael Young, intermittently from 1957 to 1959, for the Institute of Community Studies, London, and the results were published in *Family and Class in a London Suburb* (Routledge, 1960).

2. Lerner, M., *America as a Civilization*, Jonathan Cape, 1958, p. 614.

3. For this argument, see Parsons, T. 'The American Family: Its Relations to Personality and to the Social Structure', in Parsons and Bales, *Family, Socialisation and Interaction Process*, Routledge, 1956, especially pp. 16–17.

4. The study was made primarily by interviewing a selected sample of subjects. In Woodford this sample was drawn at random from the lists of local doctors employed in the National Health Service. In Menlo Park the sample was drawn similarly at random from rosters of local doctors engaged in general practice.

5. We have given fictitious names to all our informants in order to conceal their identities.

6. See Parsons, T., 'The Kinship System of the Contemporary United States', in *Essays in Sociological Theory, Pure and Applied*, Free Press, Glencoe, Illinois, 1940. And Williams, Robin, *American Society*, Knopf, New York, 1950.

7. It should be borne in mind that it was informants, and not their children, who constituted the sample. But '15 percent', for example, refers to the proportion of married children of Menlo Park informants who lived in the same house as their parents.

8. This word and others very similar are also common words for 'grandmother' in Woodford.

9. The way in which this and other kinship terms are used was discussed in Appendix 4 to *Family and Kinship in East London*, (see previous essay).

10. The truth of this Anglo–American proverb seemed to be subscribed to quite as much in Menlo Park as in Woodford.

11. Cf. Radcliffe–Brown, A. R., Introduction to *African Systems of Kinship and Marriage*, Oxford, 1950, p. 28. 'In general also, in Africa as elsewhere, grandparents are much more indulgent towards their grandchildren than are parents to their children.'

12. *Family and Kinship in East London*, op. cit., p. 163.

13. This view was stated thus in *Family and Class in a London Suburb*, op. cit., p. 85.

14. This American concern with ancestry has, of course, often been noted before, notably by Lord Bryce in *The American Commonwealth*, Macmillan, 1911, vol. 2, p. 813. What has not been done before is to compare explicitly a country in the 'Old World' with the U.S.A.

15. One of these was from Mrs. McMillan's grandfather in Georgia to his brother in Vermont just before the Civil War. Part of it went 'Dear Moses, We have separated from you politically, forever. . . . I felt as proud of my country's greatness as anyone ought to be and am still proud that I am an American born in this land of Washington, but I now feel the time has come to separate and I yield my consent. . . . On the whole people are a unit in support of the new government and they cannot be conquered, only by love, not arms. . . . We moved to Columbus January 1st and we're getting along pretty well. The fixing up of our lot covered building a Negro house, 32 feet by 16 feet. Corn is worth $1.25. I will engage my butter from you for next fall at 16 cents. What do you say to it?'

16. Dr. Millicent R. Ayoub in a private communication about some research she has done in southern Ohio confirms that similar organizations exist there. 'These families have annual reunions in some state park or so, spend the day together with a covered–dish supper, have one formal session with each sub–unit reporting marriages, deaths and births, and sometimes have family officers and family tree diagrams. In a surprising number of cases I have found people who trace their descent back to some ancestor of note, even, in one case, to the bodyguard of William the Conqueror, an Italian mercenary.'

17. We are grateful to Henry Durant of the Gallup Poll and Gerhart Wiebe of Elmo Roper and Associates for agreeing to do this work for us without any payment.

18. See Davies, W. E., *Patriotism on Parade*, The Story of Veterans' and Hereditary Organizations in America, 1783–1806, Harvard, 1955. See also Benson, L., 'The Historical Background of Turner's Frontier Essay', *Agricultural History*, 25, 59–82 (April 1951).

19. Out of the 43 Menlo Park people mentioned, 15 made their claims to ancestry through the paternal grandfather, 13 through the maternal grandfather, and 15 through both.

8

The Mortality of Widowers

> The likely durability of an institution can be assessed according to what it means to people who belong to it, and also to people who cease to belong to it. This classic paper, written with Bernard Benjamin and Chris Wallis, is on a study made into the absence of relatives—or, more specifically, into the effects of losing a wife. It appears that one death to some extent causes another. If these are the facts about mortality they suggest that the future of the family as an institution is as assured as anything can be.

Durkheim was the first well–known sociologist to stress the connection between widowhood and a particular kind of death, that due to suicide.

> The suicides occurring at the crisis of widowhood . . . are really due to domestic anomy resulting from the death of husband or wife. A family catastrophe occurs which affects the survivor. He is not adapted to the new situation in which he finds himself and accordingly offers less resistance to suicide.[1]

Sainsbury showed that suicides (causing over 5000 deaths a year, not far off the number who die in road accidents) were commoner among the widowed than the single, and that the rate was lowest among the married.[2] The Bethnal Green studies drew attention to the general psychological effects of bereavement. Marris wrote of the anguish felt by young widows, from which they only gradually recovered,[3] and Townsend of the sense of desolation felt by older widowed people of both sexes.[4] These studies suggested that the shock of widowhood might weaken the resistance to other causes of death, and not just to suicides. We report here an exploration of this suggestion.

The Mortality of Widowers

The death–rates for widowed people in every age group are known to be higher than for married people. What has not been known so far is the 'duration effect' of being widowed—we know how old widowed people were when they died, but not for how long they had been widowed. For our purpose an inquiry into 'duration effect' was clearly essential. Since a large field study was beyond the resources of the Institute of Community Studies, the opportunity to explore this question in collaboration with the General Register Office was welcomed. We had to concentrate on widowers. Widows had to be ruled out because the death certificates of men do not identify their spouses in a way that makes it possible to follow them up. Our procedure was to pick a sample of widowers who figured on the death certificates of their wives.

It was difficult to choose the age group to investigate. The figures already published show that the excess mortality of widowed over married people is greatest for younger people below the age of thirty–four.[5] Another way of putting the point is to say that widowhood seems to accelerate aging most in the younger age groups, attaching to the widowed the mortality risk of married people several years older. Perhaps younger people are especially vulnerable, because spouses often die very suddenly at these ages, many from accidents, so that the shock is greater. This suggested that an inquiry into younger people might be the most fruitful. Against this was the telling point that, for any given size of sample, the numbers of deaths would be larger for older groups. In the end expense was decisive.

The cohort chosen was of 4486 widowers of fifty–five years and older whose wives died in 1957. To allow for seasonal fluctuations, half of the group comprised those whose wives died in January, 1957, and the other half those whose wives died in July, 1957. The cohort has so far been followed up for five years, and all deaths of widowers have been noted. Mortality–rates were calculated for the first six months and second six months of duration of widowerhood, and for each year of duration thereafter, for each quinary age group at widowerhood. These rates were arrived at by dividing the deaths by the mean number of widowers at risk during the interval. The rates for the widowers were then expressed as a ratio to the rate, for the same attained age, for married men at the corresponding ages. The results are shown in the accompanying table. The average ratios, weighted for reliability, are given in the last line of the table.

All death entries of married women in the first half of the volume of such entries for January and all those in the second half of the volume for July were extracted. This secured a geographical as well as a seasonal balance. The surviving spouses were subsequently traced through the National Health Service Central Register.

Table 1. Mortality–Rates of Widowers in England and Wales by Duration of Widowerhood and Ratio to Married Men's Mortality at Same Attained Age

Age at Widowerhood	No. of Widowers		Duration of Widowerhood (Yr.)					
			0–	½–	1–	2–	3–	4–
55–59	559	(a) No. of deaths	6	12	13	15	10	13
		(b) Mean widowers' death-rate	0.0216	0.0443	0.0243	0.0288	0.0197	0.0262
		(c) Married men rate (at attained age)	0.0172	0.0182	0.0196	0.0216	0.0236	0.0255
		(d) (b) ÷ (c)	1.3	2.4	1.2	1.3	0.83	1.0
60–64	694	(a)	16	10	18	18	30	23
		(b)	0.0467	0.0297	0.0273	0.0281	0.0486	0.0389
		(c)	0.0274	0.0289	0.0312	0.0342	0.0372	0.0403
		(d)	1.7	1.0	0.88	0.82	1.3	0.97
65–69	827	(a)	25	18	41	52	47	40
		(b)	0.0613	0.0454	0.0537	0.0725	0.0704	0.0632
		(c)	0.0429	0.0450	0.0481	0.0523	0.0566	0.0608
		(d)	1.4	1.0	1.1	1.4	1.3	1.0
70–74	921	(a)	41	25	82	71	65	52
		(b)	0.0910	0.0576	0.101	0.0962	0.0970	0.0850
		(c)	0.0641	0.0665	0.0701	0.0749	0.0798	0.0846
		(d)	1.4	0.87	1.4	1.3	1.2	1.0
75–79	818	(a)	54	39	74	66	75	57
		(b)	0.137	0.105	0.108	0.107	0.137	0.118
		(c)	0.0902	0.0965	0.106	0.119	0.131	0.144
		(d)	1.5	1.1	1.0	0.90	1.0	0.82
80–84	503	(a)	49	42	62	62	47	48
		(b)	0.205	0.194	0.163	0.194	0.177	0.221
		(c)	0.154	0.161	0.173	0.188	0.203	0.218
		(d)	1.3	1.2	0.94	1.0	0.87	1.0

The Mortality of Widowers

85–89	139	(a)	18	22	20	15	13
		(b)	0.227	0.229	0.267	0.263	0.295
		(c)	0.230	0.247	0.261	0.275	0.289
		(d)	1.2	0.93	1.0	0.96	1.0
90+	25	(a)	5	7	2	2	2	2
		(b)	0.434	0.824	0.167	0.200	0.250	0.333
		(c)	0.296					
		(d)	1.4					
Total	4486	(a)	214	167	314	306	291	248
Weighted average of ratio (d) at ages between 55 and 89*			1.39	1.06	1.04	1.04	1.04	0.94

*Weights are reciprocals of variance of ratios shown at (d).

Out of the ratios set out in the table, the only ones that are significantly and consistently greater than unity are for those dying within six months of being widowed. There are three points to be made about the six months' ratios.

First, if we ignore age differences we have:

Actual deaths	214
Expected deaths (based on married men's mortality)	148 ± 12
Excess	66

$$t = 5.5 \quad p < 0.0001$$

Second, taking the age groups separately, the ratios are significantly above unity for age groups 60–64, 70–74, 75–79, and 80–84. Third, all the age groups have *positive* deviations from unity. If there is no real excess mortality positive and negative deviations would be equally likely and the chance of getting 8 positive deviations together would be $(\frac{1}{2})^8 = 0.004$, which is very small. If we look at the ratios for the later deviations (taking all ages together) we find that none of these is statistically significantly different from unity.

The conclusion is that the excess mortality in the first six months is almost certainly real. In other words, widowhood appears to bring in its wake a sudden increment in mortality–rates of something like 40% in the first six months. This increase is eventually followed by a fall back to the level for married men in general.

We naturally do not know for certain what happens to mortality–rates subsequently. All that is clear is that the widowers' rates cannot remain at the low level they reach after four years. If they remained the same as for married men, the overall ratio of widowers' mortality to that of married men would, having regard to the duration structure of all widowers in the general population, be about 1.05 at most ages. But the observed ratio is above 1.4. If this figure is reliable there must be a further differential rise in mortality at later durations of widowhood.

On the other hand, the overall ratio of 1.4 may be inflated for two reasons. The first is that the average age of widowers in any age group is older than the average age of married men in the same age group.[6] There is a difference of about a year in average age. But this does not go very far—not more than one quarter of the way—towards explaining the 40% mortality excess. The second reason is that widowers may be under–enumerated in the census or over–recorded among the deaths.[7] But such information as there is does not suggest this can possibly explain more than a very small part of the 40% excess mortality. It therefore seems that there must be a rise in mortality at later duration of widowhood.

This could come about, for example, as a result of the progressive selective remarriage of the fittest men. The annual remarriage rates of widowers in 1961 were as follows:

Age	Annual remarriage–rate per thousand
45–49	100.1
50–54	72.3
55–59	57.7
60–64	44.3
65–69	25.4
70–74	16.7
75+	4.2

If the widowers who remarried were so healthy that we may consider them as withdrawn only from the denominator of the death–rate for widowers and added only to the denominator of the married men's death–rate, then at ages 55–59, for example, this would in five years create a widower/married mortality differential of the order of 30%. At ages 70–74 the differential thus created would, however, be only 10%, so that at older ages where the observed 40% mortality differential persists, selection on remarriage cannot be by any means the full explanation. Moreover, selection cannot serve to explain the similar mortality differential observed for widows, since their chances of remarriage are much less than the chances of widowers.

The results show that there is a problem to investigate; they do not in themselves either confirm or deny the suggested explanation put forward at the beginning of this paper. The sudden short–run increase could conceivably also be due to other possible influences such as:

Homogamy. It is known that there is a tendency for the fit to marry the fit, and the unfit the unfit. Downes has, for instance, found a marital disease association, in a study on couples over 45 years of age, for hypertensive vascular disease and for arthritis.[8] But although homogamy might have a small influence, it could hardly produce such a large increment as quickly as seems to happen.

Common infection. Both spouses may die from the same infectious disease. Ciocco, in his study of the causes of death among a sample of 2571 husbands and wives who dies in Washington County, Maryland, found significant tendencies for spouses both to die of tuberculosis, influenza, pneumonia, heart diseases, and cancer.[9] Mutual infection could obviously arise, at any rate with the first three of these.

Joint unfavourable environment. Kraus and Lilienfeld suggested that the unfavourable environment which brought about the death of one spouse might do the same for the other.[10] Death in a common accident, where the husband survives a little longer than the wife, is a particularly obvious example.

Loss of care. Widowers may become malnourished when they no longer have wives to look after them. They may also go to their doctor and take their medicine less diligently when they no longer have someone to prod them—although the reverse is also possible. Widowers may consult their doctors more often and expose themselves to more infections and other hazards as a consequence. Having to adapt to a changed social role as the result of losing a spouse may itself impair resistance to disease.

All these are possible influences. But we still consider that the first suggestion we made about the 'desolation effect' of being widowed, may be at least a good part of the explanation. The grief precipitated by the death[11] is almost certainly associated with changes in the function of the endocrine and central nervous systems. Tears, slowed movements, and constipation cannot be the only bodily effects, and whatever may be the other effects, they could scarcely fail to have secondary consequences for resistance to various illnesses.

Only further study will make it possible to attach 'weights' to these various possible influences. Further cohort studies of the kind described here would be helpful. But perhaps the most useful course from now on would be to pay special attention to the immediate physical 'causes' of death. The Registrar General has recently given some information about the 'causes' of death in widowed people.[12] This shows that tuberculosis of the respiratory system, syphilis, cancer (especially buccal cavity, larynx, and testis for widowers, cervic uteri for widows), diabetes, iron–deficiency anemia, vascular lesions of the central nervous system, degenerative and hypertensive heart disease, cirrhosis of liver, diseases of pancreas, and suicide, are particularly responsible for the higher mortality of the widowed as compared with the married.

A first step would be to analyse the groups divided by duration of widowhood according to the diseases responsible for death and according to age to see if there were any pattern. But it would obviously be better to design a field inquiry of a kind which might be undertaken, say, by the College of General Practitioners. Detailed records of widowers who did not die immediately, as well as of those who did, should make it possible to sort out the influence of the factors listed above, as well as others, such as the presence of children, and perhaps point the way to more effective 'treatment' of bereaved people.

REFERENCES

1. E. Durkheim, *Suicide*, Routledge, 1952
2. P. Sainsbury, *Suicide in London*, Chapman, 1955
3. P. Marris, *Widows and Their Families*, Routledge, 1958
4. P. Townsend, *The Family Life of Old People*, Routledge, 1957
5. Registrar General's Statistical Review for England and Wales for 1958; part 3, commentary, 55
6. Registrar General's Statistical Review for England and Wales for 1959; p.166
7. 1951 Census; General Report, Chapter 2
8. J. Downes, J. Milbank Memorial Fund Quarterly Bulletin, 1947, 25, 334
9. A. Ciocco, Hum. Biol., 1940, 12, 508
10. A. S. Kraus and A. M. Lilienfeld, J. Chron. Dis., 1959, 10, 207
11. J. Bowlby, Inf. J. Psycho-Anal., 1961, 42
12. Registrar General's Statistical Review for England and Wales for 1959; commentary

9
Leisure and the Family

One of the main themes of *The Symmetrical Family*, again written in conjunction with Peter Willmott, was put in our minds by Dan Bell. It was referred to in the opening essay in this book. Following de Tocqueville, Bell said that 'What the few have today, the many will demand tomorrow'. As an aid to forecasting we dressed up this idea and called it the Principle of Stratified Diffusion, meaning that what the richer classes do today the poorer will do tomorrow. In this essay the Principle is applied to leisure habits, as revealed by a field study made in the London metropolitan region.

Forty years ago the authors of the second survey of London life and labour (themselves writing forty years after the first) said that 'all the forces at work are combining to shift the main centre of interest of a worker's life more and more from his daily work to his daily leisure'.[1] The amount of leisure time had increased, as compared with the previous century. People's incomes had increased. New industries were selling mass entertainment, and in many ways what was true then has become more so. Has it all added to, or detracted from the primacy of the family?

Our interest continues to be class—this although we already know from the pioneering surveys mainly on outdoor recreation made by Rodgers and Sillitoe for the country as a whole that it does not make so much difference as age, marriage and sex. Rodgers said that for sports age is vital. 'Some (cycling, the more vigorous team games, athletics, skating) are dominated by the very young and children. Others (tennis, riding, swimming, hiking and hill–walking) persist strongly through the 24–35 age band . . . Some (fishing, camping, golf, the more expensive forms of sailing) show either a peak or a plateau of incidence in the middle age ranges.'[2] Sillitoe in the same vein said that, 'Amongst young single people the greatest emphasis was given to physical recreation. In fact, for young men, this continued as their outstanding leisure interest into early married life. . . . The changes in leisure habits that accompanied marriage took place more swiftly amongst women.'[3] There were the same kinds of variation in London. Younger people, especially the single and especially men, did more of almost everything—played more, watched sport more, went more to cinemas and other entertainments. The total number of leisure activities that they went in for at least once in the previous year (to use an index that we shall explain more fully later) was 18.8 for men aged 29 or under, 16.2 at 30 to 49, 12.6 at 50 to 64, and 8.8 at 65 or over. The figures for women ranged from 16.0 at 29 or under to 7.4 at 65 or over. The reason seems obvious enough. Young people, particularly single, have the necessary energy, time, money and inclination. Since all this is obvious and documented, we have taken it for granted in order to concentrate on our own chief concern.

We shall proceed by way of four preliminary questions:

1. What is leisure?
2. How do leisure activities vary by class?
3. Does work extend into leisure?
4. How do contacts with friends and relatives differ?

And we shall then come to the main one:

5. How does their leisure affect their families?

What is Leisure?

Many of our informants seemed to be as puzzled as us, not about work, a good, solid, worthy word that they, and we, understood, but about leisure. If we used it, in explaining what we were about, they would quite often repeat it after us as if we were both playing a sort of nursery game. 'Leisure? What's that?', 'Leisure? No, I don't have any of that', or, 'Leisure? No, my wife keeps me too busy for that', sometimes with a wry smile.

Parker[4] has recently reviewed some of the definitions employed by other authors. These have ranged from those which would presumably be adhered to by two of the three informants we have just quoted, that is, those which treat leisure as a residual activity—'free time after the practical necessities have been attended to'[5] or 'the time we are free from the more obvious and formal duties which a paid job or other obligatory occupation imposes upon us'[6]—to those which accept that it is something left over but also attempt to put some positive content into it. Kaplan, for example, put so much into it as almost to bury the word (especially in his last sentence rolling all the ingredients together into a single pie) when he asserted that[7]

> The essential elements of leisure, as we shall interpret it, are (a) an antithesis to 'work' as an economic function, (b) a pleasant expectation and recollection, (c) a minimum of involuntary social–role obligations, (d) a psychological perception of freedom, (e) a close relation to values of the culture, (f) the inclusion of an entire range from inconsequence and insignificance to weightiness and importance, and (g) often, but not necessarily, an activity characterised by the element of play. Leisure is none of these by itself but all together in one emphasis or another.

Parker did not mention another view, which is that leisure is a state of mind, of non–activity, as contrasted with the *activity* of work, as expressed, for instance, by Pieper.[8]

> Compared with the exclusive ideal of work as activity, leisure implies (in the first place) an attitude of non–activity, of inward calm, of silence; it means not being 'busy', but letting things happen. Leisure is a form of silence, of that silence which is the prerequisite of the apprehension of reality: only the silent hear and those who do not remain silent do not hear. Silence, as it is used in this context, does not mean 'dumbness' or 'noiselessness'; it means more nearly that the soul's power to 'answer' to the reality of the world is left undisturbed. For leisure is a receptive attitude of mind, a contemplative attitude, and it is not only the occasion but also the capacity for steeping oneself in the whole of creation. Furthermore there is also a certain happiness in leisure, something of the happiness that comes from a recognition of the mysteriousness of the universe and the recognition of an incapacity to understand it, that comes with a deep confidence, so that we are content to let things take their course; and there is something about it which Konrad Weiss, the poet, called 'confidence in the fragmentariness of life and history'.

We put questions to our informants which incorporated the word. If for no other reason, the disagreement between the authors drawn upon by Parker, and added to by Pieper, would have made it ridiculous to assume that it meant the same to them as to us, or that they would all concur with each other. We therefore tried to discover what they did mean in the survey by asking, 'What would you say is the difference between what you'd call work and what you'd call leisure?', as well as by requesting the diarists to label all their activities throughout the day as one or the other, neither or both. We hoped we might, by interpreting what they said, find out something about what they meant by the words.

The first point was that most people seemed to regard the key words as opposites that could properly be distinguished from each other. Leisure and work belonged (although our informants did not put it that way) to the category of words, sometimes called binary, which can be understood only in relation to one another, in this like husband which can only be understood along with wife, or woman, more generally, with man, or indeed any word out of a pair which describes two complementary actors in a role like parent–child or employer–employee, or many kinds of spatial relationship like left–right, up–down, higher–lower, in–out which are also liberally used as metaphors. These words which are lost if alone gather meaning if they have a companion. But two is company, three is none, as shown by the muddle caused by the word 'free' having two antonyms with different meanings, determined and obligatory. None of our informants suggested, like Arendt, that the opposite of work is labour,[9] though some seemed to think the opposite of leisure is obligation.

The second point was that the words were not mutually exclusive like the examples given or like the binaries resulting from the fundamental fact that human beings are in many respects symmetrical: they have two sides to them, two hands, two eyes, two legs, two breasts, and not one or three or four. One other biological opposition, of sex, is stressed by conventions and, when these change and, say, the clothes which embody the conventional binary message do not declare whether the person wearing these 'words' is a man or a woman, some observers may behave like computers anxiously looking for a program. Work and leisure were not like that. They did not arouse quite the same anxiety. But when a Lewisham postman in the sample said that, 'I get more leisure at work than I do at home', and others said the same kind of thing, it was obvious that different criteria were sometimes being used to distinguish between the two words. They could be both opposites in one context and, if the criteria varied, the same in another.

The third point is about these crucial criteria. One of them was to do with payment. What one was paid to do was work. But although most people thought that was so, it was not the sole yardstick. If it were, housewives would do none. So as well as payment there was another criterion which had more to do with the original Latin root of the word 'leisure', that is *licere*, to be permitted. The presence of relatively more autonomy, or freedom from obligation, ranked an activity as leisure, its relative absence as work. Hence the use of free time as a common synonym for leisure.

> Work is when you have to do it. Leisure is when you want to do it. (Bricklayer, Ealing)
>
> In your leisure you define all your own parameters. (Design engineer, near Slough)

Another criterion often mentioned was the degree of pleasure.

> Leisure is for pleasure. Work you think of as a drudge. (Process worker, Barking)

Boredom is not the antonym of pleasure but at least it was often used as though it were.

> Anything which makes you bored after a length of time is work. (Bank clerk, Brentwood)

Given these principal criteria, what the Lewisham postman said makes good sense. In the Post Office he was paid and that made it work, but he felt more free and perhaps had more pleasure there than he did at home. For a manual worker the postman was, however, exceptional. For most there was no ambiguity: what they were paid to do was not notably characterized by either freedom or pleasure. But middle-class people were more likely to have autonomy in their jobs. They were therefore more inclined to call paid work leisure; for them the two were more often merged. Pleasure was in this context a word they would not often use themselves, preferring 'sense of commitment' or some such puritanical alternative which allowed them the best of both worlds, an alliance of duty and pleasure.

Freedom and pleasure were also employed to distinguish between work and leisure at home. Women in overwhelming numbers regarded domestic cleaning, washing clothes and washing-up as work. These were jobs generally disliked. As for meals, routine ones were much more of a drudgery than meals for guests or the great weekly ritual of Sunday dinner. One man said he had such a fine Sunday joint that there was enough over for sandwiches for three days. Men for their part often regarded house decoration and repairs as their wives did routine meals. 'The weekend is never long enough for all the commitments' (computer engineer, Tunbridge Wells). 'Leisure time—that's a laugh. When you come home you work' (lorry driver, Ealing). 'As a houseowner, gardening, car washing and decorating are all what I regard as necessary evils, not as leisure pursuits' (service manager, Enfield). 'I've got a list of things that need doing. I ought to relay the concrete. I ought to put up more shelves. The whole place needs repainting and re–carpeting' (research chemist, Stevenage). Keenness, or at any rate, willingness to keep up the aesthetic standards of the house and maintain it in good repair belonged with home–centredness. It might be work, but the same alliance of duty and pleasure (or duty and freedom) that made for middle–class attachment to paid work could also do the same thing for the unpaid. By working at home they would fulfil a double obligation, doing something *for* as well as sometimes *with* the family. Many working–class men got more out of their work at home, even if it was tiring, because they were more free about what to do and how to do it than they were in the other department of their lives.

The fourth point to make about the two words is that they are not collectively exhaustive. The easiest binaries to deal with are the ones already referred to, like male and female: there is not yet a third sex. Work and leisure are less so because of the middle kingdom between them. In the following list we have recorded the labels that were attached by diarists to the chief categories of activity in the multi–national time budget study. Some activities were left unlabelled; the proportion was about 10 percent overall, rising to 61 percent for sleep. 'Mixed' meant that 40 percent or more of all the activities in the batch were labelled as mixed, as neither work nor leisure, or not labelled at all; 'mainly' work or leisure that 50 percent or more of them were labelled the one or the other, and 'overwhelmingly' that 75 percent or more were.

Paid work	Overwhelmingly work
Housework	Mainly work
Travel to work	Mixed
Child care	Mixed
Shopping	Mixed
Personal care	Mixed
Eating	Mixed
Sleeping	Mixed
Meals and breaks connected with paid work	Mixed
Adult education	Mixed
Civic and collective activities	Mixed
Non–work travel	Mainly leisure
Entertainment and social contacts	Overwhelmingly leisure

Sports and walking   Overwhelmingly leisure
Other leisure   Overwhelmingly leisure

As seen by our informants, and dealing still in generalities, there was apparently a spectrum from paid work at one extreme to entertainment, sport and things like TV-watching at the other, with a spread in the middle.

We shall follow our informants, regarding work and leisure as mutually exclusive in principle, as distinguished by the three criteria of payment, freedom and pleasure, and not as collectively exhaustive. We shall from now on concentrate on the kinds of activities that were considered 'mainly' or 'overwhelmingly' leisure.

In general, married men taken as a whole spent most of their time at home. It was not without reason that men said, 'My family is my hobby', 'My wife and family are my leisure time', 'Because I'm away for longish hours I hand my weekend over to my family. They dictate me.' One diarist said he always stayed home in the evenings, reporting his routine as follows: 'Made love every night. Pinned wife down and then went to bed.' If the men had not been at home so much we should obviously not be able to talk with any justification of the symmetrical family.

But what things did they do, and how did the classes differ? We gave all the informants a series of lists of leisure activities, to which we invited them to add any we had left out, asking them about the last year taken as a whole. The first was about some of the activities done at home. The counts are in Table 1 arranged in descending order of popularity.

Watching television was of course by far the most common activity, if that is the right word to apply to people like Mr. Macrae, a storeman in Islington, who said, 'On Saturday we watched television all evening till we went to bed.' Since it was an everyday business, whereas many of the activities listed in Table 1 were done much less, its importance stood out even more from the diaries. The average time spent watching it during the week as a whole (calculated as before by multiplication) is shown in Table 2. This was in the spring and summer months of the survey. In winter it would have been more prominent. Television was also cited as the leisure activity they 'most enjoyed' of any they did by one out of five unskilled workers. The proportion was minute in every other class; the others watched it but did not 'enjoy' it as much as other things.

Except for reading and gardening the differences between the classes in Table 1 are not marked, and those there are probably did not affect the family much one way or another. Hobbies could obviously cause friction at home—one man making a very large model

Leisure and the Family

Table 1. Home–based Activities
(sample: married men working full–time)

	Professional and Managerial	Clerical	Skilled	Semi-skilled and Unskilled	All
Proportion in class doing activity 12 times or more in previous year					
Watching television	95%	99%	98%	95%	97%
Gardening	70%	62%	66%	50%	64%
Playing with children	59%	63%	66%	59%	62%
Listening to music on radio, record player or tape recorder	65%	70%	52%	44%	57%
Home decorations or repairs	52%	55%	56%	45%	53%
Car cleaning	55%	44%	51%	35%	48%
Reading (books)	67%	63%	33%	28%	46%
Car maintenance	30%	25%	38%	25%	32%
Collecting stamps or other objects	14%	24%	11%	8%	13%
Technical hobbies	10%	7%	10%	4%	8%
Playing cards or chess	9%	14%	8%	4%	8%
Playing an instrument	10%	8%	5%	4%	7%
Handicrafts	5%	6%	7%	7%	6%
Model building	6%	4%	5%	4%	5%
Total number	171	70	237	110	588
Average number of activities done 12 times or more in previous year	5.8	5.9	5.2	4.2	5.3

Technical hobbies, playing cards or chess and handicrafts were activities added by informants to our original list. Activities done by less than one percent of the men in any class are not shown but have been counted in the averages.

Table 2. Average Weekly Hours of Television Viewing
(sample: married men and women aged 30 to 49)

	Men	Women
Professional and managerial	10.0	9.9
Clerical	12.8	12.2
Skilled	12.9	11.7
Semi–skilled and unskilled	13.3	13.4
All classes	12.1	11.5
Number of people	203	206

airplane in his small back garden was hardly leaving room to hang the washing—but they were less liable to than ones which took people out of it.

For active sports there was more difference. According to Table 3 people in the higher classes played more. The order of popularity was broadly the same as in the surveys conducted by Sillitoe and Rodgers, which were on this subject more comprehensive in their territorial coverage and in other ways than ours.

Going to watch turned out to be less common than playing, although a majority of the men watched on television. Association football was the most popular, both 'live' (36 percent had been at

Table 3. Activity in Sports
(sample: married men working full–time)

	Professional and Managerial	Clerical	Skilled	Semi–skilled and Unskilled	All
Proportion in each class doing the sport 12 times or more in previous year:					
Swimming	34%	25%	20%	8%	22%
Fishing (all kinds)	9%	3%	9%	5%	8%
Association football	6%	6%	8%	5%	7%
Golf	9%	11%	4%	2%	6%
Table tennis	10%	10%	4%	2%	6%
Cricket	8%	0%	6%	4%	5%
Tennis	8%	7%	2%	0%	4%
Badminton or squash	7%	6%	2%	0%	4%
Sailing	6%	0%	1%	0%	2%
Bowls	2%	3%	2%	3%	2%
Ten-pin bowling	2%	0%	2%	1%	2%
Athletics	2%	0%	1%	0%	1%
Rugby football	2%	3%	0%	0%	1%
Horse riding	0%	3%	1%	0%	1%
Motor cruising	2%	0%	0%	0%	1%
Boxing, judo, karate, wrestling	1%	0%	1%	0%	1%
Fencing, archery, shooting	1%	1%	0%	0%	0%
Motor sports	2%	0%	0%	0%	1%
Boating	1%	0%	0%	0%	0%
Water skiing	1%	0%	0%	0%	0%
Total number	171	71	239	110	591
Average number of sports done 12 times or more in previous year	1.1	0.8	0.6	0.3	0.7

Sports have been excluded from the table if done by less than one percent of the men in any class. Examples were ice–skating, rock climbing and gliding, but again these have been included in the averages.

least once) and on television (72 percent twelve times or more). Fifteen percent had been to a cricket match (30 percent had watched cricket twelve times or more on television), and 12 percent to some kind of motor sport (32 percent twelve times or more on television). The other popular sports on television were boxing (40 percent twelve times or more), wrestling (39 percent), golf (39 percent), tennis (39 percent), athletics (36 percent), horse racing (32 percent), and rugby football (32 percent).

Clerical and skilled workers went to football more and managers watched it on television rather less than other people. Managers watched rugby and tennis more often, live and on television. Working-class men more often went to wrestling and more often watched it on television along with boxing and horse racing. But on the whole people's total 'scores' (in terms either of once or of twelve times) for spectator sports or for watching on television did not vary much by class.

Asked whether they were 'a supporter of any particular team or teams', about two men out of five said they were, the great majority of these—nine out of ten—being supporters of professional football teams. There were again no marked differences between the classes. We also inquired of those who 'regularly read a daily newspaper' which part of it they read first. Most men in all classes read one regularly. But the number starting with the sports pages varied. It was 26 percent among middle–class men and 40 percent among working–class. This did suggest a greater relative working–class interest in sport.

The final set of activities was neither home–based nor connected with sport. The details are in Table 4.

Working–class men more often played darts. Managers more often went to theatres and evening classes, more often dined out, and more often did 'voluntary work'—a sort of leisure activity, by the way, which rather offends against the earlier distinctions we were making. The cinema was obviously less popular than it would have been some decades earlier. A warehouseman living in Sutton said, 'We don't go to the cinema very often. All they have nowadays is sex and Walt Disney and I can get both of those at home.'

In asking about these various sorts of things, we did not ask where people had gone as distinct from what they had done, except for one particular activity, which varied of course from person to person, the one they had 'enjoyed most'. One difference was that on the last occasion more managers had travelled further for whatever it was: 22 percent of those whose favourite pursuit was outside the home had travelled fifty miles or more as against 11 percent in other classes.

The findings are brought together and summarized in two different ways in Table 5. Sports watched on television are excluded from the totals, on the grounds that watching television, including

Table 4. Some other Leisure Activities
(sample: married men working full–time)

	Professional and Managerial	Clerical	Skilled	Semi–skilled and Unskilled	All
Proportion in each class doing activity 12 times or more in previous year:					
Going for 'a drive in a car for pleasure'	62%	51%	62%	49%	58%
Going to pub	51%	42%	54%	58%	52%
Going for 'a walk of a mile or more'	56%	63%	41%	36%	47%
Going out for a meal (not lunch)	48%	31%	25%	23%	32%
Playing darts	12%	13%	25%	25%	20%
Attending church	22%	20%	12%	7%	15%
Cinema	16%	20%	8%	13%	13%
Voluntary work	19%	10%	8%	5%	11%
Dancing	12%	14%	10%	12%	11%
Billards or snooker	6%	10%	10%	7%	9%
Theatre	9%	1%	1%	3%	4%
Evening classes	7%	4%	2%	1%	3%
Caravanning	2%	1%	5%	3%	4%
Museum	5%	4%	1%	3%	3%
Art gallery	5%	3%	0%	1%	2%
Camping	2%	1%	3%	0%	2%
Total number	172	71	239	109	591
Average number of activities done 12 times or more in previous year	3.5	3.3	2.8	2.5	3.0

Activities have been excluded if they were done by less than one percent of the men in any class, but again incorporated into the averages. These included bingo and political activities.

sports, had already been counted. The class difference for the activities which were done once or more was larger than for those which were done more often, twelve times or more, during the year. But the general conclusion is that higher–class people did more.

This run of tables has been about husbands. Most wives were less engaged in sport, as spectators or players; they knitted or sewed more than they did anything else except watch television; they less often went to pubs, played billiards, snooker or darts; and in all, outside the home, they did less things than men. It did not, to judge by most of those measures, matter whether they had paid jobs. Those who

Leisure and the Family

Table 5. Division of Average Numbers of Leisure Activities
(sample: married men working full-time)

	Professional and Managerial	Clerical	Skilled	Semi-skilled and Unskilled	All
Once or more in previous year					
Home-based	7.3	7.3	6.6	5.6	6.7
Active sports	2.2	1.3	1.2	0.7	1.3
Spectator sports	1.3	1.1	1.2	0.8	1.1
Other non-home activities	7.5	6.7	5.7	5.0	6.2
Total	18.3	16.4	14.7	12.1	15.3
Twelve times or more in previous year					
Home-based	5.7	5.9	5.2	4.2	5.3
Active sports	1.1	0.8	0.6	0.3	0.7
Spectator sports	0.4	0.3	0.5	0.3	0.4
Other non-home activities	3.5	3.3	2.8	2.5	3.0
Total	10.7	10.3	9.1	7.3	9.4
Number of people	172	69	241	109	591

Table 6. Average Number of Leisure Activities of Men and Women
(sample: married men working full-time and married women aged 64 or under; number of people in each category shown in brackets)

	Professional and Managerial	Clerical	Skilled	Semi-skilled and Unskilled	All
Men	18.3 (172)	16.4 (69)	14.7 (241)	12.1 (109)	15.3 (591)
Women	15.6 (157)	14.5 (72)	12.8 (261)	10.7 (105)	13.3 (595)

worked went to restaurants, pubs, cinemas and theatres more than those who did not. But on the crucial point for us the generalization that applied to the husbands applied also to their wives. The point is demonstrated by Table 6 which, repeating part of the previous table for men, also adds the comparable figures for married women of similar ages.

The main conclusion from these figures is about the differences not between the sexes but between the classes. Middle-class people played more sport, and went more often to restaurants and to places of entertainment like the theatre. Above all, they had a greater range of activities both in and out of the home. These findings are in line with those from some previous inquiries on both sides of the Atlantic.

Why should it be so? One explanation is that one leisure activity triggers off another. Mr. Eldon of Enfield, a painter and decorator, spent a lot of time in his local pub, saying that 'my work is thirsty work and dirty'. Once there, he played dominoes and cribbage, and was an active member of a social club based on it. He went to the club's outings. Mr. Wain, a solicitor living in Caterham, had first joined the local golf club to play. After two years he was drawn into organizing some of the club's competitions and then, because he was so efficient, the Club Committee. He was on the Social Sub–Committee and organized—and, with his wife attended—the club's dinner–dances. Thus, a person who has many interests anyway is likely to add to them. But that does not explain why anyone should have more to start with. If we knew why we should be better able to gauge whether leisure is dependent—whether we are just observing once again the influence upon the family of the greater variety of interest in work through the mediation of leisure as one of its creatures—or whether it is also an independent variable, playing its special part in either supporting or undermining the marriage relationship.

Parker has suggested that leisure is often an extension of work. To explore this we asked whether activities were in any way 'linked to the kind of work you do'. The weakness was that the word 'linked' could be interpreted in several different ways; we put it, despite that, because we wanted to follow it up by asking how. Just under a quarter of the married men in full–time jobs said there was such a link, the proportion being higher at the top. Table 7 also distinguishes the main kinds of link as they were reported.

Table 7. Links Between Work and Leisure
(sample: married men working full–time

Kinds of Links Reported	Professional and Managerial	Clerical	Skilled	Semi–skilled and Unskilled	All
Technical	9%	1%	16%	6%	10%
Interest	15%	2%	3%	1%	6%
Business–cum–social	7%	1%	1%	1%	3%
Work–based or with work colleagues	2%	5%	2%	0%	2%
Administrative	5%	0%	0%	0%	1%
Other	1%	3%	0%	0%	1%
All reporting some link	39%	12%	22%	8%	23%
No link	61%	88%	78%	92%	77%
Total %	100%	100%	100%	100%	100%
Number	168	65	235	107	575

The examples under the heading of 'technical' were of skills being used in the one sphere which were much the same as those in the other. An industrial chemist in Ealing experimented, as a gardner, with fertilizers and fungicides to see which of them would change the colour of flowers in his garden. A laboratory worker in Sutton said that he learnt a good deal about yeast in the brewery where he worked and decided to use his knowledge to make not beer but wine, at home. He was secretary of his company's wine–making group and also a member of two local wine–making clubs. His wife did not like wine and did not join in making what she did not like. An experimental engineer living near St. Albans said he had the same approach as in his work—if not exactly the same skills—to the systematic trial of plant–grafts in his garden. The hobby of a sound engineer of Islington, hi–fi, was evident from the speakers we heard in every room. A graphic designer of Enfield said that, 'The ideas I try out in my home can often be used in display advertising which I do at work. Likewise in my work I come across ideas which I use in the home.' A horticultural engineering worker near Maidstone maintained vintage lorries as a hobby. 'It's similar to horticultural engineering. Both of them involve engineering maintenance work.' 'It's similar', said a chargehand gas fitter of Watford of his do–it–yourself, 'to what I do in my job. I plumbed in the washing machine. I installed central heating.' The gas fitter was like many other men who used their skills on their homes.

The next group of men were those who said the interest, though not the skills, spilled over. A technical author living near Aylesbury told us that whenever he could he attended aircraft shows and displays. 'It's something that I enjoy. It's directly linked with my position writing maintenance manuals for aircraft.' A car salesman at Gravesend collected old motoring magazines. A fitter at Bracknell read all he could about engineering. A messenger living in Islington working for a publisher of an antique trade paper specially liked visiting museums.

The men who mixed business with social life did it in many different circumstances. An official of a trade association, living at Sutton, went to dances organized by local branches, not because he wanted to but because he had to. A public relations officer of Marlow took people to play golf, to Lords or to rugby matches. Other people spoke of things that they did, not with clients or customers but with colleagues, like playing cricket or darts for the firm's club, serving on a social committee, going fishing with workmates or just drinking with them in the pub.

Administrative experience was also used in all manner of voluntary and trade clubs and organizations. We have noted that higher–

status people more often did voluntary work. Table 8 shows that they also more often belonged to clubs and societies and that, when they did, they more often served as officers or committee members. This was sometimes quite deliberately to further their careers. 'I'm a Fellow', said an accountant living near Haywards Heath, 'and a member of the Council of the Institute of Chartered Accountants. That's a very useful thing to be in my business.' More often, they were drawn into responsibility because it was known they had the right experience. 'When one is fairly successful in one's profession,' said someone who was, an architect living in Maida Vale, 'one seems to get asked to take part in all kinds of committees and organizations. I suppose they think one is likely to be fairly competent, or maybe that one's name will help.' A civil servant in Islington said that helping to run an old people's home, as he did, was like his job in helping to run a government department. He was not apparently being ironic.

These are only examples, drawn from all classes. The transfer of technical skills was rather more common amongst skilled manual workers than amongst others and activities done with colleagues were similar in most classes. With the other kinds of link, the managers had the edge, as Table 7 showed. Their interests, the prostitution of pleasure and the other things we have mentioned multiplied themselves outside work.

The other chief connection between the binaries seems to have been almost the other way on. Many people talked about 'unwinding' or 'relaxing'.

> When I'm out sea–fishing I can relax. I don't think about work or anything. It's crazy really because it's not pleasant. At least a

Table 8. Members and Officers of Clubs
(sample: married men working full–time

	Professional and Managerial	Clerical	Skilled	Semi-skilled and Unskilled	All
Officer or committee member of at least one club or association	28%	16%	13%	4%	16%
Active member but not officer or committee member of at least one club or association	41%	35%	36%	32%	37%
Not active member of any club or association	31%	49%	51%	64%	47%
Total %	100%	100%	100%	100%	100%
Number	169	71	235	107	582

lot of the time it isn't—you might get caught in a storm or something like that. You're getting wet and blown about and wonder if you're going to get back, and yet it's a form of relaxation. (Computer manager, Brentwood)

About once every week I put on shorts and a singlet and run for about four miles in the country round here. It's a relaxation. You push your body and the mind rests. (Marketing manager, near St. Albans)

I consciously unwind when I'm gardening. I think it's sensible. In an office you're not active and you have to keep your mind on a particular train of thought. When you're working in the garden you are being active and your mind does not have to be fixed on a particular train of thought. (Works manager, Sutton)

Parker reformulated Dumazedier's[10] three functions of leisure as being the continuation of personal development, entertainment and recuperation. He argued that the extension of work into leisure was associated with the first, 'neutrality' with the second, and an 'opposition' between work and leisure with the third. We would rather say that the people whose work extends outwards are those who most loudly voice the need for recuperation. For many middle–class men it was not satisfied by sitting around in the garden or before the television. Partly, no doubt, because their work was physically less tiring than manual workers', they chose to relax in a non–relaxed way, actively engaged in something in which they could absorb themselves. The one absorption shut out the other temporarily. We did not find in the working classes as many men who were enthusiasts for a sport or hobby, in compensation for the relatively greater dreariness of their work, as we did amongst other classes who (one would think) needed the compensation less.

So much for the job. What about its concomitants, and especially income, education and car ownership? The money that people got from their employment was obviously a good handmaiden. Among the managers, richer men more often went sailing, played golf and tennis, and went to theatres, art galleries and museums. Likewise, managers with more education were keener on sports, perhaps because they had played them at school; they also read more.

As for the ownership of cars, this appeared to have a more pervasive effect. Within occupational classes the richer and the better educated did not have a much wider total range of activities than other people. But car–owners did: they had consistently higher general scores, as Table 9 shows. Working–class car–owners were like people with cars in other classes. They played sports more, for example, and ate more meals outside their home. It seemed to be true that in general they followed a more middle–class style of life.

Table 9. Average Number of Leisure Activities According to Occupational Class and Car Ownership
(sample: married men working full–time)

	Professional and Managerial		Clerical		Skilled		Semi–skilled and Unskilled		All	
	No Car	Car	No Car	Car	No Car	Car	No Car	Car	No Car	Car
Once or more in previous year	14.1	18.8	13.2	17.1	12.6	15.7	10.3	13.8	12.1	16.7
Number of people	21	150	18	52	69	168	52	58	160	428

Table 10. Additions Made by Five Attributes to Men's Average Number of Total Leisure Activities in Previous Year
(sample: 760 men working full–time)

Average number of activities of men without any of the five following attributes	11.23
Addition made by	
1 Age 29 or under	3.78
2 Car owned by household	3.23
3 Professional or managerial class	1.93
4 Annual income £2,000 or over	1.71
5 Educated to age 17 or over	1.59

To hold class constant and consider income, education and car ownership one by one, as we have just been doing, is a perfectly good approach. But it leaves an important question unanswered. These characteristics are not independent of each other. They are interdependent, bound up together. Managers have more money and more education and more of them have cars, and the combined effect of all this is obviously important. But it is still worthwhile trying to disentangle the elements in the combination to see which matters most. The technique we adopted for this purpose was a multiple regression analysis. A very large number of relationships between the four factors, like that between car ownership and the range of activities *within* classes, were by this means summarized in a single set of indices. Age had to be brought in as a fifth factor because it made more difference than anything else.

The findings are summarized in Table 10. Men working full–time without any of the five attributes as we defined them for the computer analysis—that is not under 30, not with a car, not a manager, not with £2,000 a year or more, not educated beyond 16—had done a total number of 11.23 leisure activities at least once during the year. The additions to the score made by first one and then another attribute were as listed. The conclusion is that after age— or rather youth—car ownership added most, more so than our other big three, class, income and education.

Our index of leisure has its limitations, of course. One of the most vital was that people's scores could be inflated by a kind of multiple counting, because car cleaning and repairing were considered separate activities. But when we re–did the regression with both cleaning and repairing left out, the independent influence of the car—adding 1.97 activities—was still about the same as that of class—adding 2.07. With the spread of cars down the income scale in accord with the Principle it looks as though in one respect they have become as important as class. It follows that those who are both poor and without a car suffer from a doubly severe deprivation. There can evidently be no classless society if some but not all members of it are carless. We do not want to overdo it. We have only been talking about the range of activities, which the car can multiply just by adding to a person's geographical stretch. After this finding had emerged we retraced our ground and analysed by car as well as class almost everything we have mentioned so far in the book, and much that we have not, to see whether our findings about occupational class could still stand. Within each class car owners were more likely to call themselves middle class and vote Conservative. But that apart, the main finding stood up. In almost all respects class mattered more than cars. The main conclusion of the chapter so far also stands. The more varied and less routinized work of middle–class people was, in general, matched by their more varied leisure.

We have been looking at leisure in terms of activities rather than relationships. To add to our account of what people did with their time we needed also to consider them from this second point of view. The one is, of course, usually the other. People on walks are often unaccompanied unless by a non–human animal. But men who competed in sailing races could not do so alone, or avoid the others afterwards in the club house, even if they had wanted to. On their parents' wedding anniversaries people took them out for a treat. Irish porters piled into houses in Islington on Saturday nights. Sustaining such relationships was itself a major leisure activity which we could not list like billiards or sewing.

The information we have on this topic is not at all systematic. Many people obviously belonged to a series of social 'circles', as they would sometimes call them, meaning that their members all knew each other. It seemed that middle–class people belonged to larger numbers of these circles or networks, although the ones they did belong to were not so tightly knit as those of people who had fewer distinct circles in total. Here are a few examples.

> It's mainly relations and they all know each other. There are no others really because my best friend married my husband's brother. (Bus driver's wife, Islington)

> Our friends are mainly local friends and most of them know each other, either through living locally or through meeting here. We have made friends mainly through the children—their children went to the same school. We go round to spend an evening with one family or another occasionally. There are a few couples that the wife and I knew before we were married. (Administrator in nationalized industry, Lewisham)

> They fall into categories. First, there are our Scottish friends living in the London area—they know each other. Then the Caterham friends know each other. They come from the tennis club, the Wives' Fellowship and some are school mothers I've met through my child being at school. And then there are the business friends and my husband's friends—they link up with our Scottish friends, but otherwise the different groups don't know each other. (Accountant's wife, Caterham)

We naturally listened to what people had to say of this kind, but we could not think how to put questions about it in a large survey like ours which would in our judgment mean sufficiently the same thing to different people to produce properly comparable answers. (At least we could not see how to without confining the survey largely to that.) All we could manage in the time was to ask about particular people, identified as friends or relatives other than those our informants were actually living with, who had been met socially in the week previous to the interview.

The first point was about their sex. We have been arguing that relationships within the family have been becoming more symmetrical, with roles more interchangeable than they were. But there was still a women's world and a men's, in social contacts as in other ways. Table 11 shows that in all classes men had more men friends than women friends and vice versa.

The sheer numbers of relatives and friends are compared in Table 12. Each person is, of course, counted as one; a mother seen four times in the week by her daughter appears only once, so that the table does not give any indication of the amount of time spent

Table 11. Sex of Friend Met Socially
(sample: married men working full–time and married women aged 64 or under; total number in each category shown in brackets)

	Professional and Managerial	Clerical	Skilled	Semi–skilled and Unskilled	All
Men, proportion whose last seen friend was a man	86% (166)	79% (63)	85% (218)	86% (98)	85% (545)
Women, proportion whose last seen friend was a woman	86% (152)	86% (68)	89% (242)	92% (93)	87% (555)

Table 12. Average Number of Relatives and Friends Seen in Previous Week

(a)(sample: married men working full–time)

	Professional and Managerial	Clerical	Skilled	Semi–skilled and Unskilled	All
Local friends (living within ten minutes' walk)	2.8	1.8	2.8	3.8	2.9
Work friends	3.0	0.3	0.8	1.1	1.4
Other friends	5.2	2.1	2.7	2.2	3.3
Total friends	11.0	4.2	6.3	7.1	7.6
Total relatives	2.6	3.2	3.9	3.7	3.4
Total friends and relatives	13.6	7.4	10.2	10.8	11.0
Number of people	168	69	238	107	582

(b)(sample: married women aged 64 or under)

	Professional and Managerial	Clerical	Skilled	Semi–skilled and Unskilled	All
Local friends (living within ten minutes' walk)	2.6	1.6	2.5	2.1	2.4
Work friends	0.3	0.3	0.3	0.1	0.3
Other friends	3.4	1.1	1.3	1.3	1.9
Total friends	6.3	3.0	4.1	3.5	4.6
Total relatives	2.9	3.8	3.8	3.3	3.5
Total friends and relatives	9.2	6.8	7.9	6.8	8.1
Number of people	156	70	258	104	388

If work friends lived within ten minutes they were counted in the category of local friends. There were in fact very few such people in any class.

with others, nor the number of occasions on which they were seen. For what it is worth, however, it does show that among both men and women the people at the top end of the occupational scale saw more friends and rather fewer relatives. The others, lower down in the scale, were in one sense at least more family–centred, if family is taken for the moment to refer to the extended rather than to the immediate family. The difference between the sexes is also marked, women in general seeing fewer work friends, fewer non–local friends and less people in total.

Table 12 also shows that managerial–class people had more friends living at a distance. Among the friends most recently seen by the men, 19 percent of those of managers lived twenty miles or more away, compared with 5 percent among other classes. Their relatives, too, were more dispersed geographically. The proportion of managers' most recently seen relatives living twenty miles or more away was 42 percent; among clerical men, it was 17 percent; among skilled, 14 percent, and among semi–skilled and unskilled, 5 percent. Managers had therefore to spend more of their leisure time, even travelling by car as they ordinarily did, in order to meet both friends and relatives. Since they also went further for 'activities' in the way we were treating them before, it follows that higher–class people spent more time altogether on travel during their leisure just as they did on their journeys to work. Among the men diarists, the total average time spent in travel of all kinds during a week ranged from thirteen hours among managers to under eight hours among the semi–skilled and unskilled.

Wives saw rather less people in total than their husbands. But the couple were usually together as they travelled around their networks. This is shown in Table 13 which reports the presence of wives on the last occasion when married men had met a relative or a friend. There was a class difference, if a fairly small one: the middle–class men were more often with their wives. The question for the last

Table 13. Presence of Wife at Meeting with Relative or Friend
(sample: married men working full–time; total number in each category shown in brackets)

	Professional and Managerial	Clerical	Skilled	Semi–skilled and Unskilled	All
Wife present at last meeting with relative	83% (159)	81% (64)	75% (220)	73% (98)	78% (541)
Wife present at last meeting with friend	68% (164)	60% (63)	58% (214)	51% (98)	60% (539)

section is whether the same could be said of leisure generally as of that part of it which involved friends or relatives.

Nearly all families were home–centred, and some were more so than others. Managers, as we have seen, did more things outside the home. Were there strains caused by their leisure as well as their work, even though when they went visiting they went with their wives?

In some families there certainly were. Mr. Simpson of Reading was a skin–diving enthusiast. He went away to the sea almost every weekend during the summer, leaving his wife to spend a good deal of her time with her mother, rather as many husbands in Bethnal Green used once to do with their wives when they went off to the pub rather than the sea. Her diary recorded what happened on the Monday morning. She had gone to bed the night before, leaving a note for her husband on the kitchen table.

6:30 a.m.	Woke up and found that Derek was not home so I phoned Bill (his friend) to say that Derek would not be able to drive him to work this morning. Then went back to bed. Wondered how many other husbands led such free lives!
7:45–8:45	Called the children, cleaned shoes, plaited their hair, gave them breakfast and got their satchels ready. Saw children off to school and waved from the window as they went down the road.
9:20	Derek arrived home—he had apparently missed the tide and had to wait for the next one.
9:35	He had breakfast and then a bath while I set to work washing up the dishes.
10:20	Saw Derek off to work and went upstairs to make the bed.

Mrs. Simpson wondered how many other husbands led such free lives. Not many. In all classes married men spent much of their time at home; and for most of the time that they were away, doing the kind of things that we have been discussing, they were also with their families. They took them along when they visited friends or relatives, or (as we shall see) when they engaged in some of the most popular sports, or to watch cricket or rugby matches, or to the theatre, or to a restaurant for a meal, as well, of course, as on the holidays which were for almost everyone times when the family was together. We tried out many different comparisons between classes according to the amount of time that husbands spent with their wives and children when they were out of the home; according to the extent to which husbands had been out with and without their wives; and according to whether the wife accompanied them when they went out to engage in the leisure activity they enjoyed most. Although wives were somewhat less in evidence in the higher classes, the differences were always small.

To try and get further we adopted three other expedients. The first was to re–interview more intensively the small number of diarists who had done at least one kind of sport twelve or more times in the previous year and also recorded it as their most enjoyed activity. Higher–class people were particularly keen on sport, and this could set up tensions of its own, as the Simpson story illustrated. Fifty–one people were re–interviewed, of whom forty–one were men.

As well as men, the top social class was predominant. Among married men in the sample aged 30 to 49, 29 percent were managers; among the male sports enthusiasts the proportion was about half (20 out of 41).

The most common sports for managers were sailing (four), golf (three) and tennis (three); among the rest of the men, fishing (five) and swimming (four). The others, including squash, cricket, table tennis, motor racing and ice–skating, were done by one or at the most two people. Clearly some of these could more easily be family affairs than others. Swimming was almost always, as were camping and walking (which in this context did not mean just 'going for a walk'). Tennis, squash or table tennis could, and so could sailing, if the boat was big enough. Golf was played by wives less often than husbands and seldom together. Fishing was predominantly for men and so were motor racing, pistol shooting, cycling, football and athletics, unless the wife and children came along as spectators and supporters.

Some of the ways in which the family could be affected are worth illustrating.

Family Takes Part:

> There's no question of tennis interfering with my family. I make sure it doesn't. My wife loves it and plays too, and our nine–year–old boy is keen. As a matter of fact it was my wife who started me playing tennis again. I used to play at school. When I was first married I was playing cricket, hockey and rugby. They were my games. Then the first baby came and those games didn't fit in with my family life. My wife loved tennis and I switched to that. (Manager, chemical company, Marlow)

> There's no problem over swimming. It's the opposite. My wife likes to swim herself. So do my two sons and daughter. We all go together. (Wire maker, Stevenage)

Family Does Not Take Part but Appears to Tolerate:

> My wife doesn't play golf herself and doesn't come, but she's all for it. She likes to see my card and see how I've done. (Draughtsman, Brentwood)

> She's quite pleased, when I go fishing, to get rid of me for an hour or so. She's happy as long as I bring home something to eat. She looks on it as something that keeps me more amenable—something to occupy my mind, like. (Plumber, Southwark)

Family Does Not Take Part:

> I like sailing very much but my wife and daughter don't like it, so they're left behind. It means that I can't go as often as I'd like. The garden suffers too—they always say you can tell a sailing man by his garden. *Wife commented:* Yes, just look at ours. (Schoolmaster, Gravesend)

> My bowls sometimes interferes with the outings or with the household timetable. It's not serious, but it does affect them. (Store manager, Sutton)

> Jobs do get neglected at home because of my running. I do cross-country in the winter, track running in the summer and road running in between. My wife thinks a man should have an interest but she sometimes gets fed up. She thinks I'm mad. (Electrician's mate, Dagenham)

The numbers were, as we have said, very small. But they suggested that senior people were more likely than others to be in one of the extreme categories. With them it was rather more common for the family to suffer (if that is not too strong a word) *or* for the sport to be a family affair. In the sample as a whole nearly two-thirds of managers took part in a sport twelve times or more during the previous year. So the number of families affected must be fairly large. Sport could unite or divide. But Mrs. Simpson was clearly not alone. Leisure was sometimes a duel rather than a duet.

The second expedient was to look at men diarists who had, apart from their time at work, spent four hours or more out of their homes on their own during the period for which the diaries were kept. The proportions were roughly similar, about a third, in all social classes. Middle-class men did three main kinds of things. One was, again, sport:

> Mr. Jordan, a pathologist living in Tunbridge Wells, went home

for a meal, then drove six miles to his tennis club on a Wednesday evening, played there and talked to friends for just over three hours and then drove home.

Mr. Stewart, a factory manager working in Slough and living in Reading, drove straight from work on Thursday evening to play in a cricket match with colleagues from his firm. He had drinks in a pub afterwards with six of them and arrived home by 10:30 p.m.

Another was cultural activities:

Mr. Greenberg, a schoolteacher, went home after school on a Tuesday, had tea with his wife and went out at 7 p.m. He travelled from his home near Aylesbury to Watford and from 7:30 until 9 p.m. 'rehearsed with the Choral Society'. He had a drink afterwards with a friend and arrived back home at 10:30 p.m.

Mr. Posner, a sales manager, on a Thursday evening drove from his home in Gravesend to Rochester, where he played the viola in an orchestra. He was away from home for three and three-quarter hours, about an hour of that being spent in driving to and from the concert.

Others did voluntary work:

Mr. Welsh, a solicitor in High Wycombe, spent three and a half hours on Wednesday evening 'attending a committee meeting' at his local church.

Mr. McPhipps, an insurance broker from Ealing, 'dug out the undergrowth in the Garden of Rest' on Monday and Wednesday evenings, and went to a meeting of the parochial church council on Thursday. His church activities took up about ten and a half hours during a week, of which about half was with his wife or his wife and daughter and the rest alone or with other people.

The manual workers, when away from home and family, were watching or playing football, 'doing repairs for a friend' or in the pub.

Mr. Miller, an Islington electrician, went to the local pub on Friday evening (two hours) and Sunday lunchtime (three hours). On Saturday evening his wife went with him.

The proportions of men who were out of the home may have been much the same in all classes. But the nature of the engagement was not. The impression was that the brokers and solicitors and the like were more fully absorbed and that they were taking their leisure almost as seriously as their work, sometimes with a similar kind of professional attitude. Given that, the long arm of their leisure could intrude into the family as much as that of their job.

The third thing we did was to lean on a question about leisure similar to the one about work referred to earlier. Most people did not consider that the demands of their family 'interfered' with other things they would like to do in their leisure, as Table 14 shows. But managers and clerical workers were more inclined to. Here are four illustrations:

> I would like to play more golf, get more exercise generally. I'd like to go to more functions. But it would be selfish to my family. (Deputy manager, near Aylesbury)

> I'd like to play golf all Saturday and Sunday. I don't like shopping or decorating. My wife doesn't play golf or tennis. (Telephone manager, Caterham)

> I'd like to take up sailing, gliding, skiing but it's just not on for a family man. There's no point in starting something you can't finish. My wife hasn't got the interest. So you tend to compromise on something that everyone wants to do. (Commercial artist, Enfield)

> Without four children I could be doing a lot of things I'm not doing now. Every now and again you feel you'd like to rush off and do something different. (Accounts clerk, Ealing)

Some people talked about the constraints that home and children put upon what they could do as a couple, rather than individually.

> It's so rarely that we have any leisure time and even more rare that we can do something together. (Estate agent, High Wycombe)

Table 14. Interference of Home or Family with Leisure
(sample: married men working full–time)

	Professional and Managerial	Clerical	Skilled	Semi–skilled and Unskilled	All
Proportion saying that home or family interfered with leisure	25%	27%	14%	7%	18%
Total number	169	71	237	109	586

> Children inevitably put some limitation on what you can do. We haven't been out for six years. We can't go out for the day, because it is too long for the children. For most of the time we are at home at the evenings and weekends. (Draughtsman, Ealing)

We should now, as we have done before for other subjects, say something about the implications of our Principle of Stratified Diffusion. Leaving detail aside, the main conclusion is that, to judge from the higher classes, leisure will become more varied and more active. Television viewing and other passivities are likely to take up less of people's time. Participation in almost everything else is likely to increase, particularly in the sports which have been spreading their hold downwards ever since the Old Etonians team lost the Football Cup to Blackburn Olympic in 1883. The same thing has happened, and probably will happen, to the search for culture in museums and art galleries, painting and sculpture, playing musical instruments and adult education. Such a projection is very different from the common one that the amount of leisure time will expand dramatically, and that people will increasingly fill it with bingo and television viewing. Apart from holidays, the trends suggest no great increase in leisure time and less passivity rather than more.

It follows that the plans for the environment will need to allow for growth of many different kinds. Among sports, golf, tennis, badminton and squash are likely to become much more popular, along with sailing, water skiing, swimming and the other water sports which grew so rapidly in the 1960s. The demand for camping, caravanning, walking and driving in the country will also grow.

All in all, there will be a large extra call upon land for sport and recreation, and for people to travel about on. With the aid of their cars, others will follow the middle classes into more dispersed networks, and fling the outerworks of the region wider than ever.

If the car is going to matter so much to those who have one, it will matter even more to those without. Given the likely patterns of leisure, and given the emphasis on mobility by car that will go with it, the plight of the transport poor will in relative terms become all the worse. Even though there will be less of them, the ascendance of private transport at the expense of public threatens to isolate the minority from the main, moving stream of society. Without more equality in general and without priority for public transport in particular, more and more kinds of leisure will be shut off from the poor and the carless, young and, even more, old.

As for the majority, if the trend towards more varied leisure continues unchecked, what is this going to mean for the family? We have seen that most of our informants thought freedom to be one of the endearing characteristics of leisure. It could be excluded by obligation. But as far as we could judge from the very limited evidence we collected, the obligations generated by the family were not resented. Most people spent a great deal of their leisure time at home, and appeared to be content with it, or, if they left the precincts by car, they did so together.

Once again the higher classes hinted at a different outcome. The greater variety that they enjoyed (or suffered) in their working lives went with greater variety in their leisure and a greater geographical spread in their activities and their networks of relatives and friends. They spent more time travelling about, because they had more to travel about to. Most of them strained to prevent the greater complexity from interfering with their families, especially by taking their wives with them when they went out. But some of them brought something of the same sort of professionalism into their leisure as they did into their work, finding the one, particularly if it required skill and devotion, more of a counterpoint to the other. For such people it was sometimes not easy to reconcile their own needs and those of their families. If leisure meant to them not furious activity but what it meant to Pieper perhaps there would have been less of a conflict. But as it was . . .

REFERENCES

1. H. L. Smith, *The New Survey of London Life and Labour*, vol. VIII
2. H. B. Rodgers, The Pilot National Recreational Survey: Report No.1, University of Keele, July, 1967
3. K. K. Sillitoe, *Planning for Leisure*, Her Majesty's Stationery Office, 1969
4. S. Parker, *The Future of Work and Leisure*, MacGibbon and Kee, 1971
5. H. P. Fairchild, *Dictionary of Sociology*, Littlefield Adams, 1964
6. G. A. Lundberg et al., *Leisure: A Suburban Study*, Columbia University Press, 1934
7. M. Kaplan, *Leisure in America*, Wiley, 1960
8. J. Pieper, *Leisure: The Basis of Culture*, Faber, 1952
9. H. Arendt, *The Human Condition*, Doubleday, 1959
10. J. Dumazedier, *Toward a Society of Leisure*, Free Press, 1967

PART IV
Sociology and Politics

10

The Meaning of the Coronation

This essay was written, with Edward Shils as the first author, just after the Coronation of Queen Elizabeth. It is concerned with the part played by one of the institutions, in the form of a family on the throne, which do not change. The tone is again conservationist. The Monarchy reinforces the moral values which bind society together and makes the conflicts between the political parties less bitter.

The heart has its reasons which the mind does not suspect. In a survey of street parties in East London nothing was more remarkable than the complete inability of people to say why they thought important the occasion they were honouring with such elaborate ritual, and the newspapers naturally took for granted the behaviour on which this essay is a comment. What is perhaps more strange is that on the monarchy, at a Coronation or any other time, political science and philosophy too are silent. About this most august institution there is no serious discussion at all.

Some political scientists, as if sure that the end of so many nineteenth century reformers has been achieved, tend to speak as if Britain is now an odd kind of republic, which happens to have as its chief functionary a Queen instead of a President. It seems that even the most eminent scholars lose their sureness of touch when they enter the presence of Royalty. Sir Ivor Jennings has nothing to say in his volume on *Parliament*,[1] and in his *Cabinet Government*,[2] pausing only to note that the Sovereign still possesses considerable influence on legislation and that the King is also an important part of the 'social structure', he gives nearly all his space on this subject to an historical treatment of the Victorian period. The late Professor Harold Laski was more discerning, even though his preferences belong to the more rationalistic phase of recent intellecutal history. 'Eulogy of its habits',

177

he says, speaking of the monarchy, 'has reached a level of intensity more comparable with the religious ecstasy of the seventeenth century, when men could still believe in the divine right of kings, than of the scientific temper of the twentieth, which has seen three great imperial houses broken, and the King of Spain transformed into a homeless wanderer'.[3] For the rest, while lightly attributing this change in attitude to the imperial propaganda conducted since Victoria was proclaimed Empress of India, he too devotes himself to constitutional history, with special reference to the tangled events of 1911 and 1931. Recent British political philosophy is as applicable to a republic as it is to a monarchy, whose place in a modern society is a subject most studiously avoided.

Kingsley Martin is almost the only modern political writer to concern himself[4] with the theme to which Walter Bagehot gave such prominence when he set out in 1867 to trace 'how the actions of a retired widow and an unemployed youth become of such importance'.[5] Begehot firmly recognized that the role of the Crown was not so much constitutional as 'psychological'. He supported the monarchy for the precise reason that republicans opposed it: because it enabled the educated ten thousand to go on governing as before. By commanding their unbounded loyalty, it tamed the uncouth 'labourers of Somersetshire' who, in their simplicity, needed a person to symbolize the State. In this way 'the English Monarchy strengthens our government with the strength of religion. . . . It gives now a vast strength to the entire constitution, by enlisting on its behalf the credulous obedience of enormous masses.'[6] Mr. Martin in our day, does not, of course, share Bagehot's outlook. But up to a point he puts the same stress on the psychological functions which the Sovereign performs so well because of the sacredness with which he is invested. Once this assertion is made even he falls back, for in the greater part of the book, on the amusing story of the relations of the Sovereign with Lord Melbourne, Lord Beaconsfield, Mr. Gladstone, and the glittering host whose lives are the constitutional history of the realm.

The careful avoidance of the monarchy's role in British life appears, to the authors of this essay, to be the consequence of an 'intellectualist' bias. It is avoided because the monarchy has its roots in man's beliefs and sentiments about what he regards as sacred. The decline in the intensity of religious belief, especially in the educated classes, has produced an aversion towards all the sentiments and practices associated with religion. They do not acknowledge the somewhat alarming existence of these sentiments within themselves and refuse to admit that these are at work in others. They are acknowledged only when they are derogated as 'irrational'[7]—a charge which is both true and misleading, because it serves to dismiss them from further consideration.

The frequency with which the Coronation was spoken of by ordinary people as an 'inspiration', and as a 'rededication' of the nation, only underscores the egregiousness of the omission. This essay, using the Coronation as a point of departure, seeks to advance, in some slight measure, the analysis of a neglected subject.

In all societies, most of the adult members possess some moral standards and beliefs about which there is agreement. There is an ordering and assessment of actions and qualities according to a definite, though usually unspoken, conception of virtue. The general acceptance of this scale of values, even though vague and inarticulate, constitutes the general moral consensus of society. Only philosophical intellectuals and prophets demand that conduct be guided by explicit moral standards. In the normal way, the general moral standards are manifested only in concrete judgments, and are seldom abstractly formulated. Persons who conduct themselves in accordance with rigorous and abstract schemes of moral value, who derive and justify every action by referring it to a general principle, impress most others as intolerable doctrinaires. To the doctrinaires, of course, the ordinary man is even more shocking; they would shake the *homme moyen sensuel* from his spiritual slothfulness and elevate him to a higher plane of which he would act knowingly only in the service of the highest good. To the doctrinaire, to the ideological intellectual, the ordinary sociable man is a poor thing—narrow, unprincipled, unmoral. The ordinary man, is, of course, by no means as poor a thing as his educated detractors pretend. He too is a moral being, and even when he evades standards and dishonours obligations, he almost always concedes their validity. The revivalist reassertion of moral standards in highly individualistic frontier groups, or among detribalized primitive societies in the process of yielding before the pressure of a modern economy, are instances of the respect vice pays to virtue. The recourse to the priestly confessor and the psychoanalyst testify to the power of moral standards even in situations where they are powerless to prevent actual wrongdoing.

We do not claim that men always act in conformity with their sense of values, nor do we claim that the measure of agreement in any society, even the most consensual, is anywhere near complete. Just as no society can exist without moral consensus, without fairly far-reaching agreement on fundamental standards and beliefs, so is every society bound to be the scene of conflict. Not only is there a clash of interests, but moral and intellectual beliefs too are in collision. Yet intertwined with all these conflicts are agreements strong enough to keep society generally peaceful and coherent.

What are these moral values which restrain men's egotism and which enable society to hold itself together? A few can be listed illustratively: generosity, charity, loyalty, justice in the distribution of opportunities and rewards, reasonable respect for authority, the dignity of the individual and his right to freedom. Most people take these values so much for granted that argument about them seems neither necessary nor possible. Their very commonplaceness may seem to place them at the very opposite pole from the sacred. Yet these values are part of the substance of the sacred, and values like them have sacred attributes in every society.

Life in a community is not only necessary to man for the *genetic* development of his human qualities. Society is necessary to man as an object of his higher evaluations and attachments, and without it man's human qualities could not find expression.[8] The *polis* or community is not just a group of concrete and particular persons; it is, more fundamentally, a group of persons acquiring their significance by their embodiment of values which transcend them and by their conformity with standards and rules from which they derive their dignity. The sacredness of society is at bottom the sacredness of its moral rules, which itself derives from the presumed relationship between these rules in the deepest significance and the forces and agents which men regard as having the power to influence their destiny for better or for worse.

Man, as a moral creature with the capacity to discriminate among degrees of rightness and wrongness, feels not only safe but also terribly unsafe in the presence of the abstract symbols of these moral rules. *This is one reason why there is a recurrent need in men to reaffirm the rightness of the moral rules by which they live or feel they ought to live.* The reaffirmation of the moral rules of society serves to quell their own hostility towards these rules and also reinstates them in the appropriate relations with the greater values and powers behind the moral rules.

The need to reaffirm the moral rules comes then, not only from their sacred character, which requires that they and their sources be respected in the most serious manner, but also from the struggle against morality being continuously enacted in the human mind. Dr. Ernest Jones, in a perceptive essay,[9] has pointed to the fundamental ambivalence in the attitude to authority—first towards the parents, then towards the wider authorities of State and Church, and finally towards the rules which emanate from these authorities. This ambivalence can be overcome in a number of ways, of which reaction–formation and displacement are the most prominent. In order to curb an impulse to contravene a moral law, men will sometimes put all their energy into the fulfillment of the contrary impulse. Connection with the symbols of morality or proximity to them helps in this exertion and reinforces the strength which the individual can muster from his own resources to keep the moral law uppermost. It re–establishes the preponderance of positive devotion to the moral rules to enter into contract with them in their purest form. Contact with them in their most sacred form—as principles, or when symbolized in ritual activities, or when preached in moving sermons or speeches—renews their potency and makes the individual feel that he is in 'good relations' with the sacred, as well as safe from his own sacrilegious tendencies.

If this argument be accepted, it is barely necessary to state the interpretation of the Coronation which follows from it: that the Coronation was the ceremonial occasion for the affirmation of the moral values by which the society lives. It was an act of national communion. In this we are merely restating the interpretation, in a particular context, of a more general view (which can apply to Christmas, Independence Day, Thanksgiving Day, May Day, or any other great communal ritual) expressed by a great sociologist. 'There can be no society,' said Durkheim, 'which does not feel the need of upholding and reaffirming at regular intervals the collective sentiments and the collective ideas which make its unity and its personality. Now this moral remaking cannot be achieved except by the means of reunions, assemblies and meetings where the individuals, being closely united to one another, reaffirm in common their common sentiments; hence come ceremonies which do not differ from regular religious ceremonies, either in their object, the results which they produce, or the processes employed to attain these results. What essential difference is there between an assembly of Christians celebrating the principal dates of the life of Christ, or of Jews remembering the exodus from Egypt or the promulgation of the decalogue, and a reunion of citizens commemorating the promulgation of a new moral or legal system or some great event in the national life?'[10]

The Coronation is exactly this kind of ceremonial in which the society reaffirms the moral values which constitute it as a society and renews its devotion to those values by an act of communion.

In the following pages, this interpretation of the Coronation will be illustrated by a brief analysis of the Service itself and of some aspects of public participation in it.

The Coronation Service itself is a series of ritual affirmations of the moral values necessary to a well–governed and good society. The key to the Coronation Service is the Queen's promise to abide by the moral standards of society. The whole service reiterates their supremacy above the personality of the Sovereign. In her assurance that she will observe the canons of mercy, charity, justice and protective affection, she acknowledges and submits to their power. When she does this, she symbolically proclaims her community with her subjects who, in the ritual—and in the wider audience outside the Abbey—commit themselves to obedience within the society constituted by the moral rules which she has agreed to uphold.

This intricate series of affirmations is performed in the elaborate pattern which makes up the Coronation ceremony.

The Recognition

When the Archbishop presents the Queen to the four sides of the 'theatre', he is asking the assembly to reaffirm their allegiance to her not so much as an individual as the incumbent of an office of authority charged with moral responsibility and for which she has the preliminary qualifications of a *blood–tie*. The 'People' who signify their willingness to 'do homage and service' were once the actual members and representatives of the Estates whose participation was necessary for the security of the realm. Now, those within the Abbey, although many of great power stand among them, are no longer its exclusive possessors. The 'homage and service' of the entire society is far more important than it was in earlier Coronations and their offering is no more than a dramatic concentration of the devotion which millions now feel.

The Oath

The Queen is asked whether she will solemnly promise and swear to govern the people of the United Kingdom and the Dominions and other possessions and territories in accordance with their respective laws and customs. When she does so, she clearly acknowledges that the moral standards embodied in the laws and customs are superior to her own personal will. The Queen agrees to respect justice and mercy in her judgments, and to do her utmost to maintain the laws of God and the true profession of the Gospel. In doing this, she acknowledges once more the superiority of the transcendent moral standards and their divine source, and therewith the sacred character of the moral standards of British society.

Apart from the momentary appearance of the Moderator of the General Assembly of the Church of Scotland, the Church of England administers the entire ceremony (though the Duke of Norfolk—a Roman Catholic—organised it), and yet there is no indication that this was regarded as anomaly in a country where only a small proportion of the population actively adheres to that church. Britain is generally a Christian country, it is certainly a religious country, in the broad sense, and in the Coronation Service the Church of England served the vague religiosity of the mass of the British people without raising issues of ecclesiastical jurisdiction or formal representation. As with so much else in the Coronation Service, behind the archaic facade was a vital sense of permanent contemporaneity.

Presenting the Holy Bible

When the Moderator presents the Bible to the Queen, the Archbishop says that this act is performed in order to keep Her Majesty 'ever mindful of the Law'. The Bible is a sacred object which contains in writing the fundamental moral teachings of the Christian society. Since this Bible is to go with her always, her moral consciousness is to be kept alive by means of continuous contact with the Book in which God's will is revealed. As the Moderator says, 'Here is Wisdom; This is the royal Law;[11] These are the lively Oracles of God.' The Bible which is handed to the Queen is not simply a closed and final promulgation of moral doctrine. It is the 'lively Oracles of God', in which moral inspiration and stimulus for the mastery of constantly emerging new events are to be found. The Bible is the vessel of God's intention, a source of continuous inspiration in the moral regulation of society.

The Anointing

When the Queen is divested of her regalia, she is presented as a frail creature who has now to be brought into contact with the divine, and thus transformed into a Queen, who will be something more and greater than the human being who has received the previous instruction. When the Queen sits in the saintly King Edward's Chair she is anointed by the Archbishop with consecrated oil which sanctifies her in her regal office. When he makes the cross on both her hands, her breast and the crown of her head, he places her in the tradition of the Kings of Israel and of all the rulers of England. He anoints her saying 'And as Solomon was anointed king by Zadok the priest and Nathan the prophet, so be thou anointed, blessed, and consecrated Queen over the Peoples.' It is not merely an analogy; it is a symbolization of reality, in conformity with sacred precedent. She shows her submission before the Archbishop as God's agent, kneeling before him while he implores God to bless her.

Presenting the Sword and the Orb

The Queen is then told that she will be given power to enforce the moral law of justice and to protect and encourage those whose lives are in accordance with the law. She is commanded to confirm what is in good order, and to restore to order what has fallen away from it. The sword is an instrument of destruction. It is as dangerous as the sacred foundations of the moral rules themselves and its terrible power, for evil, as well as good, must never be forgotten by the Queen. To stress this dual potentiality of authority, it is, throughout the rest of the ceremony, carried naked before her by the peer who redeemed it. In this way, the terrible responsibilities and powers of royal authority are communicated to the Queen and the people. The people are thus made aware of the protection which a good authority can offer them when they themselves adhere to the moral law, and of the wrathful punishment which will follow their deviation. She is next invested with the bracelets of sincerity and wisdom and is dressed in the Robe Royal, which enfolds her in righteousness. With these dramatic actions, she is transformed from a young woman into a vessel of the virtues which must flow through her into her society. Thus transformed, she is reminded of the wide sphere of her power, and of the responsibilities for its moral and pious use, by the Orb which she takes in her hand and places on the altar which is the repository of the most sacred objects. In doing this, she resanctifies her own authority. She is told to execute justice but never to forget mercy.

The Benediction

The communal kernel of the Coronation becomes visible again in the Benediction when the duties of the subjects are given special prominence by the Archbishop. In his blessing, he says: 'The Lord give you faithful Parliaments and quiet Realms; sure defence against all enemies; fruitful lands and a prosperous industry; wise counsellors and upright magistrates; leaders of integrity in learning and labour; a devout, learned, and useful clergy; honest, peaceable, and dutiful citizens.' The circle of obligation is completed: the Queen to God's rule, and to her subjects on the light of God's rule, and then, her subjects to her by the same standard.

The Coronation Service and the Procession which followed were shared and celebrated by nearly all the people of Britain. In these events of 2nd June the Queen and her people were, through radio, television and press and in festivities throughout the land, brought into a great nationwide communion. Not only the principals and the spectators inside the Abbey, but the people outside also, participated in the sacred rite. There is no doubt about the depth of the popular enthusiasm. Only about its causes is there disagreement. Some claim that it is the product of commercially interested publicity, others that it is the child of the popular press, others simply dismiss it as hysteria or 'irrationality'. There are those who claim (with rather more justice)

The Meaning of the Coronation

that the involvement in the Coronation was no more than an expression of an ever–present British love of processions, uniforms, parades and pageants. Still others see the whole affair as a national 'binge', or an opportunity for millions of people to seize the occasion for a good time. The youth and charm of the Queen and the attractiveness of her husband and children are also cited to explain the absorption of the populace.

Which of these explanations is correct? All of them, it seems to us, are at best partial answers. They all overlook the element of communion with the sacred, in which the commitment to values is reaffirmed and fortified. As we said earlier, the rationalistic bias of educated persons in the present century, particularly those of radical or liberal political disposition, is liable to produce abhorrence towards manifestations of popular devotion to any institution which cannot recommend itself to secular utilitarianism.

The collision between the latter viewpoint and the devoted gravity of the popular attitude was revealed most strikingly in the uproar which followed the publication of Mr. David Low's cartoon in the *Manchester Guardian* on 3rd June. This cartoon showed a Blimp–like figure, 'the morning after', a paper crown awry on his head, the remains of the tinsel and crepe paper of a gay party littered about him, a television receiver in the corner and over it all a grim reminder that £100,000,000 had been spent on the spree. It was in the radical 'debunking' tradition. It called forth a storm of denunciation. Moral sentiments had been affronted by Mr. Low's frivolity at a time when they were at a high pitch of seriousness. The first flood of letters expressed indignation that a cynical reference to monetary costs should intrude upon a state of exhilaration, of 'inspiration', or 'uplift', upon 'a unique and inspiring experience' of 'heartfelt national rejoicing', upon a 'spirit of service and dedication and the inspiring unity of all the people who rejoiced together (and who rededicated themselves) on this wonderful occasion'. The second stage of the correspondence was no less significant. Although the anti–Low letters continued, the outburst of sentiment affirming the sacred character of the national participation in the Coronation made the more sceptical uncomfortable. Some of those who sprang to Low's defence found the expression of such intensely serious moral indignation 'frightening'.

The solemn sense that something touching the roots of British society was involved found expression in many other ways as well. An experienced observer of the London crowd said that the atmosphere on 1st June was like that of Armistice Day 1918 and of VE and VJ Days 1945: there was an air of gravity accompanied by a profound release from anxiety. The extraordinary stillness and tranquillity of the people on the route all through the early morning of

2nd June was noted by many who moved among them. Churches received many persons who came to pray or to meditate in the quiet, and in at least one famous London church—All Hallows Barking—communion services were held every hour.

Just as the Coronation Service in the Abbey was a religious ceremony in the conventional sense, so then the popular participation in the service throughout the country had many of the properties of the enactment of a religious ritual. For one thing, it was not just an extraordinary spectacle, which people were interested in as individuals in search of enjoyment. The Coronation was throughout a collective, not an individual experience.

W. Robertson Smith in his great work, Lectures on the Religion of the Semites,[12] points out that acts of communion (of which the Coronation can be regarded as an example) are never experienced by individuals alone: they are always communal occasions. They are acts of communion between the diety or other symbols of the highest values of the community, and persons who come together to be in communion with one another through their common contact with the sacred. The fact that the experience is communal means that one of the values, the virtue of social unity or solidarity, is acknowledged and strengthened in the very act of communion.

The greatly increased sensitivity of individuals to their social ties, the greater absorption of the individual into his group and therewith into the larger community through his group, found expression not only on the procession route but in the absent people as well, notably through their families. The family, despite the ravages of urban life and despite those who allege that it is in dissolution, remains one of the most sinewy of institutions. The family tie is regarded as sacred, even by those who would, or do, shirk the diffuse obligations it imposes. The Coronation, like any other great occasion which in some manner touches the sense of the sacred, brings vitality into family relationships. The Coronation, much like Christmas, was a time for drawing closer the bonds of the family, for re–asserting its solidarity and for re–emphasizing the values of the family—generosity, loyalty, love—which are *at the same time* the fundamental values necessary for the well–being of the larger society. When listening to the radio, looking at the television, walking the streets to look at the decorations, the unit was the family, and neither mother nor father were far away when their children sat down for cakes and ice cream at one of the thousands of street and village parties held that week. Prominent in the crowds were parents holding small children on their shoulders and carrying even smaller ones in cradles. In all towns over the country, prams were pushed great distances to bring into contact with the symbols of the great event infants who could see or appreciate little. It was as if people recognized that the most elementary unit for entry into communion with the sacred was the family, not the individual.

The solidarity of the family is often heightened at the cost of solidarity in the wider community. Not so at the Coronation. On this occasion one family was knit together with another in one great national family through identification with the monarchy. A general warmth and congeniality permeated relations even with strangers. It was the same type of atmosphere, except that it was more pronounced, that one notices at Christmas time when, in busy streets and crowded trains, people are much more warm–hearted, sympathetic and kindly than they are on more ordinary occasions. Affection generated by the great event overflowed from the family to outsiders, and back again into the family. One correspondent of the *Manchester Guardian*, reporting the Coronation procession, observed: 'The Colonial contingents sweep by. The crowd loves them. The crowd now loves everybody.' Antagonism emerged only against people who did not seem to be joining in the great event or treating with proper respect the important social values—by failing, for example, to decorate their buildings with proper splendour. A minor example of the increase in communal unity was the police report that, contrary to their expectations, the pickpockets, usually an inevitable concomitant of any large crowd, were entirely inactive during Coronation Day.

An occurrence in a new housing estate on the outskirts of London provides another instance. There the organizer of a street party had for many months been engaged in a feud with a neighbour so violent that they had at one time summoned each other to the local court. The origin of the feud—a minor quarrel about trespassing by children—was forgotten, and there were continuous outbursts of aggression which reached a climax in May when the neighbour poured hot water over the fence onto some flowers which had just been planted. The neighbour's children were not enrolled for the Coronation party until near the day itself. Then the neighbour came to the organizer and asked in a very humble way whether her own children might be included. They were accepted, and the two who had not exchanged friendly words for so long began to greet each other in the streets as they passed. On the day itself, the organizer, out of her generosity for everyone, went so far as to ask the neighbour to come in and watch her television set. When the neighbour had been in the house for half an hour she asked whether her husband, who was waiting alone next door, could join them. He came in, and when the Service was over, the long standing feud was finally ended over a cup of tea.

Something like this kind of spirit had been manifested before—during the Blitz, the Fuel Crisis of 1947, the London smog of 1952, even during the Watson–Bailey stand in the Lord's cricket-match or Lock's final overs at the Oval—and to some extent the broad reasons were probably the same. There was a vital common subject for people to talk about; whatever the individual's speciality, the same thought was uppermost in his mind as in everyone else's, and that made it easier to overcome the customary barriers. But not less important then the common subject is the common sentiment of the sacredness of communal life and institutions. In a great national communion like the Coronation, people became more aware of their dependence upon each other, and they sensed some connection between this and their relationship to the Queen. Thereby they became more sensitive to the values which bound them all together. Once there is a common vital object of attention, and a common sentiment about it, the feelings apt for the occasion spread by a kind of contagion. Kindness, met with on every side, reinforces itself, and a feeling of diffuse benevolence and sympathy spreads; under these circumstances the individual loses his egoistic boundaries and feels himself fused with his community.

The need to render gifts and sacrifices, so central in religious ceremonies, was also apparent in various forms. Many persons sent gifts directly to the Queen, and the vast scale of individual and collective gifts to persons known and unknown has been the occasion of much comment. Very many municipalities arranged 'treats for old folks', local authorities gave gifts to schoolchildren and gift–giving within and between families was very widespread. The joint viewing of the Coronation Service and Procession on the television called forth many presentations. The universal decorations attest not merely to the sense of festivity but also to the disposition to offer valuable objects on such an occasion of entry into contact with the sacred values of society. Low's cartoon in the *Manchester Guardian* certainly portrayed one aspect of the truth when he saw the whole thing as 'one gigantic binge'. But it was not just a 'good time' or an 'opportunity for a good time', as some persons grudgingly said in justification for giving themselves up to the Coronation. There was an orgy, in a certain sense, but it was not just one of self–indulgence. Students of comparative religion have shown that an orgy following an act of communion with the sacred is far from uncommon. It aids the release of tension and reduces the anxiety which intense and immediate contact with the sacred engenders. Moreover, what appears to be simply an orgy of self–indulgence is often one of indulgence with goods which have been consecrated or which have some sacred, communally significant properties.

Surcease from drabness and routine, from the commonplaceness and triviality of daily preoccupation, is certainly one reason for the exaltation. There is surely wisdom in the remark of a philosophical Northern villager: 'What people like is the sheer excess of it. We lead niggling enough lives these days. Something a bit lavish for a change is good for the soul.'[13] But he did not go far enough. The British love of processions, of uniforms, and ceremonial is not just simple–minded gullibility—it is the love of proximity to greatness and power, to the charismatic person or institution which partakes of the sacred. The crowds who turned out to see the Queen, who waited in the rain in quiet happiness to see the Queen and her soldiers, were waiting to enter into contact with the mighty powers who are symbolically and to some extent really responsible for the care and protection of their basic values and who on this day had been confirmed in these responsibilities. The crowds who clamoured for the Queen outside Buckingham Palace or who lined the streets on the days following Coronation Day when she made her tours of London were not just idle curiosity–seekers. They were, it is probably true, looking for a thrill but it was the thrill of contact with something great, with something which is connected with the sacred, in the way that authority which is charged with obligations to provide for and to protect the community in its fundamental constitution is always rooted in the sacred.

Let us now assume that this interpretation of the Coronation is at least plausible and perhaps correct. Why, then, should it have taken place in this way in Great Britain at this time? Not all coronations, British or foreign, have drawn such deep sentiments of devoted participation. Whereas a century ago republicanism had numerous proponents in England, it is now a narrow and eccentric sect. Although the stability of the British monarchy became well established in the course of the nineteenth century, persons who have lived through or studied the four coronations of the present century seem to agree that the Coronation of Elizabeth II stirred greater depths in the people than any of its predecessors.

Over the past century, British society, despite distinctions of nationality and social status, has achieved a degree of moral unity equalled by no other large national state. The assimilation of the working class into the moral consensus of British society, though certainly far from complete, has gone further in Great Britain than anywhere else, and its transformation from one of the most unruly and violent into one of the most orderly and law–abiding is one of the great collective achievements of modern times. Whatever its origins, the past century has certainly witnessed a decline in the hostility of the British working and middle classes towards the symbols of the society as a whole and towards the authorities vested with those symbols and the rules they promulgate and administer.

It is true that the discredit into which the British 'ruling class' fell as a result of the First World War, the General Strike and the Great Depression, diminished this moral unity. But consensus on fundamental values remained. The Second World War greatly contributed to the strengthening of attachment to society. The care which officers, junior and senior, took to avoid the waste of life, the provision for families at home, the steadiness of the emergence of victory, made for widespread solidarity and for absence of rancour even across gaps in that solidarity. The subsequent General Election was soberly fought. Following that, the Labour Government, by its concern for the underprivileged, by its success in avoiding the alienation of the middle and upper classes, and by the embodiment of certain prized British virtues in its leaders, brought this moral unity of British society to a remarkably high level. Moreover, many British intellectuals who in the 1920s and 1930s had been as alienated and cantankerous as any, returned to the national fold during the War. Full employment and Government patronage on a large scale, as well as a growing repugnance for the Soviet Union and a now exacerbated but hitherto dormant national pride or conceit also played their part in this development. The central fact is that Britain came into the Coronation period with a degree of moral consensus such as few large societies have ever manifested.

The combination of constitutional monarchy and political democracy has itself played a part in the creation and maintenance of moral consensus, and it is this part which we shall now briefly consider. The late John Rickman and Ernest Jones have argued that the deep ambivalence towards authority and towards moral rules has promoted the widespread acceptance of the monarchy in Britain and in other countries where constitutional monarchy has become firmly established. Whereas the lands where personal or absolute monarchy prevailed were beset by revolution, countries of constitutional monarchy became politically stable and orderly, with a vigorously democratic political life. Hostility against authority was, it is said, displaced from royalty onto the leaders of the opposition party and even onto the leaders of the government party. Constitutional monarchies and their societies were fortified by drawing to themselves the loyalties and devotion of their members while avoiding the hostility which is always, in varying measure, engendered by submission to morality. When protected from the full blast of destructiveness by its very *powerlessness*, royalty is able to bask in the sunshine of an affection unadulterated by its opposite. The institution of the constitutional monarchy is supported by one of the mechanisms by which the mind defends itself from conflict, namely, by the segregation of mutually antagonistic sentiments, previously directed towards a single object, onto discrete and separate objects.[14]

It might therefore be said that the vigour of British political life is actually rendered possible by the existence of the constitutional monarchy. But the aggressiveness which is channelled into the political arena is in its turn ameliorated and checked by the sentiments of moral unity which the Crown helps to create. Here it is not only the symbolism of the Crown but also the painstaking probity of Kings George V and VI in dealing with the Labour Party, both when it was in opposition and when it formed the Government, which have helped to weld the Labour Party and its following firmly into the moral framework of the national life.

An effective segregation of love and hatred, when the love is directed towards a genuinely loveworthy object, reduces the intensity of the hatred as well. Just as the existence of a constitutional monarchy softens the acerbity in the relations between political parties, so it also lessens the antagonism of the governed towards the reigning government. Governments are well known to benefit whenever the virtues of Royalty are displayed.[15] It appears that the popularity of the Conservative Administration was at least temporarily increased by the Coronation, and at the time much newspaper speculation centred on the question whether Mr. Churchill would use the advantage to win a large majority for his Party at a General Election.

Thus we can see that the image of the monarch as the symbolic custodian of the awful powers and beneficent moral standards is one weighty element in moral consensus. But the monarch is not only symbol. Personal qualities are also significant. Hence it is appropriate at this point to refer to the role of the Royal Family in attaching the population to the monarchy. Walter Bagehot said: 'A family on the throne is an interesting idea also. It brings down the pride of sovereignty to the level of petty life.'[16] More and more has this become true since then. Where once to mention the family of the King, like Charles II or George IV, would have provoked laughter, it is now common form to talk about the Royal Family. The monarchy is idealised not so much for the virtue of the individual sovereign as for the virtue which he expresses in his family life.

Devotion to the Royal Family thus does mean in a very direct way devotion to one's own family, because the values embodied in each are the same. When allowance is also made for the force of displacement, if it is accepted that a person venerates the Sovereign partly because he is associated, in the seat of the emotions, with the wondrous parents of phantasy, and if it is accepted that there is also a sort of re–displacement at work, whereby the real parents and wives and children are thought of more highly because they receive some of the backwash of emotion from their Royal counterparts, it is easy to see that the emotional change is a reciprocal one, and all the more powerful for that. Some aspects of this relationship become clear in the Christmas broadcast in which the Sovereign year after year talks about the Royal Family, the millions of British families, and the nation as a whole, as though they are one. On sacred occasions, the whole society is felt to be one large family, and even the nations of the Commonwealth, represented at the Coronation by their prime ministers, queens, and ambassadors, are conceived of as a 'family of nations'.

In other ways the monarchy plays on more ordinary occasions the same kind of role as it does at a Coronation—only in a far less spectacular way. Thus British society combines free institutional pluralism with an underlying moral consensus. The universities, the municipalities, the professional bodies, the trades unions, the business corporations—all seek to enforce and protect their internal standards and to fend off external encroachment. Yet they coexist and cooperate in a remarkable atmosphere of mutual respect and relative freedom from acrimony. There are many reasons for this. In the present context we wish only to stress the unifying function of the monarchy and the orders of society which derive their legitimacy from connection with it. Every corporate body which has some connection with the sacred properties, the *charisma*, of the Crown thereby has infused into it a reminder of the moral obligations which extend beyond its own corporate boundaries. It is tied, so to speak, to the central value system of the society as a whole through its relationship with Royalty. Quite apart from the Armed Forces, with their multiplicity of royal connection, by fleet, regiment and squadron, a thousand institutions of all kinds are also recognized by the presence of a member of the Royal Family as Patron, President, or Visitor. Royalty presides over such diverse organizations as the Royal Society and the Royal Institute of British Architects, the Royal Academy and the Royal College of Veterinary Surgeons, the British Medical Association and the Institution of Civil Engineers, the Marylebone Cricket Club and the Lawn Tennis Association, the Red Cross and the National Playing Fields Association, St. Mary's Hospital and the Royal Yacht Squadron, the Royal Forestry Society and the University of London. There are the Royal Charters, the patronage of charities, the inaugural ceremonies of hospitals and ships, gardens and factories. The monarchy is the one pervasive institution, standing above all others, which plays a part in a vital way comparable to the function of the medieval Church as seen by Professor Tawney—the function of integrating diverse elements into a whole by protecting and defining their autonomy.[17]

Even where the monarchy does not assume ceremonial offices of the type just referred to, the function of holding together the plurality of institutions is performed in some measure by the peerage and the system of honours. In all institutions and professions, all forms of individual achievement and merit are recognized and blessed by this system. The outstanding actors and pets, doctors and scientists, leaders of trade unions and trade associations, scholars and sportsmen, musicians and managers, the brave, the brilliant and the industrious, all receive confirmation of their conformity with the highest standards of society by an honour awarded by the Sovereign. The Sovereign acts as agent of the value system, and the moral values of the society are reinforced in the individuals honoured.

To sum up: A society is held together by its internal agreement about the sacredness of certain fundamental moral standards. In an inchoate, dimly perceived, and seldom explicit manner, the central authority of an orderly society, whether it be secular or ecclesiastical, is acknowledged to be the avenue of communication with the realm of the sacred values. Within its society, popular constitutional monarchy enjoys almost universal recognition in this capacity, and it is therefore enabled to heighten the moral and civic sensibility of the society and to permeate it with symbols of those values to which the sensitivity responds. Intermittent rituals bring the society or varying sectors of it repeatedly into contact with this vessel of the sacred values. The Coronation provided at one time and for practically the entire society such an intensive contact with the sacred that we believe we are justified in interpreting it as we have done in this essay, as a great act of national communion.

REFERENCES

1. 'Of the King we need say nothing. His part in the process of legislation has become little more than formal.' *Parliament*. Cambridge, 1939, p. 3.
2. *Cabinet Government*. Cambridge, 1947.
3. *Parliamentary Government in England*. Allen & Unwin, London, 1938, p. 389.
4. *The Magic of Monarchy*. Nelson, London, 1937.
5. *The English Constitution*. Oxford, 1936, p. 30.
6. Ibid., pp. 35, 39.

7. See, for instance, Percy Black. *The Mystique of Modern Monarchy.* Watts, London, 1953.

8. *The Politics of Aristotle,* trans. by Sir Ernest Barker, Oxford, 1946, p. 2.

9. Jones, Ernest. 'The Psychology of Constitutional Monarchy' in *Essays in Applied Psychoanalysis,* Vol. I. Hogarth, London, 1951.

10. *Elementary Forms of Religious Life.* Allen & Unwin. London. 1915, p. 427.

11. It is the law which is to govern Royalty, and only in this way does it refer to the law made by Royalty for the government of society.

12. *Lectures on the Religion of the Semites,* Black, London, 1927.

13. *Manchester Guardian,* 3 June 1953.

14. Anna Freud. *The Ego and the Mechanisms of Defence.* Hogarth, London, 1937.

15. The Secretary of the Labour Party once told one of the authors of this essay that he had always been confident that Labour would win the hotly contested Gravesend by-election in 1947 because the then Princess Elizabeth had been married a short time before.

16. Op. cit. p. 34.

17. 'Religion . . . the keystone which holds together the social edifice . . .' *Religion and the Rise of Capitalism.* John Murray, London, 1926, p. 279.

11

Small Man, Big World

A pamphlet published by the Labour Party in 1948, this was an early reaction against the creation of so many large new organisations by a government which was at that time extending nationalisation in every direction. The leaders of the party allowed publication because they (like the author) recognised that they were impaled on a dilemma. Efficiency required bigness, democracy smallness. Aneurin Bevan, the political godfather of the National Health Service, managed to create that and also declare that 'Bigness is the enemy of humanity'. The author was clear which side of the fence he was on, well before Fritz Schumacher took up the same theme in the 1970s. In 1969, following up on the pamphlet, he started the Association for Neighbourhood Councils which remains active in the 1980s.

One daughter hunts round in the cupboard for the box containing last year's decorations. Another goes to Woolworth's to buy balloons and miniature candle–holders. Mother is at the market looking out a nice tree. Father gets the ladder from the scullery, and holds it steady by the front window while the son goes up with a hammer to tack up the big yellow streamer with its fluffy orange bells. 'Not in the plaster, you fool.' The daughter fetches from the yard the big flower pot for the tree; she washes it clean at the tap outside before sticking on the coloured paper. 'Shall we put the tree in the corner this year?' 'No, it's better by the fireplace.' 'But the corner is best, surely?' 'Oh, I've just remembered—we've forgotten the candles. Go out and get some, will you? I'll finish off the streamers.' 'But Dad. . . .'

Of course, no family is always cooperative and contented, and some families never are. At least one man who won at the Pools did not sit down around the fire with the family and ask where they should all go for a celebration holiday; he packed his wife and children off to Southend while he went to Blackpool. But in most families things are done together. Things are talked over together. Things are often decided together. In preparations for Christmas or a picnic, every member will have a say and a part. When the son, about to leave school, is wondering where to look for his first job everyone will talk it over and give advice before a decision is taken. If the mother has to go into hospital, the others will in discussion decide how each is to help in keeping the home going while she is away.

There is no doubt that democracy can most easily flourish in the family and in other small groups built to the scale of the individual. All the members there meet face to face; if a decision has to be made, all can have a direct and personal part in making it, and all can perceive the results of their decisions.

Democracy therefore seems to require smallness. But efficiency, promoted by the growth of science, often requires bigness. This is the great dilemma of modern society.

A high standard of life demands large–scale organisation. In a primitive economy a small group of families led an independent, but often starved existence. Today men obtain a high standard of life by cooperating with thousands of other unknown and unseen people in a vast division of labour. The farmer of the United States, the peasant of Normandy, the worker in the iron–ore mines of Sweden, the riveter in the Clydeside shipyard and the miner in a Welsh pit all cooperate with each other in producing and exchanging, importing and exporting, the goods which keep them alive. This vast division of labour we cannot abandon either in the world, the nation or the factory. Indeed, in some ways we must seek still larger organisations. The economic problems of the modern world can be solved only by national and even international planning, and the best hope of permanent peace is to match the world economy with world Government.

There is no salvation in going back to some misty past in which the small man lived in a small world, no salvation in putting multi–coloured maypoles in every city square or even substituting William Morris for the Morris car. Destroying bigness would not only reduce the standard of living; it would also destroy democracy. In fact economic expansion, resting on the twin foundations of full employment and a rising standard of life, is an essential condition of extending democracy.

But higher efficiency has not been gained without social cost. In the small group like the family everyone can have an active part in making decisions and carrying them out; in the big group like the nation not everyone can have a direct and continuous say in the way it is run. The common purposes of a small group are more easily understood; in the large society the individual cannot so well see its common purposes or understand its complex working. In the small group all the members are well-known to each other; in the large group the people at the top tend to get out of touch with those at the bottom and the small man to regard those at the top as 'they,' the impersonal authorities with mysterious power over himself. In the small group—in the family, amongst friends at work or in the pub, in the little ships of the Navy—the person has a feeling of comradeship and a sense of belonging: the individual matters and his self-respect is supported by the respect of his fellows. But in the large group the individual is only too likely to be and to feel powerless and insignificant.

How can the individual be made to matter more? How can the human advantages of the small group be combined with the technical advantages of the big? There are three main answers, which will be discussed from various angles in the rest of this essay:

1. By securing the right kind of democratic leadership.

2. By establishing close two-way communication between those at the bottom and those at the top.

3. By reducing the size of organisation wherever it can be done without harming efficiency.

What will be the common purpose of this new democracy?—a question sharply posed by the experience of war. The small groups in civil defence based on the Warden's Post, grim in function, were yet in many ways models of what are needed in peace. For many danger itself was welcome. I remember an elected marshal of a large shelter in the East End who even in a prolonged lull used to talk of the big Blitz with genuine longing and regret.

It would be wrong, and it would be idle, to hanker for the same conditions in peace. 'The problem of modern society,' said William James, 'is to find a moral equivalent for war.' But is this true? Such an all-pervasive purpose as prevailed in the war cannot and should not be permanent. In peace we need a more relaxed atmosphere, less fervour, a less uniform patriotism allowing more variety and divergence. The loyalties of peace should be multiple, pinned not only to the State—and to the World—but to the home, the neighbourhood and the workplace. But it is true that in peace as in war we do need more active groupings between the State and the family to nourish the one and to release the social energy from the other. The links between all the different groupings need not be so direct as in war, but they do need to exist within a broad framework of commonly accepted purposes. Full employment, a rising standard of life, social justice and equality of opportunity for individuals to fulfil all their great and as yet untapped capacities, social ownership of the keys to social power, joy in life and pride in work, democracy in the community and democracy in industry—these, the purposes of democratic socialism, should become the common purposes of peace linking people together in a free and integrated society.

The best definition of democracy is 'government of the people, for the people, by the people,' and the pith of it is government *by* the people. All groups—from nations to families—have to have methods of governing their common affairs. But it is only in the small group that government can be continuously conducted by the people who compose it. In the large group, if only because decisions must be taken speedily, day–to–day government cannot be carried on by all the members all the time. It is necessary to choose leaders who will act for the members. In any large organisation the choice of leaders is therefore crucial.

Election is the normal democratic method of choosing leaders. The members of a group can decide how they want to be governed by electing a leader whose views or whose personal qualities suggest that he will govern as they desire. They possess a powerful sanction to compel him to do as they wish: if he does not do so, they can refuse to re–elect him. However autocratic his inclinations, someone who depends for his authority on election by the people cannot afford to ignore their wishes. He must govern by consent of the governed or, in the long run, he cannot govern at all. 'It is,' says Harold Laski, 'fundamental to the conference of power that it should never be permanent. . . . Responsible government in a democracy lives always in the shadow of coming defeat; and this makes it eager to satisfy those with whose destinies it is charged.'[1]

The larger the body, the more power do the elected leaders wield. In the small group, like the ward association in the Labour Party, the ordinary members, meeting frequently together, decide policy in some detail and so give specific and frequent instructions to their elected executive officers. But the affairs of the large group, such as the nation, are so complex that the citizen cannot give frequent, detailed instructions to the leaders whom he elects. There cannot be a daily referendum. At a General Election he can choose between the policies put forward by the Parties, and the Party favoured by the majority is returned to power. But, having given a broad mandate, he has to leave its execution to leaders elected for a period of years, during which the issues may change.

The danger is obvious. The people may only be able to take part in their own government at election times. At elections the citizen is a ruler; between elections he is ruled by those whom he has elected.

But democracy should so far as possible be a continuous process. 'Ballot–box democracy,' said Mr. Morrison at the Scarborough Conference of 1948, 'where people go and vote—if they can be bothered and persuaded and shoved around to go and vote—every few years and do nothing much in between, is out of date. We must have an active, living democracy in our country.'

So the elected leaders, if they believe that democracy means government by the people, have a great responsibility to behave between elections as democrats should. Share power with the people on the widest possible scale. Give the people the greatest opportunity to contribute to their own government. Consult. Keep in touch continuously with what the people want. Make it possible for citizens to play their part and to exercise wise judgments by giving them the fullest information—these are their duties as democrats. In other words, democracy in any large group requires a continuous two–way traffic of contribution to government from below and information about government from above.

The personal responsibility of the appointed leader is even greater. He too should govern with the consent of the governed. He too should give those he leads the greatest possible opportunity to take part in their own government. In a democracy, this is the first duty for those holding power by appointment as well as by election, whether they be in industry, the civil service or elsewhere.

It may be possible to use election to fill many more offices in the future, especially if the method whereby the choice of the electors is limited to a panel of properly qualified candidates is more widely practised. But election may be quite unsuitable for certain posts. Sometimes the technical qualifications for a job can only be judged by experts. Continuity of administration cannot always be guaranteed by election. But even though appointed, leaders should always behave as democrats, because this is their moral duty to their fellows and, incidentally, because it is the best way of securing the human cooperation which is the secret of good management anywhere. This has been realised by some of the best administrators. David Lilienthal, ex–chairman of the Tennessee Valley Authority, has said, for example, 'There is nothing in my experience more heartening than this: that devices of management which give a lift to the human spirit turn out so often to be the most "efficient" methods.'[2]

There are important lessons here for selection and training methods. For jobs giving power over people, bossy persons who believe the best committee is a committee of one should be avoided. So should all people who have no humility. The parson–politician of the U.S.A. was one of these. 'O Lord,' he prayed, 'we ask thee for a Governor who would rule in the fear of God; who would defeat the ringleaders of corruption, enhance the prosperity of the State, promote the happiness of the people—O Lord, what's the use of beating about the bush? Give us George W. Briggs for Governor! Amen.'

Training should give administrators of all kinds knowledge about methods of enlisting cooperation. The Ministry of Labour's Training Within Industry course for foremen is an example of what might be done, with adaptation, for civil servants and many other officials in and out of industry. There are far too many people with authority who know nothing of applied psychology.

Since the quality of leadership is so important, it follows that leaders must be given every chance to get the cooperation of their own groups. This is impossible unless they have proper status. A foreman who has to refer everything to a Departmental Manager is not going to be respected by the rank-and-file workers. The men will soon want to bypass the poor foreman and put their case to the Departmental Manager. But if no one in the factory has authority—if many matters have to go to some distant Head Office—it will become impossible for the management, whether democratically inclined or not, to function effectively. The obvious conclusion is that in any large organisation there should, to foster democracy if for no other reason, be the greatest possible delegation of authority to the official actually in touch with the rank–and–file. This official should have power to settle most of the questions raised with him by the people for whom he is immediately responsible.

Industrial democracy has sometimes been equated with Joint Production Committees. This is a superficial view. J.P.C.s or similar bodies are certainly needed in every factory, mine and office. So much has been written and spoken about them that I shall not go over that ground again. But two points must be stressed here.

First, joint committtees for a whole factory may be of slight value unless supported by joint consultation at every level within the factory. The committees, perhaps after a preliminary flare of excitement when first set up, may become humdrum and fall victim to that disease of remoteness which is cultivated by bigness: they may, like all other consultative bodies, get out of touch with the rank and file. Once again, the worker in one particular shop will not feel that he is being personally consulted merely because his representative is. Reporting back will help. But what is most needed is consultation in each shop between the individual and his foreman, both informally and through a shop committee, with links leading upwards from there to the J.P.C. Wherever there is anyone with managerial power over others, there should be consultation.

This is above all important in the small working group of half a dozen or a dozen people at the very bottom of the industrial pyramid.

In such a small group formal consultation may be as unnecessary as the habit of informal consultation is necessary. This can only work where the charge–hand, foreman or equivalent official is ready to consult, in other words is a man with the necessary horse–sense about people, and enough humility to be prepared to take advice from others. We are thus brought back sharply to the importance of selecting the right kind of leaders if democracy is to flourish.

Second, the nationalised industries should be models of industrial democracy which can later be followed elsewhere. In these industries, consultation does not have to battle with private profit. In privately owned industry workers have naturally been reluctant to cooperate in increasing production if the shareholders have been the only gainers. In a publicly owned industry this barrier does not exist. Cooperation between management and men becomes that much easier to achieve. But it does not follow the horse will leave the stable just because the door is opened. And much progress has yet to be made before there is full industrial democracy in these industries.

Their disadvantage from this special point of view, is, or could be, their size. It is all to the good if some necessary functions are performed for an industry as a whole; technically, indeed, a comprehensive plan of industry–wide development is most desirable. But size is a handicap if necessary authority is removed from the manager on the spot and transferred to a more remote office. The manager must be given proper status; he should have at least enough authority to enable him to take decisions about most matters normally raised in consultation with the workers. These public–owned industries can do a very great service by demonstrating how the necessary minimum of central control can be combined with the necessary maximum of power at the periphery in a form which will secure both technical efficiency and industrial democracy.

The need to delegate power and reduce size is borne out by an interesting recent study—by a survey conducted on the attitudes of building workers by the Building Research Unit of the Medical Research Council at the request of the Ministry of Works.[3] Norah Davis reports that good feeling and trust between managers and operatives bore a direct relation to the amount of personal contact between them. Sometimes there is very little. In large organisations the boss may even be quite unknown to the worker. A friend of mine was once in a large public office with a junior official. A man passed them on the stairs and nodded to my friend. 'Who was that?' 'The boss of your department'—the official had worked there ten years and had never even seen his boss!

Norah Davis suggests that morale was lower on the larger building sites and in the larger building organisations. 'The large organisations and the large working groups,' she says 'did not seem to have been welded into socially integrated units, and, as the lines of communication laid down were inadequate or circuitous, those framing policy were necessarily out of touch with the needs and wishes of the lower grades. The latter, in their turn, felt that the methods of communication made it difficult, if not impossible, for them to express their opinions and felt that "It's no good making complaints to Head Office. They just pass the buck and nothing gets done." As a result, grievances became magnified out of all proportion to their original cause and the operatives came to believe that those in authority neither knew nor cared about their existence.' This report once again stresses the need for the two–way traffic of joint consultation in the large working unit.

From the strictly psychological point of view, bigness is a liability. Certain British and foreign companies, realising this, have in effect divided up their factories into a number of sub–factories. One example was given at the Eighth International Management Congress in Stockholm in 1947. A factory in Sweden, the Scania–Vabis vehicle plant, departed from the orthodox method of manufacture by processes, where all machine tools of a certain type are located together, with a department for turret lathes, another for milling machines and so forth. Instead, departments were organised by products—to make a complete component from start to finish with the required number of turret lathes, milling machines, etc., for the purpose. Workers could then see more clearly how their part fitted into the whole. Using an orthodox method a department merely turns out a 'lathe operation' or a 'grinding operation' and it is only human that there is less appreciation of the function of the finished component. For this psychological reason the number of rejects was much smaller than with the old method.

This result suggests the division of labour may sometimes have been taken so far that it is, for psychological reasons, defeating its own object. In certain circumstances, we should realise, smallness is more efficient than bigness.

The division of labour too often produces niggling little jobs which give not the slightest satisfaction to the workers. A routine clerical job, for instance, may pass through dozens of subdivided processes, killing any sense of responsibility and initiative by the clerks who have to carry it out. It is the same with machine processes. Often it may be well worthwhile to drop the subdivisions and build a real job which a man can take an interest in. Any apparent loss of technical efficiency may be made up by the worker producing more just because he is keener.

Industrial democracy requires that every worker should have the opportunity to contribute his utmost to the running of the place in which he works. But what if no one wants to use the opportunity? Often there seem to be far more opportunities than people wishing to take advantage of them.

It is obviously not enough for the manager to say one day 'I want your suggestions about ways of increasing production.' His initiative may merely be met by apathy and distrust: 'there is a catch in it somewhere,' and often there may be. This distrust and apathy, allied as they are, have to be removed. What numerous experiments have shown, and in this they merely reinforce common sense, is that in a group which has not been run democratically the first step is to demonstrate to the members that they are respected and trusted.

Establishing joint consultation is itself one method of showing people in industry they are trusted. Another is to take joint consultation a stage further by transferring actual responsibility to the members of a working group. A demonstration of trust on this scale does seem to uncover the wish to contribute in return. This may best be explained by a few examples.

(a) A company making bearings allotted £30,000 out of annual profits for distribution among the workers in such ways as the Works Council resolved. The Council decided to use part to cover the possible loss which might be caused by abolishing clocking on. Previously amounts had been deducted from a worker's pay for each quarter of an hour he was late. With the abolition of clocking on, no deductions could be, or were, made. Each worker thus had responsibility for his own timekeeping. Being given responsibility, the workers had a sense of responsibility; and a rough check showed that after a period timekeeping had actually improved.

(b) Rate–fixers who determine piece–rate times have always been distrusted. I am told that in Czechoslovakia after the coup at the beginning of 1948 there was almost a clean sweep of rate-fixers, all purged by the workers' committees. In some British factories, in contrast, workers have been asked to do their own rate-fixing. For instance, in a large firm making steel tubes in Birmingham, a scheme of redeployment involved the introduction of a new system of piece–rate payments. To measure the times on which these payments were to be based, the workers elected two of their number who were then trained in methods of assessing proper time–rates for the jobs. The scheme was successfully tried out in a single department before extension to the whole works. It was not hurried, and the conviction of its fairness grew slowly but steadily, until eventually other departments were clamouring to be included in the scheme.

(c) The U.S. Steel Union, like several other U.S. unions, takes responsibility for raising production, employing its own technical experts to cooperate with the union members in the plant and with the management in a plan to improve output. In one rail mill output rose by 50 percent after the Union and management set up their cooperative plan.

It seems that if human relations are improved within industry, not only will production but also happiness and even health be improved. A recent official Report suggested this.[4] It found that 10 percent of a cross-section of typical war-time workers studied suffered from a disabling neurosis, defined as 'any psychological or mental illness, i.e., any disability for which there was apparently a psychological cause or partial cause.' Neurosis, moreover, caused between a quarter and a third of the absence from work due to illness. This high degree of neurosis was partly the result of faulty working conditions. Thus it was more frequent amongst those who were bored, particularly those whose job required less intelligence than they possessed, and among those with jobs offering little variety. One conclusion was that it might be more necessary to make jobs interesting than to make them foolproof. Another and more important conclusion was that 'The human relations within a factory can have an important influence on output and they are likely to have at least an equal influence on the health of the worker.'

The kind of job influences the whole character of life out of work. It is partly a matter of status. A person in a job where he feels important feels good about it. In recent years miners and builders have, for instance, 'moved up in the league,' and this is a social gain for them. Norah Davis, in the building survey referred to above, reports one builder saying: 'There's better dignity in the building trade now. Before the war you didn't like to tell a girl you were in the building trade. But now it's important.' Likewise, some experiments in joint consultation have shown how people themselves could be changed when they began to feel respected in their work. In the famous Hawthorne Experiment in the U.S.A. a group of girls in part of a factory were fully consulted about and committed to the experimental project before it started. Not only did output rise but the girls became more friendly to each other. If tired, a girl was 'carried' by the others who worked extra hard to make up for her poor performance. In another case recorded by Elton Mayo, effective consultation was introduced in a Philadelphia textile mill.[5] Morale rose, outside as well as at work. One worker told the investigators that to his great surprise he had begun taking his wife to the cinema in the evenings, something he had not done for years! Would it be too much to hope that by fostering the growth of industrial democracy, the quality of life for millions could be transformed?

The attack on hugeness applies as much to the pattern of living outside work. The great city, for instance, is giantism run mad. Needed more obviously than in industry is a reduction in the scale of organisation until it comes within the compass of neighbours. Communal activities should be based on neighbourhoods small enough to be felt as such by the people who live in them. 'This sense of solidarity among neighbours, living in the same environment and using the same complex of local services, is,' said the Webbs 'a valuable social asset which Socialism aims at preserving and intensifying.'[6]

As in industry there are many growing points for democratic advance. For example: (1) Cities are too large and should, it is commonly agreed, be made smaller. This can be done partly by dividing cities into small neighbourhood units not traversed by traffic roads and containing all the essentials of local community life. Community spirit is not something which can be created, but it can certainly be encouraged, by the right combination of necessary buildings and open space. Partly it can be done by accommodating people from the cities in the small New Towns which the Labour Government has bravely launched. Where these are being built with the enthusiastic cooperation of the people who are going to live in them, a completely new kind of democratic community—making will be seen.

(2) Community associations are springing up all over the country in places which may one day be fully fledged neighbourhood units. They often focus on an existing or hoped—for community centre. It is notable that some well—equipped centres laid on by benevolent local authorities without consulting the local citizens have been complete flops; no one has bothered to use them. In other places where the initiative has come from enthusiastic local citizens they have built their own makeshift centres, which have been of more value than the fine buildings erected *for* and not *by* the people.

(3) Some of the 7,200 parish councils have shown remarkable vitality in the last few years. Their powers are wider than usually realised; they can provide libraries, swimming baths, washhouses, village halls and playing fields, maintain and repair public footpaths, sponsor adult education, assist old people's welfare and encourage rural crafts. They can make recommendations to other local authorities on housing, water supplies, schools, roads, town and country planning, health services, child welfare and fire services, and act in various ways as agents of rural district councils. More and more parish councils are today coming to life. Herbert Morrison answered the critics of parish councils in a speech to the National Association of Parish Councils in October 1947. 'It has,' he said, 'been fashionable for some time to treat the parish pump as a symbol of pettiness and triviality, and to use "parochial" almost as a term of abuse. . . . Some things can only be done properly in a big way, but let us not forget

that it is equally true that other things can only be done intimately by people who know just who they are dealing with.'

(4) The Local Government Boundary Commission in its report for 1947 suggested the possible development in built–up areas of 'urban parish councils' which would do the same job as the most lively parish councils in the countryside. These urban parish councils could be neighbourhood councils for the new neighbourhood units.

(5) It would be farcical to suggest that these neighbourhood councils should become the chief instrument of local government. There are very many functions that can only be performed efficiently on a big scale by major local authorities. But if neighbourhood councils were to flourish and to attract energetic councillors they would have to be given worthwhile jobs to do. In part, these could be new jobs not at present done by any other authority. In providing new and richer opportunities for leisure there is great scope for expansion. They could build and run community centres where old and young could dance and sing, act and paint, attend classes and play games. They could open new playing–fields, children's playgrounds, swimming pools and bowling greens. They could establish restaurants, local museums and galleries. Certain existing functions could also be delegated to them by major local authorities. Responsibility for management of the local schools within the neighbourhood unit could be transferred from School Managers or Governors to the neighbourhood councils, which would encourage Parent–Teacher Associations. So could responsibility for the day–to–day management of local health centres and municipal housing estates. The new councils would also, like the parish councils, make recommendations to the major local authorities. If these lost anything at all in powers they would gain from the lively interest in local government which the neighbourhood councils would foster. Local government at all levels should flourish more than ever before in the new democracy.

(6) The neighbourhood councils would not replace, but would assist with premises, the myriad voluntary associations which already exist. It would be fine if these associations, particularly those concerned with the arts and adult education, expanded in number and scope. It should be Labour's policy to encourage them.

The guiding aim of the neighbourhood councils would be to give most people an opportunity to play an active part in some small democratic group additional to the family.

Is it Utopian to put one's faith in an integrated socialist democracy? Can the small man ever be sovereign? Some may think there is too much bad in men for them to be their own rulers, and consider that socialists, from Robert Owen onwards, have taken too rosy a view of human nature. These are matters about which it is difficult to argue. But it is worth noting that the more optimistic view as well as the socialist belief in democracy are beginning to receive powerful support from the new social sciences of psychology, sociology and anthropology.

Some of the social scientists, with the psychologists in the lead, are analysing from a new standpoint the complex motives of man. They tell us that two of man's deepest needs, as fundamental emotionally as the need for food is physically, are to love, or contribute to the good of others, and to be loved, or receive the affection and respect of others. Not that everyone is an angel under the skin. There are aggressive impulses in all of us. But in every human being there also is a need, however latent, however much distorted by grim experience in childhood or after, to contribute to the good of others.

The strength of democracy is that it can so fully satisfy these human needs. First, it satisfies the need to love since it gives opportunity for every person to contribute what he can to the welfare of his fellows. Second, it satisfies the need for the respect of others. It is quite possible for the members of an autocratic group to receive respect from their leader. But this respect is likely to be relatively unsatisfying because in an autocratic group, where the leader decides what is to be done, credit goes to the leader and the member does not have the opportunity to *earn* the respect of others. But where the member, acting on his own initiative, makes a positive contribution to the well–being of the group he is far more likely to feel that he deserves the respect which he gets from others.

Third, democracy allows aggressiveness to be released in a constructive manner. Compare autocracy. In an autocratic group, the members are ordered about. These orders some may feel as a slight to their own self–esteem. The slight arouses antagonism against the leader. But the members may not dare to express hostility to him. They therefore vent their aggressiveness on a scapegoat who may be either other rank–and–file members of the same group or members of other outside groups. In the case of autocratically run factories everyone is liable to blame everyone else: management blames the workers, workers blame the management, white–collar workers blame the manual workers, manual workers blame clerical workers, workers in one department blame those in another. In the case of nations governed by a dictator the chief scapegoat is often another nation; the dictator usually takes good care, in order to maintain internal unity and transfer to others the hostility which might otherwise be expressed against himself, that other nations are held out as a constant threat; and indeed even the dictator is himself only too likely to be taken in by his own propaganda. On the other hand, a democratic society allows the continuous release of aggressiveness within itself. Hostile impulses are not forcibly repressed and canalised against scapegoats. People are allowed to criticise and oppose without being penalised, and the criticism serves a useful social purpose. The result is that cooperativeness—peace—within and without the group is fostered.

The social sciences are doing more than stress the theoretical virtues of democracy. They are also beginning to demonstrate in workplace and community how democracy can be made to work more effectively in practice. But much more research is needed. Research based on field work in the social sciences is every bit as—in my personal view much more—important than research in the natural sciences. Yet the former is probably not getting 1 percent of what is being spent on the natural sciences. All of us, in our workplace, and schools and communities, can try out new methods of making democracy work better. But only the Government can finance the full-scale research that is required.

Social scientists have spotlighted the family and the school as the groups within which as children our social skills are acquired. It should soon be possible to spread widely the informed advice they can give to parents and to teachers; this will supplement the first-class physical health services which the National Health Service is so grandly building up. Beyond the home and in adult life, we look to social science to devise procedures for choosing leaders who will behave as democrats. Since industry is the test case for democracy, first attention should be given to the selection and training of people for management.

This new knowledge will enrich socialism as it will enrich the new society which socialists are making. British socialists have been broadly of two kinds—the Fabians with their emphasis on efficiency and social justice, and their devotion to facts; and the idealistic socialists, inspired by such men as Robert Owen and William Morris, with their emphasis on the dignity of man and of labour. The time is coming when the two strands can blend. If the Fabians are ready to follow the facts—the new knowledge about human relations which the social scientists are producing—they may find they are led to conclusions which differ little from those of the socialist idealists. If the latter are ready to restrain their more impractical ideas and compromise with efficiency, idealism need not lead to economic collapse and democratic disaster but to a society, built on the model of the family, which is not only more comradely but more efficient. In this new society human nature itself will increase its stature and the small man at last come into his own.

This new synthesis, shadowy as it still may be, can nowhere be more hopefully achieved than in Britain. Great Britain has the advantage of size over the two great United States of East and West. It is not so big that it will be impossible to form an integrated society within the ken of the individual. Moreover, our country is already the most mature democracy in the world, in its traditions as well as in its constitution. Tolerance, the very sinew of democracy, is part of our character. We have a generally accepted code of decency. Our sense of humour is a deadly barb for autocrats. These assets must not be left in store. They must be used to the utmost extent so that we pioneer again, not in the world of power and wealth, but in the new frontiers of the human spirit. 'None of us may live to see the complete building, and perhaps in the nature of things the building can never be completed: but some of us will see the flag or the fir tree that the workers will plant aloft in ancient ritual when they cap the topmost story.'[7]

REFERENCES

1. H. Laski, *Liberty in the Modern State*, Allen & Unwin, 1948
2. D. Lilienthal, *TVA: Democracy on the March*, Penguin, 1944
3. Norah M. Davis, 'Occupational Psychology', April, 1948
4. Russell Fraser and others, 'The Incidence of Neurosis Among Factory Workers', Industrial Health Research Board Report No. 90, His Majesty's Stationery Office, 1947
5. Elton Mayo, *The Social Problems of an Industrial Civilization*, Harvard University Press, 1945
6. S. & B. Webb, *A Constitution for the Socialist Commonwealth of Great Britain*, Longmans, 1920
7. L. Mumford, *The Culture of Cities*, Secker & Warburg, 1938

12

The Chipped White Cups of Dover

This pamphlet was submitted for publication by the Fabian Society in 1960, when Shirley Williams was its General Secretary; it was rejected. The suggestion that a new progressive party might be formed and that it would compete only too effectively with the Labour Party was anathema. The pamphlet had to be published privately by the author. This was almost exactly twenty years before the new progressive party was in fact established, as the social democratic party rather than the consumers party, but with much in common between them. At the beginning of 1983 the stock of the Alliance of social democrats and liberals stood at the same figure in the Gallup polls as the imaginary consumers party had done in 1960 and the Alliance got almost exactly 25% of the vote at the General Election in June, 1983.

To say that the Labour Party is used to staggering from one conference to another is more a tribute than a gibe. The Party still exists because it has (perhaps for the same reasons) powers of recovery almost as remarkable as those of Britain itself. People imagined the Party would be destroyed in 1914, in 1924, in 1931; people thought it would be finished by the Bevanite civil war. But the sick man has always recovered. Any socialist with a sense of history would warn us against a cataclysmic view of the present. When the drums roll for another General Election, will not all life–long Labour supporters forget their quarrels and unite to drive the Tories out? 'A sense of perspective, comrades, please,' says the old man who remembers Ramsay Mac, 'in a pinch our people will always be loyal to Labour.'

Such a point of view is understandable. Loyalty to the Party is still its greatest asset. But on this occasion, speaking as a life–long Labour supporter who spent six years of his life inside Transport House, I believe this optimistic view to be mistaken. The difference between the present crisis and the others is that the Labour Party is no longer the undisputed party of reform. In all the other crises it was. The present one is so serious because the Party is ceasing to be the only party of reform; for the first time in my life radicals and left–wingers are seriously thinking of giving their support to other parties and—as all the public opinion studies have found—so are young people in general. The Labour Party now has to reform itself before it can carry conviction as a party which could reform society.

The danger is twofold. The first, and more obvious danger, is the Liberal Party. For a quarter of a century socialists have assumed that when Liberals gave way to Labour they were eventually bound to disappear as a serious political force. This can no longer be taken for granted. At the 1959 General Election the Liberal Party was the only one which increased its share of the vote: while the share of the two main parties declined, the Liberals increased their strength, from 2.7 percent to 5.9 percent. This was, of course, partly because they fought more seats, but not entirely. The average Liberal vote in seats they contested rose from 15.1 percent to 16.9 percent, even though they were contesting many seats less favourable to them than at the previous General Election. Butler and Rose comment on their 'striking advances,' and conclude their book by saying:

> Political change comes slowly in Britain, and the forces that make for the continuance of the existing battle between Conservative and Labour are very strong. But the 1959 election at least opened up the possibility that the old demarcations of the two–party struggle are obsolescent.[1]

One does not have to be a clairvoyant or even a psephologist to forecast that the showing of the Liberals in by–elections in the next year will open up this possibility still further. If they could break through far enough to convince people, or at any rate a good many more people, that they might become such a political force that a vote for them was not a 'wasted' vote, their gains would begin to be cumulative.

I say 'if', and it is a big one. The British do not believe in reincarnation, and, that being so, the Liberals suffer from two serious handicaps. First, their greatest days were so long ago. Although a country can live on its past—Britain is a perfect example of that—this is very much more difficult for a party. Secondly, the Liberals have not had a distinctive constructive programme of their own since they last enjoyed power, or at least since the Yellow Book. They have teetered between the other two parties like a drunken referee who despite his size is constantly trying to separate the heavyweights and fell each of them with a blow which is neither a left nor a right. They have struggled to attack the Tories but never on the same grounds as Labour; and to attack Labour but never on the same grounds as the Tories. And it is still doubtful whether, with so little room for manoeuvre and with numerous entrenched supporters who are not exactly radical in terms of the contemporary world, they will be able to find an attractive independent programme.

The second and more fundamental danger is an entirely new party. More and more people are beginning, vaguely but insistently, to sense the possibility. I have heard of three separate attempts to form new parties in the last month and have been formally invited to join one of them, the 'New Progressive Party.' Its printed manifesto is just a ragbag of proposals, from the abolition of capital punishment and the introduction of a sort of syndicalism to the final objective which is 'to be first on the moon.' It is not clear whether the New Progressive Party wants to be the first party on the moon, or merely that one of its members should be the first crank to get there. Such a Party will not be a threat to Labour. But others could be.

The underlying reason for this talk is obvious enough. Everyone can observe the agonies of Labour; everyone can observe the faint but unmistakeable signs of a Liberal revival; and everyone who bothers to think about it can see that a new reforming party, free from the disadvantages I have already mentioned, should do even better than the Liberals. This is not just speculation. In a later section I present the results of a public opinion poll which was conducted, admittedly on a very small scale, in June of this year. This poll suggests that a new party would at once surpass the Liberals and become enough of a political force to alter the whole balance of political power.

Such a new party, claiming to be the party of the second half of the 20th century, would at the very least be a great danger to the party which was new in 1900.

Will this danger materialise? The Labour Party's hope of holding the progressive vote depends on whether it can satisfy the conditions that any genuine party of reform needs to satisfy. The two essential conditions are:

1. That the party of reform should be an internationalist party.
2. That its domestic policy should be concerned with the problems of today.

Has not the Labour Party always been internationalist? Certainly it was until the war. But from 1939 on a change has set in. The war and the power that followed it seem to have shrunk the Labour Party not just into a nationalistic party but more, into a Little Englander Party. Witness Labour's attitude to Europe both before and after 1951.

This change is more startling because the trend of events is all the other way. Now that satellites swing over the heads of a hundred million people before Big Ben strikes another hour, science is making national boundaries into a shoddy farce. More people are travelling to Europe every year, and not just the middle class; to verify this, stand in any European town and watch the buses drive in from Birmingham and Bolton. More people see the world, too, without setting foot outside the country. Television does not bring only American films and features into the home (the cinema did this too), it also brings programmes from and about Europe, and presents foreign news more vividly than it has ever been presented before.

The effect of improved communications on the kind of news that many people prize most has been particularly dramatic. Up till the war sport was mainly a domestic affair, or at most, with cricket or rugby, a Commonwealth one. The post–war improvement of communications has enlarged the circuits of competition; the excitements of relegation to the Second Division are already giving way to the greater excitements of the European Cup. After you have seen Real Madrid beat the Wolves on television the local team, even if it is in Division I, does not seem exactly glamorous. After you have joined 300 million other people on Eurovision to watch British failures at the Olympic Games from your kitchen, it does not seem worthwhile to make a long journey to observe the great annual walking competition around Regent's Park.

This growing awareness of the world outside Britain has two important political consequences. More people than ever before recognise that Britain is *inferior* in many ways it should not be to other countries in Europe and America. More people than ever before recognise that in certain respects Britain is *superior* in many ways it should not be to other countries in Asia and Africa. Britain is too drab in relation to Europe, and too selfish in relation to Asia and Africa. I shall discuss each of these consequences in turn.

We go on arrogantly refusing to learn the languages of Europe— I wonder how many members of the National Executive Council know the French for nuclear disarmament or the German for common ownership? We go on making ourselves ridiculous by talking English a little louder when we get to Orly. Yet the old joke about the Continent being cut off is too painful to be any longer funny, and any traveller not an Empire Loyalist is almost bound to return to the chipped white cups of Dover with more of a sense of shame than of relief. There are many reasons for shame—on one level, Britain's low rate of economic growth and its relatively poor performance in exports, on another level, the inferiority in industrial design, which is rather strikingly recognised by the pride of Britain's largest motor manufacturers in the Italian styling of their cars.

But the main reason (football, perhaps, excepted) is the growing realisation that almost all West European countries outside the Iberian Peninsula far excel Britain in the standards of what might be called their public amenities—their town planning, their architecture, their roads, the scope they offer for the enjoyment of leisure.

> The great plans for the rebuilding of city–centres drawn up by Abercrombie and others seem to have been realised less in Manchester or London than in Rotterdam, West Berlin and Milan; and the most striking new suburbs have been created not on the banks of the Clyde or the Thames but outside Stockholm and Marseilles. The disastrous new Shell building on the actual site of the Festival of Britain is the ironic symbol of the New England.
>
> Europe has been criss—crossed by great motorways while Britain has squeezed out only one since the war. A motorist can travel from Ostend to Cologne on a summer Saturday in less time than it takes to navigate the Exeter bypass.
>
> Everywhere in Europe you can have hot food and cold drinks in the open air or indoors, in the evening or the daytime, on Sundays or weekdays, and usually in a clean cafe. Whereas everywhere in Britain . . . well, you only have to observe the expressions on the faces of incoming tourists: the Frenchman looking down at his plate of meat and two veg.; the German as he alights from his train in the main station of any British city; the Italian woman as she sits shivering by the warming pans hanging *on the walls;* the American as he comes out of the 'rest room' of a Midlands garage.

This new relationship to Europe has been more galling than British inferiority to the U.S.S.R. and the U.S.A. A British sputnik has been so impossible that few people (outside the New Progressive Party) have seriously proposed it, and Conservative backbenchers who roared like tigers over Suez failed even to yelp like Pekinese when Blue Streak was abandoned for the vague promise of the American Skybolt. But we cannot plead shortage of resources as a reason for being behind Sweden or Holland. To recognise that we are backward is to acknowledge that Britain is second–rate in something more important than economic strength. We have been failing in will, in the will make the best use of such resources as we do have.

Why has there been so little protest about Britain's decline? One reason is that people who hold a tragic view of national destiny—grimly attractive as it is to many other fatalists besides the sort who study Gibbon—have failed to make a vital distinction between a first-rate *Power* and a first-rate *Nation*. Whether a country is a first-rate Power depends upon the number of submarines and aeroplanes, rockets and war-heads it can dispose of. In this sense Britain probably cannot (even if it wanted) be a first-rate Power again. But it can still be a first-rate (or, if you like, a great) Nation. Whether a country is a first-rate Nation depends on the vitality of its arts, on the quality of its sciences, on the quality of its industry and education, on the concern it shows for the weak and unfortunate, on the tolerance shown to enemies and eccentrics, on the sensitivity of its citizens to each other, on the efficiency of its government, on the aesthetic sense which pervades the large design of cities and the small design of homes, and above all on the vigour and honesty of its intellectual life.

When this distinction is made, one can see that there is no necessary connection between power and greatness. But in practice, the shock of the loss of one may affect the other. A people zealous in imposing themselves, their beliefs and their institutions upon others, as the British were in the last century, may lose heart when they can impose themselves no longer. They may find it difficult to do without a sense of national purpose, yet be unable to find a satisfying substitute for the grandeur they have lost. In such a situation a whole people may freeze into insularity, like a melancholic who has withdrawn into himself. But if Britain has had an excuse for retreating into the past, it has one no longer. Nearly fifty years have passed since power began to swing away from Britain. It is time we found a new sense of national purpose to replace, finally and for good, the sentiments of imperialism.

This means holding to a world outlook and using it as a spur for making improvements in British society which are urgently necessary anyway. It means recognising that Britain needs Europe even more than Europe needs Britain. It is out of the dialectic relationship between discontent in Britain, and union with Europe, that progress will come, towards a more lively country and a more closely integrated world.

In some ways it should be easier to strike up a new relationship with Asia and Africa than with Europe. They are in some part English-speaking Continents, and we know more about them. All over Britain there are men who have worked in India, Malaya or Ghana;

women whose fathers were in the Rajputana Rifles or a Burmese Harbour Board; children whose fathers served at Khartoum, in the counting houses of Clive Street or the Courts of Kano. Every industry in Britain is employing men who gained administrative experience in overseas civil services before they were fully 'Indianised', 'Malayanised' or 'Nigerianised'. In Australia it is said that on people's mental maps of the world the British Isles are anchored close inshore in the Australian Bight; and their 'Near North' is still called the 'Far East'. In Britain the mental maps of many people still place Bombay in the Bay of Biscay, many miles nearer than Rome, and Cairo not far off the Scillies, much closer than Bonn.

Many of these associations are with the past of an empire which is better left buried. Even so, they constitute an asset in terms of knowledge whose value to the modern world could be immense. No other country could recruit for some great international project in Africa or Asia as many experienced people, as little beset with homesickness, even when their main link with 'home' became the *Illustrated London News*. Despite the wrongs that were done under the Union Jack, Britain also has more millions of friends in Africa and Asia than any other Western country. If they were approached in the right spirit, these people would enthusiastically work with us in the development of their own countries. With assets so great, why has Britain not played more of a leading part in what is far and away the greatest task of this century?

It is partly because the British have a great liability: so many of us still believe in the 'effortless superiority' not just of the traditional 'Balliol man' but of all British men and some women. This terrifying attitude is not confined to Bournemouth. Many solid working–class people have it too, Labour voters as well as Tory. When I made an opinion survey at the time of Suez, not in Notting Hill or Tiger Bay but in the quiet decorum of Hornsey, I was dismayed by the number of manual workers who backed Eden wholeheartedly, talking of Wogs, Dagoes and Gyppies as vituperatively as they did when they were 'seeing the world' in the Army.

To this wooden–headed jingoism, which was reprehensible enough in Palmerston's day but is today suicidal as well as morally disgraceful, the main counterweight is the socialist element in the Labour Party—the belief that we are all responsible for one another. This sense of moral concern, or at any rate the practical form which has been given to it, has been Labour's greatest contribution to modern political thinking. It has led 300 years later to the acceptance, in theory a wholehearted acceptance, of Rainborowe's notion that the 'poorest he that is in England hath a life to live as the greatest he'. What Labour has not done is to persuade the people of Britain, including their own supporters and the people I mentioned earlier in Bournemouth and other places who could be such an asset to the world if they would give up the pretence of racial superiority, that the 'poorest he that is in the world' has as much right as anyone else to the good things of life; that the modern proletariat is less in Britain than in Asia and Africa; and that this proletariat, consisting of two thousand million peasants, is always close to actual starvation.

The infuriating thing is that such statements have become platitudes: people shrug their shoulders. They would not dare deny that we *ought* to spend far more on investment overseas, especially in the public domain; yet they do nothing about it. One way, I think, in which a party of reform could bring home to the people the need for action would be to involve people here in Britain much more directly in world reconstruction. I will give three illustrations of the sort of thing I mean, starting with an example from education.

At present we fail on two counts—we do not train enough British experts, particularly agriculturalists with knowledge about the tropics, and linguists of all sorts, and we do not give a good enough training to the students who come here from the underdeveloped countries. Indians and Nigerians and Arabs too often have to put up with racial prejudice in their leisure time and with indifference in their places of study. We have not taken the trouble to devise special courses suited to their needs which are (in many subjects) quite different from ours. One way to show we are ready to change with the times would be to make some of Britain's new universities overseas universities, with overseas students in a majority, and British in a minority, with as many staff as possible who know Africa and Asia as well as they know Yorkshire and Sussex, and with teaching related as intimately as possible to conditions in the countries to which students will return. Let us have an 'Asian' university in York and one 'African' university in Brighton, and another in Swansea, where pioneering work has already been done on these lines in the social sciences. Research is as important as education, and here what is needed is a gradual switch of research effort from perfecting more destructive weapons and more refined electronic equipment to the problems of agriculture and the means of controlling the growth of population in Asia and Africa.

It would also be worthwhile to form an International Service Organisation modelled to some extent on President Roosevelt's Civilian Construction Corps, in place of National Service. In the last few years young men from Britain have volunteered, on a small scale it is true, to do manual work alongside Africans and Asians in their own countries—the first time that some of these Africans and Asians have seen a white man doing manual work of any kind. An International Service Organisation could do the same on a much larger scale, appealing for volunteers from amongst young men and women who have not yet embarked on their careers, to go abroad for a year to help build the Volta Dam, drain swamps in Malaya or start schools in Nyasaland. An obligation would be laid on employers, as it has been with National Service, to keep open the jobs of men who volunteered. The Organisation could also employ the older trained people who go abroad to perform more technical tasks, and if it was thrown open, as it should be, to people of any nationality who wanted to help 'the poorest he' become a little less so, it could be the beginning of a great international experiment.

I have argued that a party of reform with a world outlook would try to make Britain less drab in relation to Europe, and less selfish in relation to Asia and Africa. There is a still more important task, to lead the movement towards world government. World government is now something more than an idealist's dream—though it is still that; it is becoming clearer every day that without it the terror of nuclear destruction will never be lifted. But it has not yet become clear to the Labour Party. Left–wing reformers have been busy for half a century pressing for the surrender of British power—all the way from Ireland and India to Egypt and Nyasaland; in harmony with this, though less consistently, they have pressed for the surrender of British military power as well—twenty-five years ago for outright pacifism and today for nuclear disarmament. This attitude has been responsible for one of the benign miracles of the century. De Valera, Nehru, Nkrumah, Zik, Makarios and Banda have been sent from H. M. Prison to H. M. Government House by the first large empire to surrender without fighting all the way. The consequence is that a free association of peoples has replaced a system of world domination. But the weakness of the left is that we have hardly ever questioned whether the 'Balkanisation' of Continents was desirable and we have always been more ready to give in to nationalism than to foster internationalism. This one–sidedness will not do much longer. The long campaign against the Empire may soon be concluded and if the campaign for nuclear disarmament is successful as far as Britain is concerned, the left will no longer have so much of the traditional anti–militarism to rely on either.

It is high time we turned away from our obsession with imperial power and began to create new power units, this time not British but truly international ones. Union with Europe would be one great step forward, revitalising the Commonwealth another—this would mean expelling South Africa to make it crystal clear that racial equality is the cornerstone of the Commonwealth and would have to be the cornerstone of any wider association as well—and setting up some organs of common government for the Commonwealth as a whole. But the most important step would be to devote all Britain's influence to strengthening the economic and military arms of the United Nations. The U.S.'s nucleus of an 'International Police Force' has saved the situation twice, in the Middle East and in the Congo. This is an immensely hopeful development, and would be more hopeful still if a permanent U.N. Force were now raised, with U.N. soldiers stationed in U.N. bases, owing allegiance not to any individual nation but to the Security Council as a whole. The bases could be the same as those that have been agreed at the Geneva Conference as necessary for detecting nuclear explosions. A British party of reform with a world outlook would welcome the U.N. Force to bases in Britain and urge the transfer of nuclear and other arms to its keeping.

I have put foreign policy first, giving examples as I went along of the kind of proposals which might be made, because I believe that a party of reform will only have a sufficient dynamic if it is dominated by a world outlook, not by a purely British one. As a people we could find a pride and purpose, not as the smallest of the Great Powers but as the greatest of the Small Powers, in helping to lead the world towards the renunciation of national sovereignty. By a further dialectic we might make use of nationalism in order to end it.

The second condition which a party of reform must satisfy is that its policy is relevant to the needs and problems of present–day society. There has as yet been so little serious social study that any analysis of what is happening must be partly a matter of guesswork. For myself, I would on the whole agree with the analysis made by other commentators, notably Anthony Crosland in his Fabian pamphlet.[2] But I would sum up my own interpretation rather differently by stressing one change in particular, which I think is potentially more important for politics than any other, the switch of people's interests from production to consumption. Butler and Rose did, it is true, say of the working–class man that 'He may well think of himself as a consumer first and only secondly as a worker.' But they said it in passing, without sufficiently recognising what I believe to be its revolutionary significance.

The nature of the change can be best brought out by focusing on working–class people and considering the sexes separately. This approach makes it clear that what has happened is the establishment of the family, more that at any time since the end of handicraft production, as *the* unit of society. I shall begin with men. Firstly, their weekends and annual holidays have been lengthened. This change has given men more effective time with their families than ever before. Secondly, work has become less exhausting as the heaviest labour has been taken over by machines, so that men have more energy left over for their homes. Thirdly, work has become less creative and rewarding wherever mechanical and electronic techniques have superseded skill, and the narrowing of the wages gap between the skilled and unskilled (in the vital period of adolescence, the gap is the other way round, the unskilled being paid more) has made it less worthwhile to train for the skilled and psychologically more satisfying tasks. Fourthly, by making work more abundant, full employment has reduced the necessity of thinking about it; a job will always be there—lose one, get another. Although the same full employment has strengthened the bargaining power of Unions with employers, it has weakened the hold of Unions upon their members by encouraging movement from one job and part of the country to another. The turnover of Union membership has been rising, and high turnover makes for a brittle structure.

Fifthly, the community of residence is now more separated from the community of work, by distance and by sentiment. Less and less do men reinforce the interests of the workplace by associating off the job, in the pub, in the workingmen's club or the union branch, with other men from the same industries. If the cotton town symbolised working–class life in the 19th century, the mixed–industry housing estate does so in the 20th. Sixthly, the standard of living has increased. The crucial improvement has been in housing. As long as a family is in a bad house there is little point in filling it with goods. A new cooker seems barely worthwhile in the space on the landing, and hot water systems are less desirable when there is no bathroom. But a new home eats up money. Lastly, the greater part of the increased earnings have as a consequence gone into the home. Men used to keep a substantial part of their earnings to themselves to spend on drink, tobacco, pools and sports. But as earnings have increased, the younger ones, at any rate, have become far more generous with housekeeping allowances to their wives, and have taken responsibility for hire purchase payments on television sets and the kind of durable goods which used to be the wife's affair. Affluence has not benefitted the pub but the home. What all these changes add up to is that men whose interests used to be concentrated on their work and shared with other men are now back in the family; and at home men are not men but husbands.

Changes have been as drastic for women. When men were bound to the production of goods, women were the sweated workers of the home, bound to the production of children. Only before marriage were they at all well–off; from that point they descended into increasing poverty, dependent on an allowance which their men did not ordinarily increase however many children arrived. In middle life, although by then worn out by child-bearing and by complaints which nagged continually because there was no money for doctors, they had some financial easement as their children began to earn—until a few years later they were plunged into the acutest poverty of all, in old age.[3] Things are not like that at all today; the spread of contraception and arrival of the National Health Service have at last released women from their bondage. They keep their health, their energy and their sex appeal far longer. Full employment gives them a chance of jobs as soon as their short period of child–bearing is over, and the fact that they are no longer so dependent financially on the main earner gives them a higher status in the eyes of themselves and their husbands. Women's interests, too, have shifted from a different kind of production to the same kind of consumption, centred on home and family, based on a new kind of union between men and women, far stronger than any Trade Union could ever be. Any party of reform will have to recognise and come to terms with this strengthening of the family, a process which began with the middle class but has swept the working class and is winning, fast. For thousands of years, until the coming of industry, the family was the unit of production on the land. After a terrible struggle, as acute in the Midlands as on the Steppes, industry broke up this sort of family. But it has now restored the family to another kind of pre–eminence, as the unit of consumption. This is one of those spirals of development in which Marx would have rejoiced.

All this is revolutionary because it means that the foundations of politics are changing. Even Methodists must admit that the politics of the last fifty years have corresponded with the old–fashioned Marxist analysis: they have been the politics of production. The cleavage into two major parties has reflected the cleavage into two major classes, and the class cleavage has reflected the division of people according to the work they do, manual belonging to the 'working class' and non–manual to the 'middle class'. This division is still an important one; many people still think of themselves in this way, and manual workers will in fact go on doing so (in one part of their minds) as long as there is such inequality between their wages and the incomes of those who seem to get a great deal for doing very little; and as long as they are treated as inferior to 'middle–class' employees in the workplace, wearing different clothes, being forced to arrive at the job earlier and work longer, having second–rate pension schemes or none at all, and eating in second–rate canteens. I predict that if the management staff of the British Motor Corporation, from top to bottom, were to start arriving at work at the same time as the 'employees', the time lost in strikes would at least halve within a year. But there is not much chance of this happening, nor, it seems, of the Unions pressing for this sort of improvement in conditions of work as they have for improvements in wages. That being so, productive classes will remain, and be sharply separated at work. But outside work the great divide is being bridged. The power of the present parties and of other institutions of class is still great; but it is less firm. The emphasis is slowly changing, and class based on production is slowly giving way to status based on consumption as the centre of social gravity. That, I believe, is the trend of social change in all the industrially advanced countries of the world.

The submission I am making is that politics will become less and less the politics of production and more and more the politics of consumption. Once accept this analysis as very broadly on the right lines, and the policy of a reforming party which would appeal to this new consumer interest almost suggests itself. A reforming party would, to return again to one of the themes of this essay, stand for immediate entry into the European Common Market. Despite all the advantages this would in the long run bring the consumer, notably through the greater competition it would promote, our present parties have for years cold-shouldered one of the most hopeful political initiatives of the century, and done so partly because they have been afraid to touch the famers, a producer interest which has been the pampered darling of politics for far too long. A reforming party would mount an attack on the monopolies and restrictive practices by which Britain is more ridden than any other country in the world. Why on earth should manufacturers still be able to enforce resale price maintenance, and deprive shoppers of competitive prices? A reforming party would amend the Shops Act with all its absurdities—the enforcement of early closing in the evening, early closing on half-days, and complete closing down for most shops on Sundays. When the growing number of women are at work, the shops are open, and when the women are free, the shops are shut. A reforming party would abolish licensing hours. Why should Britain be the only country in Europe where people can only get a drink up to closing time, when the nightly slaughter on the roads starts as regularly as the clock? Almost the only country where a person cannot get a drink with a meal? Removing the legal restriction on hours would not lead to the consumer consuming more alcohol—international comparisons show that—but to his consuming more pleasantly in times that suit his own convenience, not the legislator's idea of his convenience.

A reforming party would adopt the Hodgson Report's proposals for stopping the scandalous practice, which still persists, of selling consumers 'short weight, measure and number'. For fear of offending parochially-minded manufacturers and retailers the government has done nothing at all about that other recommendation of the Hodgson Report:

> We have come to the conclusion that the metric system is, in the broadest sense and in the interests of world uniformity, a "better" system of weights and measures than the imperial.'

The decimal system has the same advantages for money, and a reforming party would introduce it as well as modernise the coinage. The present parties take too lightly the irritation of people at having to carry around enormous loads of metal in their bags or pockets, yet still finding they have not enough medieval pieces of copper to feed a 20th century telephone (early 20th century anyway). A reforming party would, to take a final example, enforce the Food Hygiene Regulations. Then perhaps our cafes, restaurants and butcher's shops would stop giving us a deserved reputation as the dirtiest rich country in the world.

People are also consumers of the public services, and here the need for reform is if anything even greater. Private enterprise cannot wholly disregard what consumers want. The threat of bankruptcy preserves some respect for the customer. But there is no such sanction in the public sector. An air of charity, of *noblesse oblige,* clings to the social services; their administrators preserve an astonishing 19th century attitude of superiority to their 'consumers'. I am not, of course, talking of all—there are many fine administrators who have nothing of this attitude. But it is still true that many petty bureaucrats think they know what is best for people, and actually seem unaware of the resentment this causes. Many city architects design houses for the tenants without asking them what they want. The same applies to some aspects of town planning—planners are far more ready to forbid a man to build a shed in his garden or to add an annex to his house than to explain why. Many municipal housing managers, without consulting their tenants, impose a mass of fussy regulations on them, forbidding them to paint their houses, to touch the fabric, to alter the garden or, for example, to 'fly pigeons except between 11 a.m. and 1 p.m. on Sundays', or to have a cat if they live in a Council flat. I remember managers I have met on municipal estates who behaved exactly as they imagined a squire would behave, thoughtfully, efficiently, but with an almost intolerable assumption that the tenants existed for them to 'do good to'. Many National Assistance officials still manage to give the impression that ordinary people are trying to get money under false pretences. Many teachers, in State though not of course in private schools, treat the parents like children, keeping them out of the school, as though the parents were not the taxpayers who paid their salaries but a sort of cross between pauper and self–seeker, asking favours for their own children over all others. Some schools symbolise for me the prevailing attitude of mind by displaying outside their main gates notices like this one:

> NO PARENTS ARE ALLOWED INSIDE THIS GATE
> unless they have business with the Head Mistress.
> By Order of the Governors of the School.

Many doctors and hospital administrators are the same—'never mind the endless waiting in the Out–Patients' Department, never mind the ignorance about illness and treatment in which many patients are kept', they seem to say, 'we know best what is good for you.'

To prevent the traditional British gentry from being aped in the public services, and to instil a new attitude of 'service' into them, are, I believe, some of the main changes now needed if the Welfare State is to deserve its name. In spite of all that they said about the 'man from Whitehall', the Conservatives are so prejudiced against the public services that they have done nothing to reduce the pressure of bureaucracy. Reform means 'humanising' the public services on a great scale, simply by treating their users as human beings. The political consequences could be very great. For one thing, attitudes towards taxation might change. It is natural that you should resent giving money to a bureaucrat, for however good a purpose, when that bureaucrat, when he has the money, so often behaves as though it was his money and not yours. But if taxpayers, as the users of the public services, were treated with as much respect (or more) as they would get as consumers of ordinary commercial services, they might begin to feel they were getting better value for taxes, and be less resistant to paying them. I do not pretend that people will ever like paying taxes, but the degree of resistance is important, and if it was moderated, it would be politically easier to step up public spending. And that is becoming more and more urgent: we need to spend far more both absolutely, and relatively to private expenditure, on the many services that can only be provided collectively. To show what I mean, I will give just two examples of quite exceptional importance to consumers, namely education and urban planning.

The educational system is the agent of another great social change which should in any full perspective be placed alongside the switch in emphasis from production to consumption. I have elsewhere discussed the growth of the new kind of scientific, managerial and technical class which is being created by the schools and by higher education. This process is inevitable and should indeed, be speeded up, if Britain is to play a more respectable part in bringing aid to the underdeveloped countries. But the process enhances the importance of an old problem. The signal mark of British society is hierarchy. Its people are astonishingly sensitive to a thousand nuances of social status, whether based on production or consumption. This accounts for one of our besetting sins, the 'British Pause', the fact that we are inclined to pause in any social situation to find out how we *should* act before we act. There is a wary second–think—a lack of spontaneity—which helps to account both for the shortage of social innovators and the withdrawal of more people into the family where spontaneity is possible. What education is doing is to make the social hierarchy more clearly marked than ever; and to widen the gap between the people with the most and the least education to such an extent that communication is hardly possible between them.

The only way to counter the new sort of inequality and open a more fluid communication between people is to spend far, far more on ordinary education. We have, as a nation, to show that we can provide a first–rate education for the very few (something in which we still excel) without providing a second–rate education for the many. The tremendous levelling up of secondary schools, technical colleges, technological colleges and universities that this would entail would be a highly costly affair. We could get enough teachers if we wanted, enough to reduce the size of classes, and extend the period of education—but it would cost money. We could get better and more confident teachers if we wanted, by raising their salaries, if not to the level of Russia, where they rank among the highest paid in the land, at any rate to a good deal more than they get at the moment—but it would cost money. We could get more and better buildings, for schools and County Colleges and universities and hostels—but it would cost money. We could do justice to young people (especially when adolescents' wages are so high) if we paid 'wages' for children who remain at school beyond the compulsory age, between 15 and 18, as well as for those who get grants for university study after 18—but it would cost money. The question is whether we are prepared to find it. I believe that if the question were left to the 'consumers' of this service, the parents, they would willingly pay the taxes—as willingly as the people who increasingly turn away from the public to the private schools find the money for *their* children.

As for town planning, its urgency increases as steadily as the Conservatives' reluctance to do anything about it. This is perhaps most obvious from the point of view of the motorist. Congestion increases at the rate of 2,000 new motor vehicles a day. Our cities are strung through every day with frustration, economic, psychological and political. Yet expenditure on new roads is pitiful, despite the obvious fact that probably no spending is more immediately economic. The recent report from the Road Research Laboratory put the financial return on the cost of the M1—the results mainly of speedier passage and fewer accidents—at between 10 percent and 15 percent in 1960, rising to between 17 percent and 27 percent in 1965. Smoothing out severe bends in ordinary roads reduces personal injury accidents by 80 percent. Is there any doubt that when gains of this order can be achieved, motorists would vote the taxes if it were left to them, or even be prepared to pay turnpike tolls again if no other way could be found? But the consumers' point of view must embrace more than motorists. It would be botching the job to plan new expressways between cities if traffic were blocked at both ends by sprawling confusion. We have to find spaces for the 750 new homes which are built every day and reshape the worn–out urban centres into cities that we would be proud of—adventurous, colourful, exciting: with amenities up to the standard of the best that Scandinavia and Western Europe can offer. One thing is clear—there will be no progress as long as land speculators are allowed free play (as they have been since the 1959 Town and Country Planning Act), and as long as local authorities are deprived of the powers and the resources to plan large areas as a whole. This is a task requiring the kind of intellectual and physical effort which will only be forthcoming if the nation is roused from its sleep.

What hope is there of the existing parties making these issues their own? The present Conservative Party is obviously not a candidate. It is not only tied to producer interests—in the long run that £1½ millions spent by business to get them in at the General Election may prove a growing embarrassment. It is also saddled with the most old–fashioned attitudes to taxation and to social change generally. It seems even more difficult for the Conservatives than for socialists to adjust to the new world in which the British Empire has passed from the politicians to the historians. The Labour Party is on many counts less at a disadvantage. It is traditionally a party of reform and so less afraid of the social changes which would be required if Britain were to make the necessary leap into the twentieth century, in terms of international as well as internal politics. It is a party which has been inspired by a moral concern as relevant as ever to the needs of the 'submerged nine–tenths' of the world. It is a party which is less prejudiced against the increase in public spending which alone can modernise the apparatus of our collective life; it would be ready to find the money by introducing a capital gains tax and by raising other taxes if necessary.

But against those advantages must be set one minor handicap—

it has managed to convey an impression of surly opposition to consumer prosperity—this can surely be remedied—and two major ones. The first is that on almost any question affecting conventional 'morality', it is just as conservative as its opponents. The second is that it is linked to a producer interest even more openly than the Conservatives.

The first was brought home to me on an occasion I will never forget. Before the 1950 Election, when I was Secretary of the Party's Policy Committee and working on the forthcoming programme, I arranged for a group of socialist lawyers to present a report on law reform. The report when it arrived contained a large number of well–reasoned proposals for reform, such as abolishing the 'crime' of homosexuality, modernising the divorce laws, removing censorship of plays and films, and abolishing capital punishment. The members of the Committee were acutely embarrassed. Far from considering the proposals on their merits, they showed concern only that no word should ever get out that such a dangerous report had been received. Although no doubt attitudes have changed in a decade, and more liberal views gained ground, there is obviously a long way to go before the Party is ready to accept such eminently sensible proposals as these.

The second handicap is the crucial one. Many Trade Unionists would certainly reject my underlying analysis on the grounds that the distinction between producers and consumers is an unreal one: the one is also the other. That is true in general, of course, and when the Unions have stressed the interests of their members as consumers they have been at their most effective. Ernest Bevin once achieved a *tour de force* when he brought a docker's meagre dinner on a small plate to a Court of Inquiry. But what is true in general is not true in particular. Particular Unions, in pressing the claims of their own members, can disregard almost totally the interests of the consumers who belong to all the other Unions and to none; and the Trade Union Movement is after all not a movement of Trade Unionists in general but of particular Trade Unions avowedly devoted to the sectional interests of their own individual members. There is therefore always a danger that the Trade Unions in general, being a generality of particulars, will appear to be against the general interest of consumers. This danger is inherent in any strike, particularly if it is in an industry which directly serves the consumer, such as the railways, the buses or electric power. It is a danger which is only too apparent whenever there is a direct clash with consumers, as when Unions oppose the amendment of the Shops Act, or insist on not carrying standing passengers on buses. It is a danger against which the Unions have not adequately guarded themselves in recent years.

This is, I think, one of the reasons for the growing unpopularity of the Unions—to consumers they seem too small–minded about their own sectional interest as producers. The consequences for the Labour Party are obviously very serious. The plain fact is that if things go on the way they are going at the moment the Unions will be a growing liability to the Party, with smaller and smaller votes behind them in the country to set against their large blocks of votes at Conference. Unless there is a change, in a few years' time there may be no Party conferences for them to attend. If the Unions are to preserve their political power in anything like its present form, two steps are required.

The first step is for them to put their own house in order. The Trade Unions perform a vital function in the economy: they help the small man to improve his wages and conditions; without the Unions the small man would again be at the mercy of big business. Heaven help the consumer if the Unions disppeared! But they could be so much more effective. They are afflicted with the trouble to which all large organisations are liable—the man at the bottom feels insignificant, the leaders at the top are remote. To cure this trouble needs great powers of statesmanship on the part of the Unions. They must make democracy within their own organisations more effective; they must get for manual workers the same sort of annual wage, and the same hours and conditions of work, as office workers. Their responsibility is to induce a less rigid attitude to 'demarcation' and to take part in a really thorough reorganisation of Britain's sadly old–fashioned system of apprenticeship training; also to organise the non–manual workers, particularly in the new and growing occupations. Finally, their responsibility is the even greater one of making 'industrial democracy' mean something at the level of the workshop, in the process incorporating shop stewards and workshop officials firmly into the Union structure. These are not jobs which can be done from outside. The Government must keep out of this affair. These are jobs which must be tackled by the Unions themselves. If the Unions were ever again attacked by the Government through another Trade Disputes Act or by the law through another Taff Vale judgment, they would have to re–enter politics in full force. But unless that happens they would be serving the Party and the country best by concentrating for some time ahead on their own internal reconstruction.

The second step is to agree to a change in their relations with the Party, by making a good deal more of the link there already is between local Union branches and local constituency Parties and a good deal less of the link between the Union leaders and the Party at national level. As long as the old dreary cycle goes on repeating itself—of Union conferences marching through the year towards the autumn, one by one deciding what the Party policy shall be, often without more than cursory consultation with their own rank and file—Labour will remain so obviously a producers' party that it will fail to attract the young unattached people who want reconstruction at home and a new sense of national mission abroad. If the Unions resist the transformation of the Party, an independent party of the left will have to take up the cause of reform which Labour can no longer serve.

I discussed in my opening section the possibility of a new party, and argued that it would be a greater threat than the Liberals to Labour. In the light of the discussion, does it still appear such a fantastic idea? I have argued that there are two paramount political needs today—for a consumer appraisal at home and for an approach to world government abroad; and that neither of these needs is being satisfied today. Then why should a new party not arise? It does not matter whether it be called the Consumers' Party or not, the name does not matter, for 'consumers' is here little more than another name for individuals; whatever its name, it would be a party to press for the unity of consumers in the world and the interests of consumers at home.

Yet three obvious objections will be made. First, it will be said that consumers could never be *organised*. The consumers are everyone—how could they be brought together into a political party?—it is ludicrous. I think it is no more ludicrous than organising producers, who are also almost everyone. It is worth noting the growth in the last three years of the Consumers' Association which has expanded its membership to just on 200,000, and the Consumer Advisory Council to 65,000—this at a time when the membership of the producers' unions has been moving the other way. These associations are still small and they are firmly outside politics, with a job to do which is quite different from that of a political party. They show that consumers can be organised, not that they could be organised *politically*.

The Co–operative Movement, with its political wing, does surely show that consumers can also be organised politically. The Co–op. has lost its dynamic, for the same reasons as the Labour Movement, that it is out of tune with social and economic change; its rejection of the Gaitskell Report was a grievous blow to those who believe that the principles of consumers' cooperation are as sound as ever. But perhaps it may yet reconsider its position on this and other urgent questions and so recapture its forward momentum. Whether it does or not, it is certainly evidence that consumers can be organised politically.

But even this example does not altogether meet the objection.

There are obviously very great difficulties about organising consumers into tight pressure groups which would bear the same relationship to a new party as the Trades Unions Council does to the Labour Party of the F.B.I. to the Conservatives, and I do not think it could happen. Yet would this be such a source of weakness? Surely it would also be a source of strength. I believe that people in general are fed up, as things are at the moment, with the ceaseless jockeying for power of pressure groups: sectional interest is weak because it can so seldom take a broad and generous view of the problems of the whole nation, or of the great tottering world of which this nation is such a small part. I believe that people would welcome a new initiative on the part of a group which was no sectional. A consumers' party might appear merely acquisitive and materialist. But it need not be so. A consumers' party could take the broad view, for it is as consumers that we look out upon a much larger and more varied scene than when we are at work. A consumers' party could be internationalist, for it is not as producers that we feel sympathy for Indian or Chinese peasants—rather the reverse since other producers are possible competitors. It is as consumers that we feel for them: they too are people, whose families are dying because they do not get enough to eat.

The party would have little money, and if it had little money it would not initially have a strong political machine, with hundreds of paid officials, like the Labour and Conservative Parties. But would this be fatal? Election studies have questioned the value of the old political machine; it is liable to antagonise as much as it is to attract support. What matters now is the kind of appeal which could be projected over television at the national level and by small bands of enthusiasts in the constituencies. I do not think a new party would find itself at a disadvantage if it was a much less elaborate affair than the old parties, with less ponderous headquarters than the one where I worked, with a less tight discipline, with less insistence on conformity, with less subordination of members to the national office, and above all with more plain speaking by M.P.s emancipated from the Whips. It might be the other way round.

The second objection is that such a party could not have a progamme that made sense. I have outlined a programme in previous sections. To summarise, a consumers' party would stand in foreign policy for joining Europe, giving much more generous aid to the underdeveloped countries and for achieving world government in our time; and in domestic policy for removing restrictions on consumer freedom, for expansion of public services and for liberalising the law. Whether such a programme would draw support is something the reader will have to decide.

The third and last objection is that such a party would not win any support. I must agree, of course, that there is no hard evidence. But the Gallup Poll recently put up a question on my behalf to a representative cross–section of the adult population of Great Britain. People were asked whether they would vote for a Consumers' Party, and, since one question could not be made too lengthy, only one aspect of the policy of such a party was touched on. The results are summarised in the Table.

Extent Of Support For A Consumers' Party At A General Election
(Gallup Poll, June 1960)

			Voting in 1959 General Election			
		Total	Conservative	Labour	Liberal	Rest
Voting for a	Yes	25%	26%	21%	55%	22%
Consumers'	No	38%	40%	41%	31%	32%
Party at a new	Don't know	37%	34%	38%	14%	46%
General	% age	100%	100%	100%	100%	100%
Election.	Number	800	312	282	31	175

Informants were asked whether they would vote for a Consumers' Party at a by–election and, as one would expect, the support would be greater than at a general election.

The evidence would be firmer if finance were available to explore the subject of a new party in a much fuller survey, asking the basic question in many different ways and bringing out more of the aspects of the policy of such a party. But this poll certainly does not suggest that the prospects for a new party would be hopeless—since apparently a quarter of the voters would be for it and another third, of the undecided, would be winnable. Even if it did not become the largest party in the State it would probably still make a difference to the balance of political power and be capable of wholly altering the result of a General Election.

I submit that if a new party were founded at the proper time, it would gain substantial public support. It does not follow that it is something that progressives should work for here and now, and this brings me to my final conclusion.

Labour could still be the new progressive party—if it satisfies the conditions that any reforming party must satisfy.

REFERENCES

1. D. E. Butler and R. Rose, *The British General Election of 1959*, Macmillan, 1960
2. C. A. R. Crosland, 'Can Labour Win?', Fabian Tract 324
3. H. Tout, *The Standard of Living in Bristol*, Arrowsmith, 1938

13

Consumers and the Quality of Life

The British Consumers' Association started by Michael Young in 1957 took the leading part in establishing the International Organization of Consumers Unions which in 1983 has in membership 120 consumers organisations in 50 countries. This is the speech made by the author at the Oslo Congress of IOCU in 1964.

Each one of us, as an individual, is part of a growing movement. It is clear that this is a growing movement and there are many of its leading pioneers amongst you. From the conversations I have had, I know that many of us, looking back on our own particular stories in our own particular countries, have something of a sense of a miracle about what has happened. There was a meeting, there was a word; there were a few pounds put into a kitty; there was a faith; there was a hope; suddenly there was a demand. And what has looked small began to look big.

All over the Western world people are asking: What does this new consumer movement imply? What is this new force that has become so much more than a whisper? Where is it going to take the societies of which our movement is a part? Having been to the Kontiki exhibition yesterday and having been impressed with that, it seems to me that even though there is a wind blowing our movements are not so much a raft as a ship. We can take decisions about the kind of advantage we shall take of this favourable wind which is blowing in all the industrial countries.

I am not going to lay down the law, I am now going to try and ask what seem to me important questions and for the most part I shall not answer them, although I shall not be able to refrain from doing so altogether (particularly as one's own questions, of course, are usually the easiest to answer). I want to put before you three dilemmas, which I think are our three central dilemmas. I call them dilemmas rather than choices, because I think they represent particularly tough choices.

> *Dilemma no. 1:* the needs of the poor versus the needs of the rich.
>
> *Dilemma no. 2:* the claims of commercial products versus public services.
>
> *Dilemma no. 3:* the standard of living versus the quality of life.

First, the needs of the poor versus the needs of the rich. Whom are we serving? The rich, or at least the richer: they pay for our services and they subscribe to our publications; they support us, and by and large poorer people do not. Yet we must all know that in essence the rich do not need the kind of service we provide nearly as much as poorer people do. The rich are more educated; they know how to complain; they can afford to make mistakes.

The poor are in a much more difficult situation. It has often been said that the poor are doubly exploited in the modern economy: they are exploited because they have less money and they are exploited in a second sense because on the whole what they buy is less good value for money. I think we can go on to say that they are perhaps trebly exploited: they suffer from a third disadvantage—they do not get the kind of information service on the merits of goods and services which we are trying to present to the public.

What, then, is our choice? Are we already, or are we going to become, the hard–faced businessmen of the consumer world, always with one finger on the cash register, always counting our pennies? The wise virgins on the fringes of Madison Avenue in a sense living off Madison Avenue as a kind of parasite at one remove? Or can we take a more generous or broader view of our functions? Will we seriously devote more of our money, more of our energy, more of our time, to broad–based consumer education, to sustaining a campaign for more effective consumer laws, so that everyone will be protected, poor as well as rich?

There is another aspect to this dilemma. It has become unfashionable in the West to talk as I just talked about the rich and the poor. We prefer on the whole to mask the differences there are behind politer euphemisms, a kind of semantic hypocrisy. We talk not of the poor but of the lower income groups; not of the rich but of the higher income groups, or the better–off. And one can see that there is some sense in this because in our countries in the West the differences are perhaps less marked than they were; the poor are not as poor as they were.

On the international scene, though, the words are far less worn and have their own direct meaning. In the world of today the proletariat of the West, it has been said, are not in the West but in the underdevloped countries. Here are people who know what poverty means. Something like two–thirds of the population of the world are in some degree undernourished. They are not concerned about *what* they are going to have for breakfast, they are concerned about *whether* they are going to have any breakfast at all. These people, the greater part of our fellow human beings, have no choice.

I do hope that we will really make something of the special fund which the International Organization of Consumers Unions is being asked to set up. Perhaps once a decent practical project can be worked out in one of the underdeveloped countries, we will all be prepared to put our hands in our pockets and contribute at least one percent of our annual incomes or revenue to the particular development project which represents the best investment we can make. I know that one percent is nothing, or nearly nothing—treasurers won't agree with me, but in the perspective of the world and history it is nothing—but it would be at least a gesture. It would show that we are sometimes prepared to put our finger on the cash register for the interest of other people than ourselves and our own members, who are by and large the most privileged people this world now sustains.

Our second dilemma—claims of commercial products versus public services. We have, of course, concentrated for the most part in our work on commercial products and commercial services. There is an unbalance between the private and the public sectors of the economy. We have more and more popular newspapers, magazines and T.V. programmes and not enough schools and teachers. We have more and more equipment to put into homes and not enough homes built for people who cannot afford to buy their own. We have more and more patent medicine and not enough doctors, hospitals, nurses. We have more and more cars, but not enough roads and we have hardly begun to design the new cities we need.

If we are to avoid being killed by the car, if not in body, then in spirit, we can surely recognize that in addition to better commercial goods and services we also need a great expansion of public services, education, health, social services generally. We need to be prepared to spend a greater proportion of our national incomes and our own incomes in making the urban landscape one which is fit for the last part of this century and the next, in view of the kind of problems which modern transport presents.

Have we not as consumers in our organizations the duty to try to bring home to people that they are as much consumers of public services as of private? Have we not the duty to try and organize people, not just in our own organizations, but organize people as parents, as patients, as passengers? And have we not the duty too to scrutinize such public services as we have to make sure that their efficiency is improved, certainly in line with the efficiency of private business?

I would like to mention one suggestion which seems to me to have particular merit. I think in one country after another we have had a problem about what to do about the monopoly services, particular public monopolies where no comparison within one country is possible. The suggestion here is that we might join up, through I.O.C.U., in order to make a comparative survey, a sort of international test. Then all can be asked to take part, say, in a general survey of the telephone services, railway services or whatever it may be, in their countries, and the results on a comparative basis would be available for publication in all your journals. If they did nothing else they would certainly command a great deal of publicity.

There is yet another function I think for us to perform, one we have hardly begun, which is to get information *from* the consumer. We are in our organizations a kind of information cooperative. But so far the information has been mainly a one-way traffic. We have given information to people; by and large we have not got information from people about what they want and what they need. And until we do this we know that people will be fitted to products, whereas what we want is that products and services and the public services should be fitted to men and women. By means of sample surveys, by means of social research, we know that this job can be done, that we and others can find out what ordinary consumers do want and do need. And if we only can get the money, we can do the job. Here is a case, I think, where it would be perfectly legitimate for each of us in our respective organizations to seek aid from governments, from foundations, wherever we can. We should undertake this new function of conducting research in order to find out not only what our members think, but also what people generally, the consumers at large, think in our various countries. I believe it is only through the aid of research that we shall ever be able to speak with any authority as representatives of consumers. It is really very little use attending one more committee, whether it is of standard organizations or whatever it is, unless we know what we are talking about, and what we want to know how to talk about is what ordinary people need and want. And there is only one way we can do this, one way we can put ourselves in a seat of authority: use research in order to increase the value and increase the supply and increase the range of the information that we have, sensitive information about what men and women really want and need in all kinds of fields that we are operating in.

Now, lastly, *the third dilemma*, the most difficult I think: standards of living, as I phrased it, versus the quality of life. The great drive in all our industrial nations is towards a higher and higher standard of living. This has become the great platitude of the twentieth century. But to what end is this drive directed? So that kitchens can be packed tighter, ever tighter with labour saving equipment which sometimes belies its name? Are we in the consumers' organizations no more than servants of the washing machine? A sort of human appendage to the machine age? Is our ideal, our picture of Utopia, a housewife in a great suburban house fitted from one end to the other with humming machinery, rushing frantically from one gadget to another, re–arranging the piles of treasured consumer reports from one table to another? Is there nothing to the good life except more and more refrigerators and T.V. sets? Are we as consumers in fundamental agreement with industrialists that all that is necessary to the good life is to produce more, better and cheaper goods?

For such and more rhetorical questions each one of us must give his own answer: we shall certainly not agree. All I can suggest, by way of guidance, is that we might ask ourselves again: what is our basic purpose? Surely it is not so much that people should become endlessly richer, as that they should be able to think for themselves: make rational choices for themselves; that each individual person should be his own planner. Is not our aim the advancement of freedom, the enlargement of individual economy? And if so, we cannot end where we have begun, with the emphasis only on consumer products. Maybe people are already beginning to ask new questions; not just what to buy, but how to use their time wisely; not just what to buy, but how people can make things for themselves; not just what to produce, but how to use leisure for individual fulfillment; how to be creative; not just what to buy, but how to take delight in all the costless pleasures of life: the open air, the trees, the sky. And perhaps the time will come when people will choose not to buy: choose themselves, in their own individual use of freedom, to limit their acquisition of property in the interest of a fuller life, which may for some people also be a simpler life. And if this time comes we should be ready for them and even perhaps a little ahead of them.

I close, in deference to our hosts, by referring to Peer Gynt. He said great folks are known by the deeds they do. I would say that great movements are known by the ideas they have. We still have the chance to become a great movement.

14

Somali Radio Service

Michael Young, as Lord Young of Dartington, protested, as on other occasions, what the Conservative Government was proposing on the occasion it announced cuts in 1981 in the BBC External Service. He spoke in particular on 30 July 1981 about Somalia, where he hopes to establish a branch of the World Refugee College. The House of Lords defeated the government on this issue and the Somali service was saved.

My Lords, encouraged by what the noble Lord the Foreign Secretary said about being sad about the Somali service, and by what the right reverend prelate the Bishop of Guildford said at the beginning of his speech, I propose to concentrate on the proposed abolition of this particular vernacular service. It is a small service; it is necessarily in Somali because very few people in the Horn of Africa speak English even in what was formerly British Somaliland. It costs about £180,000 a year; it has a staff of eight and a weekly output of seven hours. Though small it is highly effective. Each one of its Somali newsreaders is known personally throughout the length and breadth of the country. Yesterday, our Wednesday was, in Somalia, as throughout the Somali-speaking world, known as 'BBC Day'. All Wednesdays are known as 'BBC Day' because of the extra coverage that is given to them. Its first transmission today, a few hours before this debate began, was listened to, as on other days, by groups of 50 to 100 people gathered around a radio set in the city of Mogadishu, in the towns of the country, by the nomads in the desert and, above all, by the refugees in the 33 refugee camps in that country. Refugees have been forced to flee across the border from Ethiopia by what the Ethiopian Army has done in the Ogaden and other provinces of Ethiopia, backed, as that army is, by Russian advisers and Cuban troops.

I have had experience myself on many occasions of the value of group listening which is so common in Africa and other continents. Some years ago I was engaged in trying to establish an open university in Northern Nigeria based on the ordinary university of Ahmadu Bello, and had occasion frequently to see what the response was to the Hausa service of the BBC in small and, as many people would think, insignificant villages throughout Northern Nigeria. It was not uncommon at all for as many as 300 people—the entire adult population of a village—to desert whatever else they were doing and gather around, say, the 10 sets that they had in the village so that they could all listen to what was the most respected and popular service in the country—the only one which had the reputation for truthfulness. At present I am trying to establish a refugee college in Somalia which will also be based on radio.

The BBC service, I maintain, matters certainly as much in Somalia as it does in Northern Nigeria, mainly because, as the noble Lord, Lord Strabolgi, said earlier, the Horn of Africa is in the utmost turmoil, suffering from extreme instability, with people waiting with foreboding for the next move by the Soviet Union. In 1977, when Russia pulled out of Somalia and switched to backing Ethiopia instead, it introduced into Ethiopia some 15,000 Cuban troops who are now just across the border from Somalia. The country has Russians and Cubans on the one side, and facing it across the sea, other Russian satellite states in South Yemen and Aden where our own British naval base was immediately taken over by the Russians when we scuttled out of there in an act of unilateral disarmament some years ago, just as the Russians would take over the BBC spot in the evening before nightly prayers at 5:30 if we now scuttle our Somali service.

No one, of course, knows what will happen next in this troubled region. Perhaps there will be another Afghanistan? But if that happens, will we be able to do with effect what we have already done since the invasion of Afghanistan in another part of the world? Two years ago it was proposed by the Government that the Turkish service should be cut. Luckily, they had second thoughts on that, and as a result it has been possible, based on an existing experienced personnel, to step up Turkish broadcasts and, as the noble Lord the Foreign Secretary said, to add Pushtu services.

No doubt we would want to do the same if there were a similar turn of events in the Horn of Africa. But would we be able to do so? The team of Somali speakers, extremely difficult to put together and mobilise, just up the road from here in Bush House would be disbanded and their like could not easily be found again. We should lose our audience—some to the Russians and perhaps some to the Americans if they decide, in view of the naval base that they have at Berbera in Somalia, that they could not allow the present Italian radio service to be the only voice of the West to reach Somali–speaking people.

In view of that, and in view of the fact that the noble Lord the Foreign Secretary has now returned to his place, I should like to ask him—and this may be a subject to refer to in the winding up of the debate—whether his staff have had discussions with the State Department about their views on the proposed abandonment of the Somali service. Above all, if we scuttled on this we should lose our sources of information within Somalia; the news–gathering network that we have could not be reassembled if, at some later date, it became urgently necessary.

This service is not only valuable in the area and not only highly popular because Somali Radio used to be under Soviet influence and lost some of its credibility, not only because when so many people are jittery they particularly need a credible, truthful, reliable source of news about what is really going on; it is because of the sheer quality of the Somali programmes—not the martial music which is the staple fare of radios in military states, but Somali folk music and Somali oral poetry, which is extremely popular and belongs to a long and honourable tradition in that country.

The BBC's weekly missing persons' programme—important when so many people have been lost track of in the great upheavals—is avidly listened to wherever Somalis gather, not only in Somalia but in coffee shops in Aden, Rhiyad, Abu Dhabi, Nairobi, Iraq, Egypt and throughout the Middle East, as well, incidentally, as by Somali students in communist countries. The BBC knows how effective this service is because it receives so much correspondence from people who have been reunited as a result of its operations. Therefore, it is hardly surprising that there have been many objections from inside the country at the closure of the service.

When the cuts were announced a presidential delegation from Somalia was in Nairobi to attend the Organization for African Unity summit and expressed its shock at what was proposed. I understand that very recently some influential Somali citizens approached the British ambassador to say the same thing. In view of this, I hope that the Government will be able to tell us that they are at least willing to consult the British ambassador again before making their decision irrevocable.

My final words go wider than the Somali service, which I am using simply for purposes of illustration. Seven times in the past eight years Labour or Conservative Governments have cut, or tried to cut,

BBC overseas broadcasts. From this Social Democratic Bench I cannot say if in the future there is a Government of a different political colour we shall reverse this decision and restore and maintain the Somali service and other services under threat, because it will never be possible to restore them in full once they are disbanded.

Of course, it is necessary to improve audibility. All that the noble Lord the Foreign Secretary said on that subject must command agreement in this House. However, as we see it from these Benches, that is no reason why it should be necessary to cut the vernacular services as well and also the transcription services. Therefore, my appeal must be to the noble Lord the Foreign Secretary to draw back before it is too late. We lost an Empire; we do not need to lose the BBC services as well. We are no longer, in general, a major power, but we are a great power in the world of broadcasting. We are still a great power with a voice that speaks of the values of civilisation. I appeal to the Government not to silence that precious voice, even in these particular services that are now under threat.

15

The Middle of the Night

When the Social Democratic Party was created in 1981 the author was one of its founder members. He subsequently set up the Tawney Society as a think tank for the new party. The essay which follows, written in conjunction with Peter Hall, is an excerpt from a Tawney pamphlet. It argues that whatever the setbacks the new party suffers in its early years, it has at least one of the requisites for success: the right fit with the changing class structure of society. The underlying hope is that a radical movement with flair and dedication will again be reborn, as it has so many times before in Britain's history.

Very rarely indeed in political history can it truly be said that a cause and a party stand at some critical juncture, the outcome of which may be decline or triumph. The autumn of 1982 is surely one of these few occasions for the Social Democratic Party in Britain. In a breathless 18 months a new party was born—the first major event of this kind in British politics for nearly a century—and went on to early and spectacular successes at the polls. It was a light in the middle of the night. Yet no one would deny that in the last six of those months some of the momentum has been lost. Unexpected outside military and political events provided the major cause for this setback. But behind that was something more basic: a questioning of the SDP's ability to provide a convincing political alternative solution for the country's present discontents.

The SDP meets for a truly momentous national conference. Before it are the first fruits of a frenetic year of policy–making: the Green Papers, representing the party's first coherent and detailed statement of its answers to the pressing problems of the economy, industry, education, urban affairs and industrial democracy. For a week the attention of the nation will once again be firmly on the SDP.

But this time the mood will be more sober, less euphoric than in the heady days after the Limehouse Declaration. The questions that will be asked will be the right ones. First: are the policies relevant to the grave and deepening problems that now affect the world and this country within it? Second: do they represent a coherent political philosophy capable of uniting diverse interests and outlooks into a common programme of action? Third: is there a sufficient appeal to distinctive groups of the electorate, not merely on the basis of the self–interest that has traditionally fuelled party politics, but inspired by a new sense of communal purpose?

The relevance of the first question is transparently obvious; the second perhaps less so, but absolutely crucial. A programme of a political party, or policy statement, needs agreement between the parts and the whole. We would think little of an economic policy that called simultaneously for expansion and restraint, or for major social programmes coupled with lower taxation. But we look for more than formal or logical agreement: we seek some informing principles or philosophy that unite the separate parts and give them a wider meaning. Long–established political parties find this relatively easy; the broad principles for which they stand, however fudged and out–of–date, are well known to all. New parties, unless they stem from some very strong organising principle, will tend to lack this central coherence. Herein lies a challenge for the SDP: it did spring out of a heartfelt wish for a new start based on philosophical principles, and its central need now is to set these down in clear and challenging form.

That, then, is the central task of this Tawney pamphlet. We seek to do something that the Green Papers in themselves do not attempt and in the nature of things could not have attempted: to ask how far they reflect a consistent political philosophy. In order to do that, we need first to ask: What is, or what should be, that philosophy? There is as yet no general agreement on this point.

One approach—and also an answer to the third question—lies not in the kinds of statement that SDP people make, but rather in the kinds of people they are. The most important characteristic of the SDP is that, in sharp contrast to the two older parties of the left and right, it is not a class party. More precisely, it does not represent the major class divisions that have so long characterised and bedevilled British society. It sets itself aside from the Tory base in landed wealth and more recently in speculative wealth. It similarly separates itself from the proletarian class solidarity of the Labour party, associated as it is with a particular kind of labour (manual work) that now represents only a declining minority of all employment. Instead, the SDP represents a union of just those elements who feel that they have no place in these older parties: scientists and technologists, entrepreneurs and managers, professionals in many varied fields, teachers and medical workers, journalists and lawyers and a thousand and one other occupations. Some work for themselves, others for private companies, others for central and local government, yet others for public organisations.

These groups represent the expanding sector of the British economy. Between 1961 and 1980 manufacturing shrank from over 38 percent of employment to just over 30 percent; services expanded from 47 to over 59 percent. Twice as many people now work in providing services as in making goods—and even in the latter, many are not on the shop floor but in offices and laboratories. It may still seem surprising but more people now work in professional and scientific services than in engineering; nearly four times as many in banking, insurance and finance as in mining and quarrying; and nearly twice as many in public administration as in textiles, once our leading staple industry.

The most important factor in British politics of the 1980s is thus the massive extension of the new middle classes. They are not of course completely new; Orwell wrote, forty years ago, about 'the upward and downward extension of the middle class', which made 'the old classification of society into capitalists, proletarians and petit–bourgeois (small property–owners) almost obsolete'. As usual, Orwell was perceptively ahead of his time. In 1941, what he called 'the intermediate stratum' was a minority; now, it constitutes a majority of the nation. A common criticism of the SDP is that its meetings contain too few manual workers on the floor or on the platform. That criticism has justice, but it tends to ignore the fact that there are no longer so many of these people anywhere. And the workers who still do manual jobs increasingly share a style of life which, for lack of a better title, could be called middle–class. In this sense, the SDP, which includes manual workers who have in their outlook left the old class consciousness behind, merely represents the vanguard of a social trend, just as the Labour party represents the rear.

However, the new middle classes have not the same homogeneity as the old working class; nor do they have the same roots in the sense of being recognisable members of a class, having a sense of class–consciousness and of solidarity. As a slogan, 'Workers of the world unite' has been robbed of some of its magnificence by its over–optimism. The traditional working–class appeal that has been the driving force behind 10,000 strikes—*one out, all out*—does not evoke the same automatic response from the new classes, even though increasing numbers of them are union members. They are specifically not manual workers. Many do jobs that did not exist thirty years ago.

They are not so open to that peculiar form of exploitation that Marx first identified: they do not merely have their labour power to sell to their employer to exploit as he thinks fit. They do not share a strong identity stemming from the work they do and their relationship to the mode of production. The work they do is highly diversified: it is divided up between new and old, professional and managerial jobs. Thus the clerk in an advocate's office in Edinburgh, or a radiographer in a hospital in Nottingham, would feel no common bond with a computer programmer in Guildford; if one is engaged in a dispute with his employer, the others are unlikely to feel instinctive sympathy.

What then do they have in common? They are mainly workers by brain rather than by manual skill; they earn their living by their own efforts, and in most cases have little inherited wealth; they are relatively highly educated, being once children who benefited from the massive post–war expansion in higher and secondary education; they earn middle incomes and have broadly middle–class styles of life. They thus cannot be defined as a class in terms of their productive role. But the fact to recognise is that alongside the shift in the economy from working–class to middle–class occupations there has been another long–term shift of people's roles and interests from production to consumption. Weekends and annual holidays have lengthened, giving men and women in paid work more time for leisure. Better houses have given people more space which they can control and do what they like with, in their many capacities as husbands and wives, fathers and mothers, gardners and cooks, carpenters and electricians, musicians and painters, do-it-yourself car repairers and window cleaners. For the great majority still fortunate enough to have paid jobs, even in the middle of the second worst recession of this century, their real life is not so much in those jobs as in what they do outside with the money they earn from them.

In this respect they are merely reasserting a distinctively English (or British) tradition. In the same 1941 essay, Orwell wrote of

> the *privateness* of English life. We are a nation of flower–lovers, but also a nation of stamp–collectors, pigeon–fanciers, amateur carpenters, coupon–snippers, darts–players, crossword–puzzle fans. All the culture which is truly native centres round things which even when they are communal are not official—the pub, the football match, the back garden, the fireside and the "nice cup of tea".

This is still true, just more so. The organisations that people increasingly belong to are not only the trade unions but a whole host of new organisations which reflect their special interests as conservationists, consumers, educationalists, motorists, citizens band enthusiasts, wine−makers, real ale fanciers, members of Amnesty International, collectors for Oxfam, supporters of local amenity societies, and a thousand and one other things. A very important part of SDP philosophy is that it recognises this essentially individually−based, voluntary, communal aspect of life and seeks to build on it.

The rise of the new middle classes already had an impact on politics before the arrival of the SDP. For both the main traditional political parties were tied to the old style of production−based parties, one dominated by the unions, the other by business. They thus helped prolong a simple two−class structure long after it failed to correspond to the social arithmetic of our society.

The really novel point, however, is this: that the new classes are not a class at all in traditional terms. As we have already tried to show, they do not have a common and clear set of class interests. But that does not stop them becoming a new *political* class. The difference is that they have not entered upon the politcal stage just to protect and to forward their own interests. Though of course self−interest will play its part, the members of the new classes are just too diverse to underpin a separate social constituency. They look beyond their own interests to those of society as a whole. We would deny that idealism and altruism were lacking in the politics of the past; these virtues played a crucial role in the formation and in the long and proud history of the Labour Party, where the shared circumstances of hardship helped forge the organisation and strategy while the aspirations provided the motivating force. Any party at any time must have its foundation both in some common interest and in some idealistic force. What we are suggesting is that in the new structure of Britain the base for the SDP must lie in a richer and more diverse set of interests which does not rule out a coherent set of shared beliefs.

The key to both is the fact about the new middle classes: that many of them work in what used to be called the liberal professions. Whether teachers or nurses or journalists, they are centrally concerned with the lives of other people to whom they relate as providers of services. This explains the apparent paradox that, perhaps for the first time, very large numbers of people are politically concerned as much about the fortunes of other people as about their own. And this sympathy extends to human beings outside the immediate orbit of their own lives, to the poor in other parts of the nation or of the world. It is to such people, and to their sympathies, that the SDP must appeal, or perish.

If their concern is to be with the common affairs of the whole polity, if they are to follow the best traditions of democratic socialism, it follows that the new groups who form the SDP's natural support must have a very special concern for—indeed, form another kind of alliance with—the people who, far from belonging to the new middle classes, have become part of another significant group of modern society: the new deprived classes. These are no longer the conventional working class: rather, they are the non–working classes. Some of the growing army of unemployed, particularly the old but also many of the unskilled young, face the prospect of never working again—or at all. Still others are witness to the changing patterns of family life in other ways than those already mentioned—notably the single parent families—and others to demographic changes—the increasing proportions of elderly people in our society. Still others are the disabled and the outworkers and the women in part–time work where they can easily be exploited; the tenants of the inner cities who are (whatever else they suffer from) underprivileged just by reason of the place where they live; and the members of ethnic minorities, who are still discriminated against in a hundred subtle and unsubtle ways.

A strange irony that neatly illustrates the changed nature of contemporary British society is that the Labour Party and the unions represent the people in full–time employment: the privileged manual workers who are still working. Yet it is possible that by the mid–1980s, allowing for the 21 percent of the voting population who are now over retirement age, plus the unemployed and the disabled and the single–parent families and other members of the marginal population, close on half the total voting population might have no immediate interest in the production of goods and services. So it is precisely the plight of the new underclass that cries out for many–sided political attention if we are to realise our aspiration to be *one* nation. A new political class, asserting its identity, will work in vain unless it faces the dismal bottom line of the new social arithmetic of late twentieth century Britain and accepts the paramount need for redistribution of income and wealth. An alliance between the new middle classes and the new deprived classes is the underpinning which could give the political Alliance the thrust it needs. The challenge to the art of politics is to show that this new alliance can be the fulcrum of a new consensus in British society to replace the ones we have lost. 'The two parties have different but complementary assets', said David Steel, but one asset they must have in common is consensus.

Fortunately, we already know something about the political beliefs that have guided the new political class and brought about the birth of the SDP. From the evidence of the books that have been published and the polls, and from the canvass of opinion among our own members, there are common principles which are shared.

First, there is an assertion of the fundamental liberal principle: that, in any contest between the rights of the individual and the interests of some larger collective body, individual rights are paramount. From this it follows that Social Democrats are first democrats: they believe that the best guarantee of individual freedoms is through the maximum extension of democratic rights, properly guaranteed through due constitutional processes, in all walks of life, and completed by the introduction of proportional representation.

There is however a most important corollary: a liberal and democratic society is based on the individual's right to choose for oneself. That extends to all aspects of life, from the largest to the smallest. Ordinary people everywhere should be free to choose the kind of housing they want to live in, the kind of work they do, the kind of education their children shall receive, the kind of car they drive or the kind of bus service they get, the health care they receive if they fall sick, the council that provides their essential services. Because we place choice at the forefront it follows that we believe in the traditional association between democracy and the market: consumer sovereignty shall apply in both. (Thus, it goes almost without saying, we accept and support the mixed economy.) But we take the principle much further than the traditionalists: we argue that governments should guarantee not merely choice in the marketplace, providing a framework for the operation of individual actions so as to have due regard for the impacts that they may have on other individuals and on society in general, but also in the delivery of public sector services. We believe that people want the best services and that the best way of achieving this is to give them greater freedom to choose what they want.

As a second principle, however, we believe that choice has an important further corollary. We are *Social* Democrats: we believe that choice for all demands redistribution of income and wealth. But we want to achieve this in ways that reduce bureaucratic interference to the minimum while actually multiplying the individual's opportunities to choose the pattern of goods and services, both private and public, that he or she finds best.

Social Democrats, then, need to recall the classic words of Colonel Thomas Rainborowe in the Army debates at Putney in 1647: 'The poorest he that is in England hath a right to live as the greatest he'. Substitute the poorest she, and that is no bad motto for the SDP in the United Kingdom of 1982. The now–famous Limehouse commitment to an 'open, classless and more equal society' remains fundamental to our purposes.

But we need to go beyond that, and ask: what is this life, that we all have a right to live? Here, Tawney himself provided the answer, in a statement from 1949 significantly titled *Social Democracy in Britain:*

> Civilisation is a matter, not of quantity of possessions, but of quality of life. It is to be judged, not by the output of goods and services per head, but by the use which is made of them. A society which values public welfare above private display; which, though relatively poor, makes the first charge on its small resources the establishment for all of the conditions of a vigorous and self–respecting existence; which gives a high place among these conditions to the activities of the spirit and the services which provide them; which holds that the most important aspect of human beings is not the external differences of income and circumstance that divide them, but the common humanity that unites them, and which strives, therefore, to reduce such differences to a position of insignificance that rightly belongs to them—such a society may be far from what it should be, but it has, at least, set its face towards the light.

Thirdly, because of their regard for the individual, Social Democrats believe that—other things being equal—the best form of economic and social organisation is one that involves small groups of freely cooperating individuals in pursuit of common ends; whether these groups are called family businesses, or small companies, or cooperatives, or clubs. They will work therefore to secure the maximum possible decentralisation of power to such small groups, alike in the social, the economic and the political spheres. We are in favour of democratic socialism but (to borrow the phrase from an SDP member, Evan Luard) socialism without the state, or at least without so much of the state as we have had to put up with in the past. Or, as Chelly Halsey has said, we want to move from the welfare state to the welfare society. We need to replace the bureaucratic providing state by an enabling state: one that manipulates the market and provides opportunities and rights outside the state rather than absorbing more and more functions into itself.

We are not so naive as to believe, with Marx, that the state could ever wither away; it represents an essential mechanism for managing the national household and for redistributing goods and services, which market mechanisms cannot on their own perform and which no other known institution is likely to do either. But we want to control it, and tame it, so that it serves our purposes rather than some remorseless purposes of its own. This will entail the decentralisation of bureaucracies, the exploration of alternative forms of state provision, the return to natural communities as pegs on which to hang the organisation of this provision, a participative style in decision–making, democratic contol of both decisions and their implementation, and a new provision for voluntary action of the kind Jo Grimond appealed for in a notable speech.

> To many people voluntary action, good deeds done for no material reward, are positively wrong. Even interest in one's fellows and curiosity about their individual foibles is withering in official organisations. Human relationships in business are frowned on by the bureaucratically minded.

No one should be able to say that about the Alliance. But all of this will not be easy; for it entails not merely changes in structure, but also the education of people into an acceptance and an appreciation of these values, so that they know *how* to participate. Jefferson said it nearly 200 years ago:

> In every government on earth is some trace of human weakness, some germ of corruption and degeneracy, which cunning will discover and wickedness insensibly open, cultivate and improve. Every government degenerates when trusted to the rulers of the people alone. The people themselves therefore are its only safe depositories. And to render even them safe their minds must be improved to some degree.

The Jefferson rule however applies just as much to our principle of choice as to our principle of participation. Both, if they are not to degenerate into manipulation and quackery, require constant concern for the education of the whole people to make them more aware as citizens, consumers and participators. It may also entail—as American experience in the present century has shown—the establishment of rules of the game so as to exclude charlatans and swindlers. This may mean additional regulatory bureaucracy; the better way, if it can be achieved, is through the growth of voluntary organisations to monitor products and services both in the private and in the public domain, together with the development of education for citizenship on a more ambitious scale than ever attempted before.

Fourthly, the acid test for a Social Democratic Alliance government will be to make a start in realising the conditions of the good life in circumstances that are less propitious than at any time since the depression of the 1930s. As Tony Crosland once emphasised with the perception that always distinguished him, to redistribute resources—whether for the sustenance of the underprivileged, or for the enrichment of all—is relatively much easier in a period of economic growth than in a period of stagnation. When times are hard for almost all but unbearable for some, the risk is that the relatively affluent may join the "I'm all right Claude" brigade and seek to pull up the ladders around their middle-class walls. It is precisely to counter that danger that the SDP came into existence.

If Britain were in a less critical condition it would make good sense to propose policies to give Britain the tranquility it has so long needed and so long lacked. But, as Keynes once wrote in a similar context, the time for all this is not yet. The SDP will succeed if and only if it first reflects the interests and concerns of the new groups in society. It must also offer reasoned, clear and practical solutions to the apparently intractable problems facing the nation today: solutions that are a true alternative to the musty orthodoxies of the Thatcherite right and the Trotskyite left. These problems manifest themselves in relative economic decline. But the repeated attempts of economists—whether calling themselves Keynesians, or Monetarists, or by any other name—have proved equally incapable of dealing with them. We hold that the problems reflect far deeper-seated social and cultural causes, and that only very radical changes in our values and our institutions will bring a revival.

An Alliance government must be prepared to tackle that task. If it does not show itself better fitted to grasp the new necessities of our time and master them better than the other parties it will not succeed, or even come into existence. Too often, in the past, such attempts have been beaten down or rendered ineffectual on the grounds that they would threaten our traditional way of life. Social Democrats should specifically reject the heresy, so prevalent and so fashionable throughout Britain's history over the last hundred years that there is something offensive and immoral about technological achievement and economic growth. On the contrary, the best features of our way of life will be those most threatened by dissension and disorder if we are unable to use economic growth to achieve social justice. Of course, we are against the darker impacts of industrialism: we want to see an end to heavy, demoralising toil, to stunted lives in bad environments. But the way to achieve this is by moving as fast as possible to embrace new technologies and new industries and services based on investment in new machinery and above all on investment in the capacities of human beings.

Fifthly and finally, Social Democrats believe that prosperity is indivisible. The welfare of each is the welfare of all. Social Democrats believe that this should be a principle governing our economic policies both nationally and worldwide. But ironically, as events on the international stage are now demonstrating, narrow self–interest gives its support to the same principle. The economic crisis that is threatening so many of the developing countries must be solved because if not it will mean a spiralling downward crisis in the entire world economic system. Social Democratic economic policy must be posited on the notion of global interdependence.

In making the criticisms we have and in putting forward our proposals we are not for one moment pretending that this is the last word, nor, of course, the first. The details all need further discussion. What we have tried to do in effect is to say why we joined the SDP. We were persuaded by hope, hope that after a sad period of exhaustion and cynicism in British politics a radical movement with flair and dedication might again be reborn, as it has so many times before in our history.

To close we would like to return to our starting point and emphasise once again the necessity for building an alliance, evident as much in international and national as in community politics, between the new middle classes and the new deprived classes. Without that alliance we do not believe that the Alliance will in fact turn out to be the lever which could edge our country out of its long–standing state of depression and into a new role in the world of ideas and the world of action which realises the enormous potential still residing in the British people. The world also needs hope; that it will not have without a recognition that the most deprived classes are not in Britain itself. Politically speaking, it is still the middle of the night—we have a few more hours before what could be the dawn.

Epilogue

This book reflects a lifetime's interest in the future, that is, in changing anticipations at different points in the century. It also expresses two dominant moods. The first is radical, restless and optimistic. For the six years from 1945 to 1951 I was the head of the Labour Party's Research Department and involved in policy making for the most radical democratic government of the century. The Manifesto for the 1945 Election, which I helped to write, was called *Let Us Face the Future*. It sounds very much a period piece, and of course it is; but it worked—the entire programme was put into action—and the experience gave me a taste both for conjecture and for acting on it. Our particular brave new world of those years was no dystopia. A better future for Britain was in the offing, and likewise for the British territories in the Indian, Asian and African Continents which the Labour Government propelled towards independence.

One chapter in this book, *Small Man, Big World,* belongs to that period. I thought that big government, like big business or big unionism, was a threat to democracy, since democracy could flourish best in small groups built to the scale of the individual. But I still had faith that one only had to hammer away at such obvious truths and in the end governments would have to give way, that is, give away some of their power.

The faith did not seem outlandish at the time. The government to which I was appealing from the party office *was* effective. Even so, it lost its momentum and was defeated at the General Election of 1951. It was succeeded by a long, drawn–out yawn. But I believed (and still do believe) that reform is both needed and possible, with the impetus coming not so much from within political parties as from without. This happened with the Consumers' Association. I wanted to copy the Consumers Union of U.S.A. but to make the copy a good deal more lively than the original—which I think it has been so far. The Association's journal, *Which?*, has become a somewhat farouche national institution. I put the proposal that such a consumer body should be established into Labour's Manifesto for the 1950 Election, and, luckily, nothing was done to implement it, leaving the way open for a private initiative. The success of the Consumers' Association has in its turn led to many new Acts of Parliament intended to protect consumers and to the naming of Ministers for Consumer Affairs in both Labour and Conservative governments. It has become one of a number of non–party pressure groups dedicated to reform, and one referred to in the paper on *The Chipped White Cups of Dover* and in the speech on *Consumers and the Quality of Life*.

I formed another, to get the Open University set up—this was unfortunately too expensive for anyone except the government to finance—but to campaign for the government to do just that, which eventually it did. The original case for it is in the essay on that subject in Part II. I was prompted to push for it partly by the satire, intended to be deadly serious as well as funny, embodied in the book, *The Rise of the Meritocracy*. The meritocratic elite of the future was to be open only to those who could as children sail through one examination after another. The Open University was, and is, to be open to anyone, with or without qualification.

These two campaigns have been successful. Not so the one launched, as a follow–up to the Open Univeristy, by the International Extension College. Its 'manifesto' on the Third World is in Part II. Under its aegis a small chain of new colleges has been started in Africa, consultancy work done in dozens of Third World countries, and a World Refugee College established in 1980 as an offshoot. But the goal was perhaps too ambitious. It was to create as an alternative to orthodox schools a dense network of 'radio colleges' which would be open to anyone and which would also not be exam–ridden. The people to benefit would be the hundreds of millions of children and adults who, as things are, get no schooling at all. But how can they be organised? If there is a way we have not found it yet. The importance of radio is stressed in the speech in the House of Lords on the BBC's Somali Radio Service.

Single–issue politics cannot, however, ever oust ordinary humdrum politics. I have never completely abandoned my hopes for the latter, and, whether with hopes or without them, the state of the political life of any nation must never be neglected. This was without any longer expecting any worthwhile general reforms to come from either of the established parties. A new progressive party was different. I put in a plea for one in 1960 and helped to found one in 1981: the Social Democratic Party. Less institutionalised than the old parties, with roots not going so deep into history, the new party should be more receptive to new thinking. We shall see.

The other mood is less aerated, less optimistic, more concerned with the prevention of further decline than with the achievement of further progress. The purpose is conservation. This mood was first struck in the essays which appear in Part III on the family. *Family and Kinship in East London* was about the threat posed by 'progress' to extended families which, until they became the victims of housing policies, had proved their resilience, as I hope they will again. The immediate family has also been under threat and, if it were not able to resist, the whole of our marvellous civilisation would crumble within a generation or two. Nothing is more important than the conservation of the family and what remains of active community life. The broader conservationist or ecological movement needs to encompass them both.

It is always difficult to remember what the future seemed to hold at any moment in the past. But futuristic memories are one of the keys to the understanding of any age. Looking back through the marches of the century to what I thought would happen, what I hoped would happen, and what did happen, I am left mainly with a sense of wonder. It has been as marvellously true of our age as of any other that, in Blake's words:

> Eternity is in love with the productions of time.

ABOUT THE AUTHOR

Michael Young, born of an Australian father and an Irish mother, is a British sociologist who is unusual not just for having produced two sociological books (*The Rise of the Meritocracy* and—with Peter Willmott—*Family and Kinship in East London*) which have persisted as best-sellers twenty-five years after their publications but also for his innovations in the world of action. He is the originator of the Open University, the Consumers' Association, the Advisory Centre for Education, the International Extension College and the Mutual Aid Centre. His life has been divided between forecasting the future and making it. Making it sometimes means trying to conserve the best of the past and carry it into the future. He is, as Lord Young of Dartington, a Social Democratic member of the House of Lords.

Index

Academic year, 28
Acción Cultural Popular Hondureña (ACPH), 83–84
Adult education, *see* Radio colleges
Age structure, and new settlements, 7
Agricultural cycle, and radio colleges, 81–82
APCO, 82
Arnold, Matthew, 49
Automobiles
  leisure activity and ownership of, 161
  Menlo Park kinship study and, 120–121
  road planning and forecasting with, 8

Bagehot, Walter, 178
Bartlett, F. C., 178
Beckerman, W., 24
Behavior, and forecasting, 24
Bell, Daniel, 20, 146
Bethnal Green family life study, 97–117
  acquaintances seen daily in, 100–102
  advantages of kinship system in, 115
  attachment to community in, 104–105
  bereavement effects in, 138
  family as link to network in, 107–108
  family influence on community life in, 106–107
  genealogical knowledge in, 134
  government housing programs and, 115–117
  home visiting patterns in, 102–103
  length of residence and kinship in, 108–109
  long-standing residence patterns in, 99–100
  mother-daughter ties in, 110–113, 126
  older generations in, 113–115
  residence of grown children in, 125–126, 128
  self-sufficiency of family in, 113–114
  travel outside neighborhood in, 105–106
  turnings and social patterns in, 103–104
Bevin, Ernest, 227
Bible, in Coronation Service, 183
Birth-rates
  forecasting in educational planning and, 6–7
  Open University planning and, 63–64
Botswana, radio colleges in, 79
Bowden, Dr., 65
British Broadcasting Corporation (B.B.C.), 71
  Somali Radio Service and, 238, 239, 240, 241
British National Plan, 24
Bruner, Jerome, 81
Buchanan Report, 8, 11
Business cycles, 19
Butler, D. E., 211, 219

256

Index

Cambridge University, 71
Canada, farm forums in, 80
Cars, *see* Automobiles
Catholic Church, 78
Census, and episodic time scale, 30
Change
   educational system and, 224–225
   forecasting and, 4, 18
Church of England, 182–183
Ciocco, A., 143
Circadian cycles, 36–37
Class
   club membership and, 159–160
   cycles and imitation of, 19–20
   differences in leisure activities and, 157–158
   educational change and, 224–225
   genealogical awareness and, 135
   home-based leisure activities and, 152–154
   leisure as extension of work and, 158–159
   Menlo Park kinship study and, 121
   new middle classes and sense of, 244–245
   other leisure activities and, 155–156
   sports activities and, 154–155
   television viewing habits and, 152, 153
Clock time, 33
Club membership, and class, 159–160
Colombia, radio colleges in, 76, 82
Communication
   forecasting and, 4
   between levels of social organizations, 197, 200–201, 202–204
Community
   Bethnal Green study of attachment to, 104–105
   Coronation and feeling of, 186–188
Community associations, 205

Competition, and forecasting, 9
Concorde (airplane), 8–9
Conservative Party, 225, 226, 240
Consumer Advisory Council, 229
Consumers and consumption
   commercial products versus public services and, 235–237
   demand cycles and, 20–21
   needs of poor versus needs of rich and, 234–235
   politics and, 222–224, 227
   quality of life and, 233–237
Consumers' Association, 229
Consumer party, 230–231
Co-operative Movement, 229
Coronation Service, 177–193
   anointing of Queen in, 183
   benediction in, 184
   Bible in, 183
   as collective experience, 186–188
   families in celebration of, 186–187
   idealisation of Royal Family and, 191–192
   institutional monarchy and, 190–191
   love of processions, uniforms, and ceremonial in, 188–189
   meaning of monarchy in, 177–178
   need to render gifts and sacrifices in, 188
   oath taken in, 182–183
   people's celebration of, 184–185
   plurality of social institutions held together by, 192–193
   reaffirmation of moral values in society and, 179–182
   recognition of Queen in, 182
   religious feelings connected with monarchy and, 178–179
   as religious ritual, 186
   sword and orb presentation in, 183–184

258 INDEX

Costs
  developmental, and forecasting, 8–9
  social, and efficiency, 196–197
Council of Economic Advisers, 15
Crosland, Anthony, 219, 250
Crowther, Sir Geoffrey, 65
Crowther Report, 7
Cycles, 27–42
  antecedent or postcedent, 40
  astronomical events related to, 27–28
  circadian, 36–37
  clock time in, 33
  definition of, 31
  dependent or dominant, 38
  different cycles with different periods simultaneously, 37–38
  duration of time sense in, 28–29
  episodic time in, 29–32
  fluctuating function of time in, 35
  forecasting and search for, 18–21
  frequency in, 34
  life cycle concept in, 31–32
  mean free time in, 34
  oscillation in, 35–36
  periodic, 34
  personal behavior routines in, 36–37
  phase in, 35
  pulsating time in, 35
  reckoning of year in, 27–28
  recurrence distinguished from, 32
  relaxation time in, 33–34
  rhythm in, 38
  synchronized or harmonized, 38
  system in, 38–41
  terminology in, 29
  time as numerical variable in, 32–34
Czechoslovakia, 203

Daughters, see Mother-daughter relationships

Davis, Norah, 201–202, 204
Dawn University, 71
Death rates, and widowhood, 139
Defence planning, and forecasting, 9
De Jouvenel, Bertrand, 17
Demand
  cycles in, 20–21
  forecasting and, 9–10
Democracy
  forecasting and, 5
  group size and, 196
  human nature and, 206–208
  leadership in, 197, 198
Demography, and forecasting, 16–17
Developmental costs, and forecasting, 8–9
Distance teaching, see Radio colleges
Divine right of kings, 178
Division of labour, 202
Doctors, forecasting demand for, 7–8
Dore, R., 91
Dumazedier, J., 161
Durkheim, Emile, 138

Economic conditions
  forecasting and time series and, 21–22
  influence of forecasting in, 6, 24
Economics
  cycles in, 35
  forecasting and variables in, 14–15
  leisure activities and, 161, 162
Educational policy, 43–95
  birth-rates and, 63–64
  cycles in demand for education and, 20
  food production and, 93–94
  forecasting on birth-rates and, 6–7
  influence of forecasting in, 24
  meritocracy and, 45–61
  Open University in, 63–72
  population growth and, 73–74

primary school strength and, 88
radio colleges and, 75–95
righting injustices from past and, 87–88
social change and class and, 224–225
teacher training in, 88
theories of equality in, 47–48
Third World alternative to, 73–95
Elections
Labour Party and, 211
participation in, 198–199
Electricity Council, 12
Eliade, Mircea, 31
Elizabeth II, Queen of England, *see* Coronation Service
Episodic time, 29–32
Equality, and meritocracy, 47–48

Fabians, 208
Factories
communication between levels in, 200–201, 202–204
size issues and, 202
Family, 97–173
Bethnal Green study of, 97–117
community and, 106–108
Coronation Service and, 186–187
idealisation of Royal Family and, 191–192
leisure and, 146–173
Menlo Park study of, 119–135
number of weekly visits in, 164–166
older generation in, 113–115
self-sufficiency of, 113–114
widowers and, 138–145
see also Father-son relationships; Kinship, Mother-daughter relationships
Family associations, 130–131
Father-son relationships
Bethnal Green study of, 111
Menlo Park study of, 128
Five-Year Plan (Soviet Union), 5
Food production, in Third World, 93–94

Forecasting, 1–42
accelerating demand in, 9–10
behavioral influences of, 24
birth-rate and educational planning with, 6–7
competitive predictions with, 9
cycles in social behavior in, 27–42
demand for, 3–4, 5
developmental costs with, 8–9
difficulties with use of, 4–5
economic plans with, 6
explanation testing with, 17–18
housing demand in new settlements with, 7
interrelated variables in, 14–15
knowledge of past in, 13–14
limits to trends with, 22
manpower, 7–8, 10, 24
multidisciplinary approach to, 16–17
production with, 12–13
publication issues in, 15–16
reliance on, 22–23
road planning with, 8
search for pattern or cycle in, 18–21
social change focus of, 18
social sciences and, 16–18
time series and national economy in, 21–22
town planning and, 10–11
validation of method in, 15
Fourier's theorem, 37, 38
Frequency, in cycle, 34

Gallup Poll, 131, 231
Genealogy, awareness of
Bethnal Green study of, 106–107, 134
class structure and, 135
Menlo Park study of, 121, 129s2–135
U.S.–Britian comparison for, 132–133
Ghana, farm forums in, 80
Goody, J., 31
Government policy, *see* Educational

policy; Housing programs;
Social policy
Green Papers, 242, 243
Grimond, Jo., 250

Hansen, Alvin, 19
Hawthorne Experiment, 204
Hodgson Report, 222
Honduras, radio colleges in, 83–84
Housing programs
    Bethnal Green study and, 115–117
    forecasting demand in, 7
    Menlo Park study and, 121
Huguenots, 106–107, 134

Illiteracy, 74
INADES, 80, 82
Income, and leisure activities, 161, 162
India, farm forums in, 80
Infectious diseases, and widowers, 143–144
Institute of Community Studies, 129
Intelligence, and marriage, 52
International Extension College, 72
International Organization of Consumer Unions, 235

James, William, 197
Jefferson, Thomas, 250
Jennings, Sir Ivor, 177
Joint Production Committees, 200
Jones, Ernest, 180, 190

Kaplan, M., 148
Keynes, John Maynard, 251
Kinship
    advantages of, 115
    Bethnal Green study of, 97–117
    Menlo Park study of, 119–135
    older generations in, 113–115
    residence and, 108–109
    see also Family
Knight, Frank, 23

Kraus, A. S., 144

Labour force, and forecasting, 7–8, 10
Labour Party, 46, 210–213, 240, 246, 247
    Asia and Africa's relationship to Britain and, 215–216
    attitude of 'effortless superiority' and, 216
    community associations and, 205, 206
    consumption orientation of politics and, 222–224, 227
    decline of Britain viewed in, 215
    elections and power of, 198
    Europe's relationship to Britain and, 213–215
    foundations of politics and, 221
    international power units and, 218–219
    Liberal Party and, 211–212
    possibility of new political party and, 212, 229–231
    production orientation of politics and, 221–222, 227
    progressive vote and, 212–213
    socialist element in, 216–217
    support for Consumer's Party and, 230–231
    training of experts and, 217–218
    unions and, 227–229
    women and social change and, 220–221
    working-class focus of, 219–220
Labour theory of value, 47
Laski, Harold, 177–178, 198
Laver, J., 21
Leach, E. R., 31
Leaders
    communication between different levels and, 197, 200–201, 202–204
    personal responsibility of, 199
    selection and training methods for, 199–200
    size of organization and, 201–202

Index

Leisure
    average number of relatives seen in, 164–165
    car ownership and, 161
    club membership and class and, 159–160
    definitions in, 147–149
    differences between classes in, 157–158
    differences in viewpoints on work and, 148–152
    educational level and, 161, 162
    forecasting in new town planning and, 11
    functions of, 161
    future research in, 172–173
    home-based activities in, 152–154
    income and, 161, 162
    marriage and changes in, 147
    meetings with friends and, 166–167
    other activities in, 155–156
    sex of friends met socially in, 164, 165
    social circles and, 163–164
    sports activities in, 154–155
    television viewing habits in, 152, 153
    transportation and, 172
    wife and patterns of, 156–157, 167–172
    work as extension of, and class, 158–159
Lerner, Max, 120
Liberal Party, 211–212
Life cycle, 31–32
Lilienfeld, A. M., 144
Lilienthal, David, 199
Limehouse Declaration, 243, 249
Local Government Boundary Commission, 206
London School of Economics, 66
London University, 66, 68
Low, David, 185, 188

Manchester Guardian, 185, 187, 188
Manpower forecasting, 7–8, 10, 24

Marriage
    Bethnal Green study and, 102
    intelligence and, 52
    leisure habits and, 147
    mother-daughter ties and, 112
    residence and, 109–110
    widowers and rates for second, 143
Marris, Peter, 138
Martin, Kingsley, 178
Marx, Karl, 47, 245, 249
Marxist theory, 221
Mauritius, radio colleges in, 79
Mayo, Elton, 204
Mean free time, 34
Medicine, and manpower forecasting, 7–8
Menlo Park kinship study, 119–135
    attitudes about residence in, 123
    automobile ownership in, 120–121
    family associations in, 130–131
    family relationships in, 128
    frequency of contacts between parents and grown children in, 125
    genealogical knowledge in, 129–135
    mother-daughter relationships in, 125–126, 127–129
    religious affiliation in, 121–122
    residence patterns of grown children in, 123–125
    Woodford study differences with, 120–123
Meritocracy, 45–61
Middle class, and politics, 244–246
Military, and forecasting, 9
Modulation of cycles, 41
Monarchy, *see* Coronation Service
Moral values, and monarchy, 179–180
Morris, William, 208
Morrison, Herbert, 199, 205
Mother-daughter relationships
    Bethnal Green study of, 110–113, 126
    Menlo Park study of, 125–126, 127–128

Mott, Sir Nevill, 65
Mumford, Lewis, 33, 104

National Bureau of Economic Research, 21
National Extension College, 69, 70–72
National Institute of Economic and Social Research, 15
National Service (Great Britain), 217–218
Needleman, L., 20
Neighborhood councils, 205–206
Neurosis, and working conditions, 204
New Progressive Party, 212
New towns, 205
  forecasting and, 7, 10–11

Oath, in Coronation Service, 182–183
Open University, 63–72, 95
  birth-rates and, 63–64
  after first ten years, 70–72
  founding of, 66–69
  on international level, 72
  research stations used in, 64–65
  television lectures in, 68, 69, 70
Organisations, *see* Social organisations
Orwell, George, 244, 245
Owen, Robert, 206, 208

Parish councils, 205–206
Parker, S., 147, 148, 158
Pieper, J., 148
Policy, *see* Educational policy; Housing programs; Social policy
Politics, 175–252
  consumption and quality of life issues and, 233–237
  consumption orientation of, 222–224
  middle classes and, 244–246
  organisation size issues and, 195–209
  possibility of new political party and, 229–231
  production orientation of, 221–222
  Somali Radio Service and, 238–241
Poor, and quality of life, 234–235
Population growth
  educational policy and, 73–74
  forecasting and, 12
Production
  forecasting and, 12–13
  politics and orientation toward, 221–222, 227
Public services, and quality of life, 235–237

Quality of life, 233–237
  commercial products versus public services and, 235–237
  dilemmas in, 234
  needs of poor versus needs of rich in, 234–235
  standards of living versus, 237
  working conditions and, 204–206
Queen of England, *see* Coronation Service

Radio colleges, 75–95
  advantages of, 91–93
  age range of students in, 90
  argicultural cycle and, 81–82
  courses in, 80–86
  examples of, 82–86
  government interest in, 86–87
  orientation to work of, 89
  planning on local level for, 78–79
  in rural areas, 89–90
  social organisations and, 78
  Somali Radio Service in, 238–241
  student population in, 76–77
  study group organisation of, 77–80
  teacher training with, 88

technology and, 94–95
value of group listening in, 239
Rainborowe, Thomas, 248
Relaxation time, 33–34
Religious beliefs
　Coronation seen as ritual in, 186
　feelings about monarchy and, 178–179
　Menlo Park study and, 121–122
　oath in Coronation Service and, 182–183
Residence patterns
　attitudes about, 123
　Bethnal Green study of, 99–100, 108–110, 125–126, 128
　of grown children and parents, 123–126, 128
　marriage and, 109–110
　Menlo Park study of, 123–125
　work place and, 220
Rhythm, in cycles, 38
Rickman, John, 190
Road planning, 214
　forecasting and, 8
　need for, 225–226
Robbins Committee, 6, 8, 64, 65, 69
Rodgers, H. B., 146
Roosevelt, Franklin D., 217
Roper and Associates, 131
Rose, R., 211, 219

Sainsbury, P., 138
Scarborough Conference of 1948, 199
School
　system of cycles in, 39–41
　see also Educational policy
Science, and manpower forecasting, 7–8
Senegal, radio colleges in, 79
Sheldon, J. H., 115–116
Shopping centres, and forecasting, 9
Shops Act, 222
Sillitoe, K. K., 146–147
Smith, W. Robertson, 186

Social change
　educational system and, 224–225
　forecasting and, 4, 18
Social class, *see* Class
Social costs, and efficiency, 196–197
Social Democratic Party (SDP), 242–252
　deprived classes and, 247
　new middle classes and, 244–246
　political beliefs as basis of, 248–252
　social organisation membership patterns and, 245–246
Social organisations
　changing membership patterns in, 245–246
　communication between levels in, 200–201, 202–204
　cycles and, 36–37
　democracy and, 296
　efficiency and social costs in, 196–197
　election of leadership in, 198–199
　human nature and, 206–208
　leisure activities and, 163–164
　meaning of coronation in, 177–193
　plurality of institutions in, and monarchy, 192–193
　radio colleges and, 78
　reaffirmation of moral values and coronation in, 179–182
　selection and training of leaders in, 199–200
　size issues in, 201–202
Social policy, 97–173
　Bethnal Green study and, 115–117
　organisation size and, 195–209
Social sciences, and forecasting, 16–18
Somali Radio Service, 238–241

Soviet influence and, 239–240
value of group listening and, 239
Sons, *see* Father-son relationships
Sorbonne, 67
Soviet Union
  forecasting in, 5
  Somali and, 239, 240
Spens Report, 24
Sports activities, 154–155
Stalin, Joseph, 5
Standards of living, 237
Study group, in radio colleges, 77–80

Tanzania, radio colleges in, 78, 79, 80, 84–86
Tawney, 71, 193, 249
Teachers
  manpower forecasting for, 8
  training of, in Third World, 88
Technology, and radio colleges, 94–95
Television lectures, in Open University, 68, 69, 70
Television viewing habits, 152, 153
Third World educational policy, 73–95
  basis for, 75
  food production and, 93–94
  illiteracy in, 74
  population growth and, 73–74
  primary school strength and, 88
  radio colleges in, 75–95
  righting injustices from past with, 87–88
  teacher training in, 88
Time
  clock, 33
  episodic, 29–32
  fluctuating function of, 35
  life cycle concept in, 31–32
  mean free, 34
  measurement of, 32–34
  as numerical variable, 32–34
  oscillation and, 35–36
  periodic, 34
  phase and, 35

pulsating, 35
reckoning of year in, 27–28
relaxation, 33–34
sense of duration of, 28–29
Totalitarian state, and forecasting, 5
Town planning, 205, 214
  forecasting and, 10–11
  road planning and, 225–226
Townsend, P., 138
Traffic planning, 8
Training Within Industry, 200
Transportation, and leisure activities, 172

UNESCO, 74
Unions, 247
  human relations within, 203–204
  Labour Party and, 227–229
United Nations, 219
University
  double shift of students in, 65–66
  research station as extension of, 64–65
  see also Open University

Water Resources Board, 11–12
Webb, Sidney & Beatrice, 205
Whitehead, Albert North, 92
Widowers, 138–145
  age groups and effects of, 139–142
  death-rates for, 139
  duration effect in, 139
  influences on, 143–144
  remarriage rates for, 143
Willink Committee, 7
Women, and Labour Party, 220–221
Woodford family life study, 120
  father-son relationships in, 128
  frequency of contact between parents and grown children in, 125
  genealogical awareness in, 134

Menlo Park study differences with, 120–123
mother-daughter relationships in, 125–126, 127–128
residence patterns of grown children in, 123–125
Work, as extension of leisure, 158–159
Workers
  communication between leaders and, 197, 200–201, 202–204
  division of labour and, 202

Working class
  Labour Party focus on, 219–220
  Menlo Park study with, 121
  size of factory and, 202
Working conditions
  character of life and, 204–206
  differences in viewpoints on leisure and, 148–152
  neurosis and, 204
  residence and, 220
World Bank, 74

Zuckerman Committee, 8